At Beetle of the Pyramid

TRAVELS

IN

UPPER AND LOWER EGYPT,

DURING THE CAMPAIGNS OF GENERAL BONAPARTE.

BY
VIVANT DENON.

TRANSLATED FROM THE FRENCH.

To which is prefixed,
AN HISTORICAL ACCOUNT OF THE
INVASION OF EGYPT BY THE FRENCH.

By E. A. KENDAL, Esq.

ILLUSTRATED BY MAPS, VIEWS, &c. &c.

IN TWO VOLUMES.

VOL. I.

DARF PUBLISHERS LTD
LONDON
1986

FIRST PUBLISHED 1802
NEW IMPRESSION 1986

ISBN 978 1 85077 098 5

THE
TRANSLATOR'S PREFACE.

THAN the Egyptian Travels of M. Denon, a book more interesting in its subject, or more satisfactory in its execution, has seldom issued from the press. The country of which it treats, and the circumstances under which it was produced, equal each other in singularity. Travelers have always intermingled adventure with observation, and their readers have perhaps been pleased to find description relieved by action; but few have had opportunities of animating their works with adventures like those in which M. Denon was engaged, and, with as much truth, it may be said that few have been capable of turning their opportunities to the same advantage. An elegant writer, an accurate and picturesque observer, a lively historian, he has brought forward a mass of information of the most varied nature, and such as only the union of his talents and situation could have permitted him to procure and afford. " This distinguished artist," says general Berthier, " followed to the cataracts the division commanded by general Desaix, partaking its fatigues and dangers,

to

to examine the magnificent remains with which the country is covered. His collection will furnish the philosopher with researches fitted to develope the history of an enlightened people, and the lover of the arts with a source of instruction and enjoyment." In truth, the war in upper Egypt is here depicted with so much exactitude, intelligence, and vividness of colour, that the reader fancies himself present at all its transactions; and this narrative, frequently as painful as it is impressive, is blended with accounts of architectural grandeur never exhibited but in Egypt, and views of nature, and of man, in like manner characteristic of that country.

Nor is it only as a book of general entertainment and knowledge that this work is capable of gratifying curiosity. It has great political value. It throws light on the prospect, behind and before. It shows what France has been in Egypt, and what she desires to be again.

The extent and more eminent features of M. Denon's travels are so amply and so ably expressed in his own preface, that they do not require to be mentioned here; but it would perhaps be regarded as negligent, if, though the fact be already public, the reader were not, thus at the threshold, reminded, that, at Thebes, he had the good fortune to find manuscripts in the antique character of the Egyptians, a discovery which may be reckoned an epoch in antient learning, and which alone would

place

TRANSLATOR'S PREFACE.

place his name among the first of benefactors to letters.

Were it necessary to pronounce a panegyric on this performance, much might also be said on that warmth and rectitude of feeling which here clothes the man with as much reputation, as industry the traveler; and, as a part of the evidence in support of this observation, there might be cited that frankness, that unqualified indignation, with which the crimes of the author's countrymen are recorded, and the miseries produced by the warfare they occasioned deplored; crimes and miseries of which men of narrow information will not fail to make large account, and the acknowledgement of which, all things duly considered, is equally honourable to its patron and to itself: but, to awaken attention to illustrations of Egypt, or operations of the French arms, must be as needless as easy; and the rest will with greater propriety be submitted to the judgment of the public: the Translator has better occasion for appeal in his own favour.

Though very universal in his taste, M. Denon traveled more particularly as an artist; and hence, in one point of view, his work might, be ranked among those Travels which are denominated picturesque: it is, however, more than picturesque; and, as should follow from what has already been said, has many recommendations independent on the large collection of designs by which it is accompanied. No doubt, the productions of a skilful draftsman,

draftsman, even when, as is here sometimes the case, they represent the least important objects, are always pleasing, and generally instructive; but the great expense which unfortunately attends the graphic arts, in almost all instances confines their enjoyment to a small number of their admirers. In valuable books, they have the additional ill quality of turning the key not only on themselves but on the stores of literature. In a word, to have preserved all M. Denon's plates, the price of the work, in the French more than twenty pounds, must, even on a very reduced scale, have far exceeded what a large number of readers could have reasonably afforded to bestow; and, the Publishers, in consequence, calling to mind that the authors of large works, restrained by this inconvenience, have usually forborne to give them similar decorations, however desirable; in short, that, for this reason, it is customary to separate books from prints; have thought that they should perform an acceptable service to an extensive part of the public, by returning to the ordinary practice, and printing a translation unincumbered with more than a few interesting plates: they believe that these plates will be found to have been meritoriously executed, and they are sure that a few thus engraved will be more grateful to the eye, and more capable of affording information, than a multitude of coarser efforts.

This arrangement, however, has imposed a task of peculiar difficulty on the Translator. A large part

part of the work, not to break the thread of the narrative, and to accompany the plates, has received in the original a detached form. To have omitted this, would have been to have deprived the reader of least half the value of his purchase; to have inserted it in long and continual notes, would have been to distract his attention from the text, involve the subject-matter in obscurity, and weary rather than gratify the mind. It is justly observed that a book with extensive notes is never wholly read; the text being neglected for these, or these for the text. The remedy proposed, was that of restoring the fragments to their natural situation, the narrative: this has been done; to give them room, the former, to the loss only of some obvious redundances, has been compressed (compressed rather than abridged); and, for the performance of all this, the Translator, after having consulted the advantage of a large class of readers, throws himself on the indulgence of the rest.

Prefixed is a short narrative of the invasion of Egypt, a subject which, if yet at all forgotten, must be revived by these Travels. Within so small a compass, that event could not be very fully detailed; but a collection of dates, and a somewhat methodical view the of whole, will probably be agreeable on a topic certainly among the most curious of modern history.

AN

HISTORICAL ACCOUNT

OF THE

INVASION OF EGYPT

BY THE FRENCH.

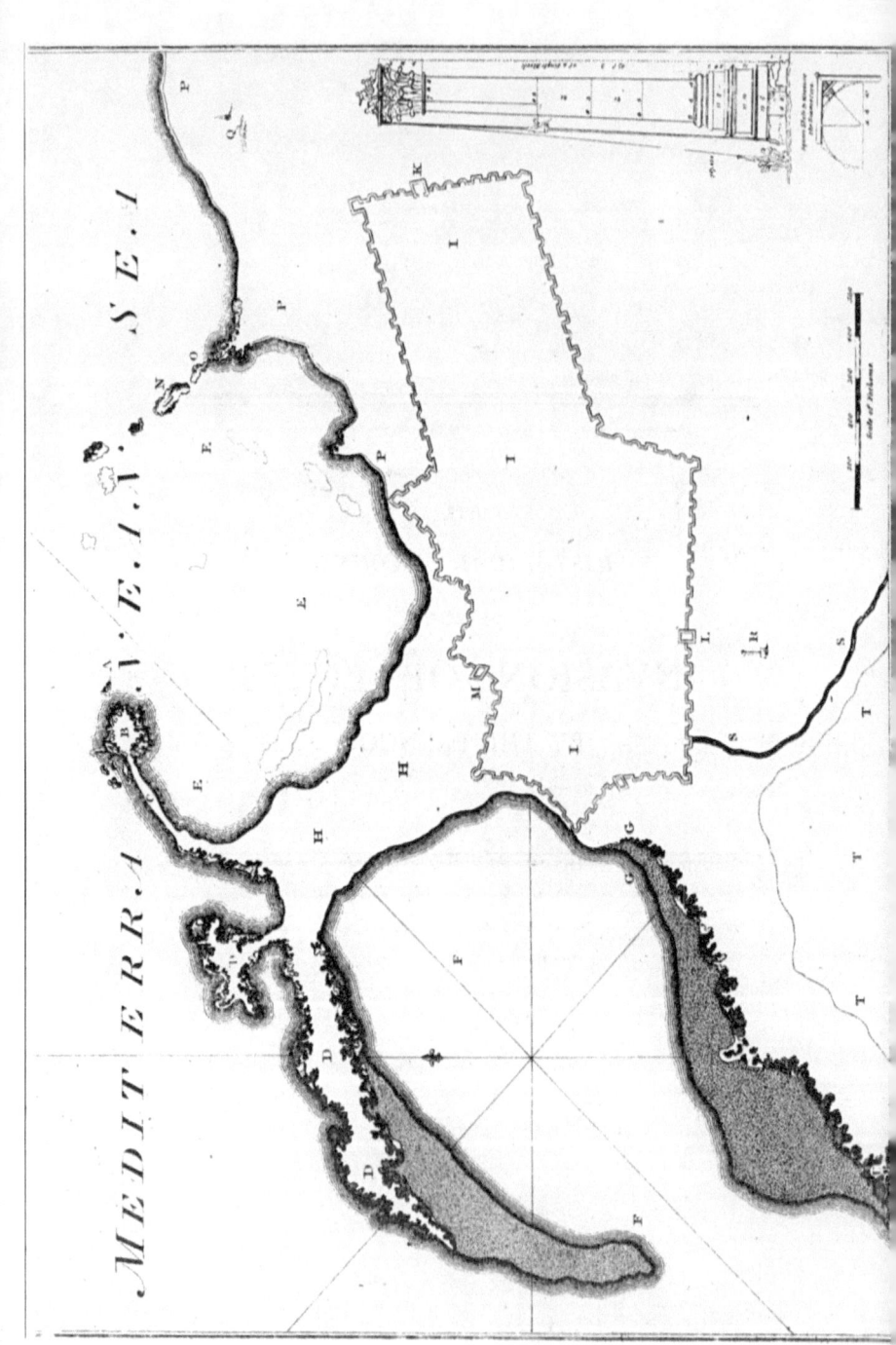

AN

ACCOUNT

OF THE

INVASION OF EGYPT.

D<small>ISTINGUISHED</small> as it was by extraordinary enterprize and atchievement, the war which followed the dissolution of monarchy in France, and between the present writing and the termination of which only a few months have passed, produced nothing the history of which will be read with stronger interest than the invasion of Egypt. The movements of hostile armies, by the scene of activity they display, the hopes and fears by which they are attended, and of which they make partakers those most of all indifferent to the issue, seldom fail to engage the attention of the mind, and as seldom to instruct the soldier, the statesman, and the philosopher; but, if these are characteristics of all military expeditions, those which more adequately distinguish this still remain unnoticed. The circumstances under which it was planned, the country to which it was sent, the general by whom it was led, the manner in which it was performed, the considerations and consequences it involved, all contribute to place it among the most triking eve nts, not of one, two, or three nations only, but of the human world. The book of Travels to which this memoir is prefixed, which sprung from this very
expedition

expedition, and which details a part of its circumstances, will naturally excite a wish to see the whole; to see at once its motives, its features, its commencement, its operations, its successes, its reverses, its conclusion; and to draw together these particulars, to arrange the scattered members, and to give the subject a form commodious for examination, is what, with the utmost brevity of manner, it is here proposed to attempt.

I. A few words will call to mind that maritime trade with Asia, and countries similarly abundant, which makes so large a consideration in the politics of Europe in general, and an equally few, that with India, making a still larger in those of Britain in particular. It is not necessary, either, to dwell on that aversion of the natives of plentiful countries from the efforts of commerce, by which Europeans, being compelled to court an intercourse which the former would never seek, and to secure, by territorial dominion and consequent monopoly, its security under governments which, at the best, regard its continuance with indifference, have been led to acquire more than mercantile advantages; or on the means or circumstances by which, of all Europeans, the British have acquired, in this same India, the empire of widest extent.

Reverting, now, to the rivalry by which, like the little republics of antient Greece, the clustered nations of northern Europe maintain themselves in perpetual agitation, it is easily seen that this indian empire must draw upon Britain the animosity of all her neighbours, and particularly of France, pre-eminent in that disposition because the nearest in this character, and because the nearest also in the amount of her prosperity and strength. France, therefore, for a long period of time, has had it for a natural object of her policy (for of every nation to depress others and, at least relatively, exalt itself, is the

natural

natural and indispensible policy), either to deprive Britain of this empire, or to gain for herself another, equivalent if not superior. To accomplish the one, or the other, or both of these, her statesmen turned their eyes, first on those powers whose immediate losses were the component parts of that empire, and who, therefore, though they might want the means of injuring, could not want motives for hating, the nation by which it was held; and next, as a possession to be obtained for herself, on a country that not less, by its natural and commercial advantages, promised positive aggrandizement, than, by its local proximity, and still more perhaps by the introduction to oriental powers with which it must furnish its masters, it equally promised to assist the collateral pursuit. This country was Egypt*; and these motives the mediate cause of the invasion.

The government by which this project was formed did not live to put it in execution; but the succeeding saw its wisdom, and adopted it for its own. It became engaged in war with Britain, as with several other powers of Europe. A period of war is a period of licence for ambition; and now, therefore, the seizure of Egypt, and the attack on the empire of Britain in India, were put into practice. There were still other immediate motives. In the course of the war, France had lost her own territory in India, and her american islands; these she might not be enabled to regain; and Egypt, the acquisition of which was the easier task, was more than a counterbalance. Inferior in naval strength, she had it more within her compass to manage a maritime expedition in the Mediterranean than in the Atlantic or the Indian ocean. If gained, the colony would also be nearer the parent country, more abundant

---

* See papers found in the cabinet of Lewis XVI.

in its benefits, and more easy of defense. Nor was it only in the event of subsequent retention that the possession of Egypt by France would give a wound to Britain. From the instant it should be attempted, it would divert her attention from european politics, it would occupy her with interests more dear to her than those by which she was bound to her allies, it would give a coolness and disjunction to the alliance, it would even indispose or disable her to act in the direction which this more immediately required, it might excite alarms capable of detaching her from the objects for which she carried on the war; and, in addition to all these considerations, in case of obtaining possession, it would be advantageous even as movement of war only, by affording a property with which to purchase peace. On the whole, the invasion of Egypt, both in its mediate and immediate motives, had, not only the raising of France, but the raising of France at the expense of England, for its direct principle; a principle uniformly avowed by the french government and its servants*, and which, by its wisdom and magnitude, appears worthy of having actuated the councils of intelligent statesmen, and of being received by history as the true origin of that event. Individuals, nevertheless, have attributed others; and, under the possibility of their truth, they have a claim to record. Some speculators†, in Britain especially, little considerate of the difficulties by which the vastest and most successful of human power is restrained, and supposing countries as easily overrun as pages, have supposed designs which their readers have admired because they seemed impracticable, and half cre-

---

* See general Berthier's letter to the directory, of the 11 *Thermidor, an* 6, and *Proclamation du général Bonaparte aux soldats* &c. *Pieces Officielles de l'armée d' Egypte.* Iier partie, p. 1.

* See *Political Recollections*, &c. and other publications.

dited

dited because they were marvelous. Not only the British were to be driven from India, but the whole turkish empire, all Germany, all Italy, were to be subjugated. More temperate, however, in their hopes, than these in their fears, it is probable that its projectors expected only to abridge the first, and for the rest confined their views on Egypt, the holding of which would at once enable France to stand a competition in the commerce of the east, and add to its general ascendancy among european powers. It is to be added, that a commander-in-chief of the army employed has stated, as an immediate motive, that the french government had, during the sixth year of the republic, obtained knowledge of the intention of its enemies to possess themselves of Malta, and Egypt itself; that it had only resolved on preventing this; and that the interests of the commerce of the Levant, the annual profits of which had amounted to nearly fifty million franks, demanded the measures it had pursued*. These assertions, however, though officially made, appear, with respect to the two former, to have resulted rather from the private view of the subject entertained by the officer from whom they proceeded, and to whom they are peculiar, than from facts absolutely authentic; and with respect to the third, which probably alludes to certain disputes in which the french merchants were involved with the beys and others, to comprehend rather subordinate than main considerations.

II. But, whatever were the motives for this undertaking, resolved on by the directory it was attempted, and a moment arrived in which policy required this or a similar measure. In the year 1797, the arms of France had almost exhausted all the employment which they could obtain on the

---

* *Le general Menou à l'armée francaise,* &c. *Pieces Officielles,* II ieme part. p. 342.

continent

continent of Europe, and yet their successes were rendered ineffectual by the superiority of Britain at sea. Deriving wealth from the war itself, and almost secure against the irruption of armies, this insular nation was able to purchase reiterated hostilities from the powers of Germany, and instigate them to encounter dangers from which the loss of money was the only injury herself could sustain. It was necessary, therefore, to change the mode of warfare; it was necessary to aim a blow that Britain was susceptible of feeling. France was without fleets, she was without seamen, she was without naval skill; she could attempt nothing by sea: and yet the sea was the basis of commerce, and commerce of the power of Britain. But France had brave and numerous armies; these were her resources, and common sense dictated their use. Fortunately, a short voyage would convey an army to a point at which Britain was vulnerable; it was fortunate also that this point, while it had the negative advantage of procuring injury to Britain, had the positive one of benefiting France. Under these circumstances an armament was ordered; Malta and Egypt were made its destination [*]; the troops of which it was composed were principally those who had been victorious in Italy, for the Rhine still required the rest, and the command was entrusted to general Bonaparte, him under whom its victories had been gained.

Here, the circumstances that are to follow, require a previous view of the political situation of Malta and Egypt at the era of this enterprize, and the order of ideas that are to be linked, that Egypt be the previous consideration.

Egypt is a province of the turkish empire, and its inhabitants though divided by the mosaic, the christian, and

---

[*] *Pieces Officielles*, II ieme part. p. 343.

the mohammedan, yet so much for the most part attached to the latter, that, in a statistical point of view, it is to be regarded as a mohammedan country. In its quality of province of the turkish empire, two considerations present themselves; the first the state of peace and alliance which had long subsisted, and which at the time of equipping the expedition still subsisted between that empire and France, and the resistance which the former might desire or be willing to make to the designs of the latter. In regard to the first, a very peculiar tenor of language, in some measure grounded on the second, was held by the government of France. This represented that, though it invaded, it entertained no hostility to the empire; and, while it entered the country by surprizal and force of arms, it spoke amicably to the sultan, and professed to have arguments worthy of ensuring his approbation on its conduct. These arguments, which might be complicated in their nature, or of which a difference of nature might be supposed, were at least certainly grounded on the sort of tenure by which the sultan holds the province.

Egypt, that province, once, though the profusion of physical blessings with which it has been endowed, the seat of one of the first empires of the earth, lost its independence under the sword of Cambyses; in a subsequent age, it changed the dominion of the Persian for that of the Greek; and by this revolution, after the death of Alexander, obtained, though not another line of Pharoahs, a release from foreign controul. The Ptolemies ended in Cleopatra; from a province of the upper roman empire, it fell to the lower or eastern; the emperor of Constantinople lost it to the successors of Mohammed; the califs were followed by the sultans, and Egypt was once more the territory of a sovereign state.

In

In the year of Christ 879, the power of the califs being on the decline, Ammed the son of Teilun, governor of Egypt usurped the sovereignty*; in the year 1249, Turan the son of Malek was assassinated by a mamluc, or, according to others †, massacred by mamlucs, asiatic slaves whom he had purchased, and of whom he had composed his garrisons and marine. From this period, or soon after, the government remained in the hands of the mamlucs, who augmented and perpetuated their numbers by fresh purchases of slaves, and the monarchy was elective in this body. The mamlucs progressively raised the aristocracy above the throne, and, about the year 1517, lost the latter to the emperor of Constantinople, Selim the Second. Depressed, however by victory, rather than destroyed by conquest, the power of the mamlucs was suffered to continue, and their whole loss to consist in that sceptre the mutual struggles for which had been the cause of their weakness. Egypt received a constitution by which, under the title of beys, twenty-four of these, chosen among themselves, were entrusted with the revenues and civil administration, subject to an annual tribute of six hundred thousand zeckins, and the partial controul of a resident pasha or governor; and on condition of spiritual subjection to the mufty of Constantinople, and acknowledgment of the sovereignty of the ottoman sultans in the prayers, and on the coin.

Political arrangements are so much governed by what is expedient rather than by what is desirable, that the wisdom of Selim in the present must, if censurable at all, be censured with caution; and, if it were really possible to have

---

* *Histoire de l'Afrique, &c. par Cardonne.*

† *Ibid.*

dispensed

dispensed with the preponderance of the mamluc body, yet its existence was well calculated to prevent the governor appointed by the Porte from assuming independence; and an enlightened statesman would perhaps have judged it an advantage the sole to be considered, that he thus secured himself against the dangers attending the existence of a sovereign power on his more immediate frontier. From this constitution, however (and Selim perhaps foresaw and disregarded the evil), it has resulted that the power of the Porte over the internal affairs of Egypt is extremely limited, and that the stipulated revenue, or tribute, has often, not by absolute refusal, but by delays and subterfuges, been withheld by the beys.

This political situation of Egypt, resulting from these circumstances, presented to the designs of the French a difficulty and a facility, both, in a great degree, peculiar to this country. It multiplied, and, at the same time, it divided, the powers against which they have to contend. Both the strength of the turkish empire, whatever it might be, and that of the beys, with all their revenues, mamlucs, and egyptian followers, were to be overcome; the beys, however, and the Porte, had many separate interests, and separate interests necessarily threw an advantage in the way of a common enemy; yet the interests of the beys and of the Porte, however various in domestic particulars, were unanimous in this, their hostility to the existence of a third power in Egypt. On the whole, nevertheless, the disunion of interests was a breach in the palladium, and a discerning enemy might enter.

The conduct of the expedition to Egypt had therefore a twofold nature; the beys were to be subdued by arms, the sultan by negociation.

Malta,

Malta, an island lying between that of Sicily and the coast of Africa, and which had committed several acts of hostility against France*, was valuable as a military outwork for the security of Egypt, and in general as a citadel commanding the Levant; it is a place at which water is taken in by vessels proceeding up the Mediterranean; and the want of water for the french fleet and convoy was to be made the immediate cause of hostilities: to subdue the order of saint John of Jerusalem, by which this island was possessed, and the essence of which institution consisted in perpetual enmity to the mohammedans, would also be an action grateful to the sultan, the design of conciliating whose favour comes next to be more distinctly considered.

The beys, it has been seen, were but indifferent subjects, and the actual possession of Egypt by the Porte, little more than nominal; on this foundation it is said to have been proposed to negociate for an admission, more or less unqualified, of the power of France into that country, where, in military and civil authority it should take the place of the beys, while, like these, but more faithfully, it should render the stipulated tribute, and acknowledge the supremacy of the mufti, and the sovereignty of the sultan. In this broad proposition several modifications might be introduced, and perhaps were intended to exist from the first; but something more plausible, more really consonant with the interests of the Porte, must surely have been designed; or the expectation of acquiescence must have been grounded upon an idea of its moral or at least physical imbecility: it could never be thought that the sultan would rely upon the continuance

---

* *Pieces Officielles*, P. I. p. 23.

of tribute from a power superior to himself, or that he would think France a better neighbour than the beys; and arguments might easily have been brought forward more respectful to his understanding. A further consideration of these arguments is impracticable within the limits of the present sketch; but, of whatever nature they were, it has been rumoured that they were agreeable to a party in the divan, which, rather than the sultan, governs the otman empire, and the conduct of that government in the actual event of the invasion, accorded, it will be found, with this supposition. In Egypt itself, it was intended to represent the arrival of the french army as a transaction equally favourable to the interests of the sultan and the inhabitants, and hostile only to the beys; the beys, rebellious to the one, and oppressive to the other.

The command, as has been said, was given to general Bonaparte. In general Bonaparte, the republic had a citizen in whose character the soldier was but an ingredient. He was hitherto publicly known for little besides military capacity, or perhaps good fortune. His enemies, proud of fighting with pygmies, spoke of him with contempt. He was, however, a lover of the arts, a scholar, and a statesman. Possessed of ascendancy over those with whom he was concerned, he had at his disposal the arrangements for his expedition; and he went out from France rather a sovereign than a general. The colour of his mind was reflected in the whole armament. Learning and science were leagued with arms. He regarded that of the bayonet as the worst and least permanent of conquests. It was only by spreading civilization and assimilating manners that he hoped to retain Egypt; and, preparing to put in practise all that theory could suggest for this purpose, he invited men of knowledge and genius in every pursuit to be his companions: sensible also of the valuable discoveries to be made in Egypt, he prepared in like manner to bring back these to Europe.

The military force, when the several detachments were united, consisted of nearly forty thousand men*; and the list of artists, men of letters, and those of science, contains the following numbers and departments: in geometry eight, in astronomy four, in general mechanics fourteen, in watch-making two, in chemistry eight, in mineralogy five, in botany three, in zoology five, in surgery six, in pharmacy three, in antiquities two, in architecture four, in drawing five, in engineering nineteen, in geography eighteen, in printing fifteen†. In conformity with the various objects attended to in this assemblage of persons, the implements of war were accompanied by those of science.

Though nothing could be more public than the collecting this armament, its destination was kept a profound secret. The peculiar features just described were thought designed only to mislead the world as to its object; and they had the good quality of calling forth the witticisms of men incapable of appreciating their value.

Toulon, on the Mediterranean, was appointed for the harbour from which the principal division should embark, while others were prepared at Ajaccio, Genoa, and Civita-Veccia; and all whose duty were to assemble at the former point repaired thither early in May 1798. On the ninth of that month, Bonaparte visited the squadron, which was decorated with flags for his reception‡. From that day till the nineteenth, the wind continued unfavourable; on this, it changed to the north-west, and the signal-gun for getting under weigh was fired‖. On the twentieth,

---

* Dodsley's Annual Register, 1799. † Norry. ‡ Norry.
‖ Ib. Denon.

the Orient, the admiral's ship, and on board of which was Bonaparte, left the harbour*, together with fourteen other ships of war, and more than two hundred sail of transports†. Addressing a proclamation to the land and maritime forces, and which he denominated the *army of the Mediterranean*, " Soldiers," said Bonaparte, " you are one of the wings of the army of England. You " have made war on mountains, on plains, and in " sieges; it remains for you to make war by sea. The " roman legions, which you have sometimes imitated, " but not yet equaled, combated Carthage by turns on this " same sea, and on the plains of Zama. Victory never " forsook them, because they were always brave, patient " under fatigue, disciplined, and united among themselves. " Soldiers! Europe has its eyes upon you: you have " great destinies to fulfil, battles to give, dangers, fatigues, " to vanquish; you have to do more than you have ever " yet done for the prosperity of your country, the wel-" fare of mankind and your own glory. Soldiers, sailors, " infantry, artillery, cavalry, be one! remember that, in " the day of battle, you will have need of each other. " Soldiers! sailors! you have been hitherto neglected; " now, the greatest anxiety of the republic is on your " account: you will be worthy of the army of which you " make a part. The genius of liberty, which, from her " birth, has rendered the republic the arbiter of Eu-" rope, wills that she shall be the same of the most dis-" tant seas and nations. ‡"

The troops were further encouraged by the promise of unusual advantages; the land to which they were going was said to be fitted, and by the republic destined, to af-

---

* Denon. † Norry. ‡ *Pieces Officielles*, &c. P. I. p. 1.

ford

ford them a permanent provision, and each was to have a gift of six arpents of land.*

The secrecy in which the object of the expedition was involved did not lessen the apprehensions of the powers against either of which it was possible that it might be directed. That it was equipped in the ports of the Mediterranean was some guide to conjecture; and Britain did not neglect to watch that sea with all the vigour and closeness which a numerous and admirable fleet could effect. With respect to the Porte, it was arranged that at the same moment in which the expedition left Toulon, a french embassador should proceed to Constantinople, to inform the sultan of the motives of the invasion of Egypt; a precaution which, from a cause, says general Menou, upon whose authority this assertion is made, that can only be suspected, was not taken†. A rumour, to which allusion has already been made, represents that the embassador at Paris was privy to the affair, that negociations had been opened with a party at the head of which was the then grand-visir, and that, in a word, the counsels of the divan were divided upon the measure.

After coasting along France, and a part of Italy, the fleet passed between Cape-Corsica and the island of Capraya‡. From the crew of an english brig, which an aviso burnt on the coast of Sardinia, it learned that a squadron was in its pursuit‖. On the ninth of June, it reached Malta, after a voyage unattended with any species of difficulty§. The soldiers had been kept in constant employment, either learning to climb the masts, or exercising the guns¶.

In the evening of the ninth, Bonaparte sent a shore one of his aide-de-camps, to ask permission of the grand-mas-

---

* See p. 14. vol. I. of this work. † *Pieces Officielles*, Pr II. p. 343.
‡ Denon.   ‖ *Pieces Officielles*, P. I. p. 4.   § Ib.   ¶ Ib.

ter to fill water at the different anchorages of the island; and the manner in which this request was answered was to settle that in which the island was to be treated. The reply was brought by the consul of the republic at Malta. It amounted to an absolute refusal; the grand-master professing himself unable to let more than two transports take water at the same time; a mode by which, upon calculation, the whole armament, to which the convoys from Corsica and Italy were now joined, and which consisted of five or six hundred sail*, would have required three hundred days for this operation†. The want of the army, says Bonaparte (as if the capture of Malta had not made a part of the original plan), was urgent, and rendered it my duty to employ force for its relief‡. He directed the consul to address a letter to the grand-master, in which after describing him as indignant that he should have given permission to water only by *four* vessels at a time, the latter invited him to propose some medium of accommodation, and assured him that the city had no hope but in the generosity of the french commander, who had given the most precise orders that the religious customs, and property, of the Maltese should be scrupulously respected‖. After some trivial resistance, the island was subdued. The inhabitants took refuge in the metropolis of Valetta, whence an heavy fire was kept up during the evening of the tenth. The besieged made a sortie, in which they lost the standard of the order. Bonaparte began to land his artillery; and, at the same time, not trusting to military efforts alone, he attempted various negociations, by the result of which this place, capable of enduring a siege of im-

---

* Ib. p. 5.   † Ib. p. 22.   ‡ Ib. p. 5.   ‖ Ib. p. 22.

mense

mense duration, was induced to capitulate on the same evening. The consul-general of the batavian republic was requested to write to Bonaparte on the part of the order: " His most eminent highness and his council, having " sent for me, have commissioned me to observe to you, " citizen general, that when they denied you entrance " into the ports, and begged to have your answer, they " pretended to no more than a perception of the depar- " ture which you required of them from the laws imposed " by their neutrality. The conduct of the order towards " the french republic, and the protection which, as well " as its people, from whom it will always be inseparable, " it has always received from the french nation, cause it " to consider a rupture as a misfortune to which it wishes " to put an end. His most eminent highness, therefore, " and his council, ask for a suspension of hostilities, and " for information concerning your intentions, which will " doubtlessly be conformable with the generosity of the " french nation and the known sentiments of the cele- " brated general by whom it is represented." During the night, a convention between the republic and the order was framed and concluded. This consisted of eight articles, by the first and most important of which the order put into the hands of the army the city and forts of Malta, and surrendered to the republic its rights of sovereignty over, and property, in that city, together with the islands of Malta, Gozo, and Cumino; by the sixth, the knights were secured in their private property; and by the seventh the people in their religion and privileges, and from all extraordinary levy*. On the twelfth,

---

* Ib. p. 32.

Bonaparte

Bonaparte wrote to the bishop of Malta, commending the pacific conduct of that prelate; begging him to assure his clergy that, not only the catholic, apostolic, and roman religion would be respected, but its ministers specially protected; declaring that he knew no character more worthy, nor more deserving of the veneration of mankind, than that of a priest, who, full of the true spirit of the evangelist, feels that his duty commands him to preach obedience to the temporal power, and to maintain peace, tranquility, and union, in the midst of a diocese; and requesting him to come immediately to the city of Malta, there, by his influence, to preserve good order and tranquility among the people: he added that he would meet him there himself that evening, and that he desired to be then presented to all the *curés* and other principal persons of Malta and the surrounding villages *. In reply, the bishop assured Bonaparte of his disposition to act in the manner of which that general had expressed his approbation, and of his intention to take no part in any thing foreign to his pastoral ministry; and professed his pleasure in being able to say that the entrance of the french troops into the city had been effected without the least effusion of blood, a blessing for which he could not but take care to render thanks to the Almighty by a solemn *Te-Deum*, which he had ordered to be sung in public and pompous procession, that very day †. During the five following days, amid a variety of military cares, as well for the conquest as for the armament, Bonaparte published a civil constitution for Malta ‡, the minute particulars of which, though interesting in the extreme, it is not possible to insert in this memoir. The

---

* *Pieces Officielles*, p. 37. † Ib. p. 38. ‡ Ib. p. 39.

civil

civil administration was vested in nine commissioners, under controul of the military commander, and each of whom were to perform the office of president for six months, alternately.

Of military stores, general Bonaparte found at Malta two vessels of war, one frigate, and four gallies, twelve hundred pieces of cannon, fifteen hundred thousand pounds of powder, forty thousand muskets, and other articles*. All the money in the treasury of Saint-John did not amount to a million franks. This Bonaparte left to provide for the expenses of the garrison, and for those of completing a ship, called the *Saint-John.*

The garrison was made to consist of four thousand men†, under the command of division-general Vaubois, the officer who had commanded the debarkation, and who had conciliated the inhabitants by his wisdom and mildness‡. By one of the articles of the constitution, or code, all slavery was abolished; and, by another, in consequence, all the turkish slaves were to become prisoners of war, " and, seeing the friendship which sub-
" sisted between the republic and the ottoman porte, sent
" home when the general-in-chief should direct the same,
" and when he should find that the beys consented to
" send to Malta all the french or maltese slaves they
" possessed"§. These Turks, and other mohammedans, were taken on board the fleet, to the number of some hundreds, together with a body of volunteers, under the denomination of the *maltese legion*‖. These recruits, in some

---

* *Pieces Officielles*, p. 8.
† Denon and others: according to Norry, 3000.
‡ *Pieces Officielles*, P. I. p. 9. § Ib. p. 44.
‖ Norry. In his letter to the directory, the general observed that he had caused the Turks to embark as sailors, but said nothing of any

some degree, supplied the place of the soldiers left in garrison, and of various persons grown weary of their voyage*.

On the seventeenth, the squadron began to leave the port. On the evening of the eighteenth, the whole got under weigh.

It has already appeared, that, at Malta, no secret was made of the destination of the armament, and its reference to the *beys*. Some disturbances being caused at Malta by the soldiery, and through misconduct of a nature to be very extensively injurious in Egypt, Bonaparte drew up a set of regulations enforcing the strictest discipline under heavy penalties, and caused them to be read on board each ship†. Among other articles, it was ordered that whoever should violate the women, or enter the houses of the mohammedans, or the mosks, should be shot; and none of these regulations, the spirit of which is so necessary for the welfare of an army, were transgressed‡. In a proclamation, published two days subsequently to the departure from Malta, ' after declaring the object of the expedition, which was to promote the general interests of civilization and commerce, and humble the naval power of England, and confidently promising, after several fatiguing marches, and some hostile encounters, complete success, Bonaparte told them they were going to live with mohammedans, the first article of whose religious creed was, that *There is no God but God, and Mohammed is his prophet*. " Do not contradict them," said

---

any other troops. Neither are the latter mentioned by M. Denon. The Annual Register (Dodsley's, 1801), however, on what authority does not appear, says that Bonaparte was joined by " some thousands of the maltese sailors and soldiers."

   * Denon.   † Norry.   ‡ Ib.

he,

he. "Conduct yourselves towards them as you have done towards the Jews and the Italians. Show respect to their muftis and imams, and the ceremonies prescribed by the koran; as you have shown to the rabbis and the bishops. Cherish the same spirit of toleration for the mosks that you have entertained for the religion of Moses and of Jesus Christ: the roman legions protected all religions. You will find here usages different from those of Europe. You will reconcile yourselves to them by custom. The people of the land into which we are about to enter differ from us in their mode of treatment of women; but, in every country, he who offers violence to the women is a monster." Bonaparte proceeded next to warn them against giving way to a spirit of plunder: "Plunder, which enriches only a very few, reflects dishonour on the whole; it dries up our resources, and converts into enemies those whom it is our interest to have for friends." In conclusion, he reminded them that the city they were going to attack was built by Alexander, and that grand recollections, fitter to excite the emulation of Frenchmen, would be recalled to their minds at every step. At the same time, orders were issued that every individual of the army who should pillage or steal should be shot; that the punishment of death should also be inflicted on every individual of the army who should impose contributions on the towns, villages, or individuals, or should commit extortions of any kind; and that, when any individuals of a division should have committed any disorders in a country, the whole division, if the offender should not be discovered, should be responsible, and pay the sum necessary to indemnify the inhabitants for the loss sustained.*

Eight

---

* The original proclamation, which appears to be the same with that alluded to by M. Norry, being omitted in the *Pieces Officielles*, and
otherwise

Eight days were employed at Malta; the voyage between that island and Alexandria was performed within twelve more*. On the thirteenth of June, the fleet was before the city. A frigate had been dispatched, to warn the consul and other frenchmen of its arrival, and gather information as well concerning the actual dispositions of the inhabitants as concerning the british fleet †. While the frigate lay in the offing, a small vessel, in spite of her efforts to the contrary, ran into the port; and, though the British had been there three days before ‡, and raised the alarm §, it was not till now that a general tumult arose, threatening the lives of the Franks. In the vain custody of some mariners of Alexandria, the consul, however, was permitted to come on board the frigate, by which he was carried to the admiral's ship.

At this point of time, a heavy sea opposed the descent; the transports were mingled with the ships of war ||, and, in this unfavourable situation, the attack of the British was to be momentarily expected. It was now late in the evening. Bonaparte ordered an immediate debarkation.

According to one account, Bonaparte placed himself at the head of the debarkation **; but, according to his own, general Menou, with his division, was the first, and himself followed, with general Kleber ††. The violence of the wind rendered the proceeding as difficult as it was dangerous; and some lives were lost in the boats. General Menou, however, reached the shore, near Marabut, within a league and an half of Alexandria; and, at eleven o'clock

---

otherwise out of reach, the above detail is given solely on the authority, and in the words, of *Dodsley's Annual Register*, for 1801.

* *Relation des campagnes, &c. par le général de division Berthier.*
† *Pieces Officielles*, P. I. p. 107. ‡ *Berthier*, p. 8.
§ Denon. || Ib. ** Ib. †† *Berthier*, p. 9.

was

was joined by Bonaparte. At day-break, a body of mamlucs and Arabs began to skirmish with the advanced-posts:

On approaching the enclosure of the old city of the Arabs, Bonaparte ordered each column to halt without the range of the cannon: desirous to prevent the effusion of blood, he attempted a parley; but horrible shouts of men, women, and children, and a cannonade from a few pieces that were immediately unmasked, declared a resolution to defend the city*. After the walls were scaled, every house was defended; but, before the end of the day, the city was calm, the two castles had capitulated, and the invaders were in entire possession of the city, its forts, and its two harbours†.

In the evening, the imams, shechs, and shereefs, promised fidelity to the government; and Bonaparte published this proclamation: " Too long have the beys who govern
" Egypt insulted the french nation, and loaded her mer-
" chants with vexations; the hour of their chastisement
" is arrived. Too long has this horde of slaves, purchased
" from Caucasus and Georgia, tyranized over the fairest
" part of the world; but God, upon whom every thing
" depends, has ordered its empire to end. People of
" Egypt! you will be told that I come to destroy your
" religion; believe it not: reply that I come to restore
" your rights, and punish the usurpers, and that I vene-
" rate, more than the mamlucs, God, his prophet, and
" the koran. Tell these that all men are equal before
" God: wisdom, talents, virtues, make all the difference
" between them. Now, what wisdom, what talents, what
" virtues, distinguish the mamlucs, that they exclusively
" should possess all that is lovely and sweet in life? Is
" there a beautiful estate? it belongs to the mamlucs. Is

---

* *Pieces Officielles*, P I. p. 107. † Ib.

" there

" there a beautiful slave, a beautiful horse, a beautiful
" house? they belong to the mamlucs. If Egypt is their
" farm, let them show the lease that God has granted.
" But God is just and bountiful to all mankind; all the
" Egyptians are called to fill all posts: let the most
" wise, the most informed, the most virtuous, govern,
" and the people will be happy. There were formerly
" among you great cities, great canals, great commerce:
" by what has all been destroyed, if not by the avarice,
" the injustice, and the tyranny of the mamlucs? Cadis!
" shechs! imams! tshorbadjies! tell the people that we are
" the friends of true moslems. Is it not we that have destroy-
" ed the pope, who said that war must be made on mos-
" lems? Is it not we that destroyed the knights of Malta,
" because the madmen believed that God willed them to
" make war on moslems? Is it not we that have long
" been the friends of the grand seignior (whose designs
" may God accomplish!), and the enemies of his ene-
" mies? Are not the mamlucs, on the other hand, in con-
" tinual rebellion against the grand seignior, whom they
" still refuse to acknowledge? They execute only their
" own schemes. Thrice happy those that are for us! they
" shall prosper in their rank and fortune. Happy those
" that are neuter! they will have time to become ac-
" quainted with us, and they will come to our side. But
" wretched, thrice wretched those that shall arm for the
" mamlucs, and fight against us! there shall be no hope
" for these; they shall perish!—I. All villages, situate
" within a line of three leagues of the places passed by the
" enemy, shall send a deputation to the general com-
" manding the troops, to inform him of their submission,
" and their having hoisted the colours of the army (white,
" red, and blue). II. All villages that shall take up arms
" against the army shall be burned. III. All villages
" that

"that shall submit to the army, shall display, with that of the grand seignior our friend, the flag of the army. IV. The shechs shall put their seals upon all goods, houses, and other property belonging to the mamlucs, and shall be careful that nothing is embezzled. V. The shechs, cadis, and imams shall continue to perform the functions of their situations; every inhabitant shall remain at his accustomed station, and prayers shall be continued as usual. Every one shall thank God for the destruction of the mamlucs, and cry, Glory to the sultan, glory to the french army, his friend! curses on the mamlucs, and happiness to the people of Egypt!"*

During the siege, general Kleber, at the foot of the wall, while pointing out to his grenadiers the place at which he wished them to scale, was struck on the forehead by a ball. He fell; but the wound, though serious, was not mortal†. He was left in command of the place‡.

On landing, the greater part of the army had entered Alexandria only to pass through it into the desert§; the remainder, with the exception of the garrisons placed in this city, and the troops dispatched under general Menou, for the reduction of Rashid ‖, commenced its march for Cairo on the sixth and seventh of July. At half past nine o'clock on the morning of the third day, it discovered the Nile at Rahmanieh. The soldiers, fatigued with their march across the desert, and fainting with thirst, threw themselves, clothed as they were, into the water. Almost

---

* *Pieces Officielles*, P. I. p. 233.   † Ib. p. 108.   ‡ *Berthier*.
§ *Denon*.
‖ Commonly called *Rosetta*. The use of a right name instead of a wrong can need no apology. Some years ago, *Abû-kîr* was written. *Bouquier*. *Rosetta* is not a synonym, but a corruption, of *Rashid*.

at the same instant, the drum called them to their colours. A body of mamlucs, to the number of about eight hundred, had advanced in order of battle; but, on the hastening of the French to arms, they withdrew, and, before Bonaparte could advance, fled before the artillery, commanded by general Desaix. The French lost one officer and a guide, and had ten infantry slightly wounded. The mamlucs had about forty killed and wounded.

Bonaparte resolved to rest at Rahmanieh during this and the following day. In the night of the latter, general Menou, who had possessed himself of Rashid without difficulty, and left it with forced marches, joined the army. He brought information that a french flotilla had happily entered the Nile, but that it ascended that river with difficulty, the water being still low. Immediately after his arrrival, the army marched towards Miniet-Salameh, where it slept, and whence it departed before day-break.

At a league before it, Murat-bey, at the head of four thousand mamlucs, had posted himself to oppose its progress. His right was sustained by the village of Jibbrish, in which he had placed some pieces of cannon. On the Nile, he had several batteries, and a flottilla composed of eight or ten large gun-boats and armed jerms*. Bonaparte, apprized of his station, had left Rahmanieh to offer him battle.

In point of cavalry, the mamlucs were greatly superior to the French; the latter having only two hundred, and those lame and harassed, while the latter, four thousand in number, were not more magnificently than vigorously appointed†.

The french flottilla had joined the army, and it was ordered by Bonaparte to proceed, keeping such a course

---

* *Berthier* p. 20. † *Pieces Officielles*, P. I. p. 110.

as might enable it to support the left of his line, and attack the flotilla of the enemy at the moment he attacked the mamlucs and the village; but the violence of the wind compelled it to gain a league upon the army, and to meet and fight the flottilla of the enemy at disadvantage. The peasants, conducted by the mamlucs, threw themselves into the boats, and into the water itself, and boarded a demi-galley and a gun-boat; two other gun-boats were taken by the mamlucs; but the french commander recaptured all, and, after an obstinate combat, in which, on the one side and the other, more than an hundred and fifty discharges of cannon were given, set fire to the mamluc admiral, and to several others of the fleet, and dispersed the whole. *

Meanwhile, informed, by the noise of the guns, of the engagement, Bonaparte forced the village, the front of which had been covered by the army of the beys: The mamlucs of which this was composed, advanced upon the wings of the French, seeking, according to their manner of fighting, a weak point in the flanks or rear, on which they might make impression; but, the line being everywhere equally strong, and receiving them with a double fire of the flank and front, after several irresolute charges, and spending a part of the day within half cannon-shot, they retreated with the loss of six hundred, killed and wounded. The French lost seventy men.

Bonaparte now advanced within a trifling distance of Caira, without further impediment, than such as a burning climate, and the want of water and other necessaries, threw in his way: but, at the pyramids, he found the beys, prepared to make one more effort for the defense of

---

* *Berthier. Pieces Officielles.*

the metropolis. His more formidable enemy was before; but he had another that continually harassed his rear: this was the Arabs; who attacked every one at the least remove from the column, and, at the distance of three hundred toises, kept the army without communication with Alexandria.

The twenty-three beys, at the head of whom was Murad, had entrenched themselves in the village of Embabeh. Their force was said to consist of six thousand mamlucs, and a multitude of Arabs and peasants. Here, a division of the mamlucs charged with the rapidity of lightning, and the individuals (for they fight individually) displayed a bravery that would have been admirable but that it was the bravery of madmen, seeking, as it were, death in preference to victory. The division imprudently threw itself between two of the french battalions; and, seizing the moment, Bonaparte immediately ordered an attack on the entrenchments and the village. The village was turned, the entrenchments forced, and the whole army routed. Murad was pursued to Jizeh; and crowds of the mamlucs, Arabs, and peasants, vainly performing prodigies of valour, fell under the bayonet, or, attempting to escape, were drowned in the Nile. Forty pieces of cannon, eighty camels, and the baggage and provisions of the enemy, fell into the hands of the French. The rich costume of the mamlucs afforded the soldiers a considerable booty. Such is the superiority of european tactics, that, in this battle, so decisive and disastrous to the beys, the French had only ten killed, and thirty wounded.

On the morning of the next day, the principal person of Caira, headed by the kia or lieutenant of the pasha of Egypt, came to offer to Bonaparte possession of the city. Bonaparte assured them of the desire of the French to be in amity with the people of Egypt and the ottoman Porte, and

and of the scrupulous respect that would be shown to the manners, customs, and religion of the country. The pasha had left Caira in the night, with Ibrahim-bey. The deputation returned, accompanied by a detachment of the army. The people had availed themselves of the defeat and flight of the beys for an opportunity to run into some excesses: the house of Murad had been pillaged and burnt; but the proclamations of the chiefs, and the appearance of the army, re-established order.

On the twenty-third of July, two months after his departure from Toulon, Bonaparte removed his head quarters into Caira. On the loss of the battle of the Pyramids, the beys had divided their forces into two parts. The one, under the command of Murad, whose office placed him at the head of the military establishment of Egypt, and whose talents rendered his superiority universal, retired into upper Egypt, while the other, under Ibrahim, the official head of the civil department, doubled into the lower, and towards Suez and Syria. The French were in need of rest, and Bonaparte felt it necessary to devote to himself the establishment of a provisory government for the city and the country: he wished, therefore, to have deferred, not only the pursuit of Murad, but that of Ibrahim also, which latter waited for the reinforcement of mamlucs that would arrive with the caravan from Mecca: nevertheless, as the neighbourhood of Ibrahim, who employed his time in raising insurrections, was an evil to be checked, brigadier-general Leclerc, after a repose of eight days, was sent from Caira with three hundred cavalry, three companies of grenadiers, a battalion and two pieces of light artillery, with orders to take a position at Canca, and observe the motions of this bey. On the sixth of August, three other divisions of the army joined in pursuit of Ibrahim, who, though unsuccessfully,

had

had attacked Leclerc on the day after his leaving Caira. Ibrahim retreated towards Salehieh, on the confines of the desert which separates Syria from Egypt. In the course of the pursuit, Bonaparte rescued several parts of the sacred caravan, the attack of which his endeavours to prevent had failed. He gave the pilgrims, the merchants, and their women, a supper, set them on camels, and furnished them with a strong escort to Caira. On the arrival of the French at Salehieh, Ibrahim continued his retreat into Syria. The rear-guard of the bey, itself three times more numerous than the advanced of the French, was still in sight. Bonaparte's infantry was a league and an half behind; but, with the few cavalry he possessed, he followed and fell upon the mamlucs. The latter fought only in the way of protecting their retreat; but, the French having forced their way between the ranks, a combat furious beyond all proportion with the number of persons engaged, ensued. Every man fought for himself, and equal courage distinguished either side. Several of the French received numerous wounds, and about twenty were killed. In their flight, the mamlucs abandoned two pieces of cannon, and fifty camels. Bonaparte left general Caffarelli to fortify Salehieh and Belbeys, and, on the twelfth of August re-arrived at Caira.*

Ibrahim-bey, who had been wounded in the skirmish, was now in the midst of a painful journey of nine days, between the canals of the Delta and the rivulets of Syria. Murad was in the valley of Fayum, anxious, for the present, rather to avoid than attack the arms of the invaders. In a word, the beys had no longer an army. Their hostile efforts had dwindled into those of insurgents; and their hopes of success were placed rather upon revolts among

---

* *Berthier. Pieces Officielles.*

the people, than in victories over the troops. The capital was in the hands of the French, repeated defeats had broken the spirits of the friends and encouraged the animosity of the enemies of the beys, every measure that could conciliate the Egyptians with their new masters was adopted; and, for every force that was to originate within the country itself, its conquest appeared to be complete. With respect to the sultan, his acquiescence was confidently expected; and the actual possession of the French was a powerful argument for its expediency.

Thus, and in this manner, had France added to her territories that portion of the earth which nature might seem to have designed for the seat of universal empire; that portion of the earth where (one, but one mighty river, more than countervailing continents of deserts) triple and quintuple harvests offer food for a countless population; where the productions of the tropics might be innocently reared; where the trade between India and Europe was antiently conducted, and where nothing but its government prevents it from being resumed, to the manifest benefit of mankind; where, in a word, the junction of two seas, and of Africa, Asia, and Europe, form a point of communication between the whole world.

But, in whatever degree Egypt is a wealthy or important territory, in whatever degree its possession could aggrandize France, and, still more, in whatever degree it could injure Britain, in that it behoved the latter to oppose its change of possessors. The conquest of Malta had discovered the destination of the french armament; and, from that moment, with a policy and activity the reverse of which would have been folly and indolence, this government strained every nerve to render its labours fruitless. A division of the british fleet stationed in the Mediterranean,

nean, under the command of rear-admiral sir Horatio Nelson, had been in search of it from the moment of its leaving Toulon. This reached Malta two days after it had sailed for Alexandria. Seeing the tri-coloured flag on the forts, the fleet had steered directly for Candia. It passed within six leagues of the armament; and, not finding it at this island, proceeded to Alexandria. Here, it landed a dispatch for India*, and it declared itself in pursuit of the French†. It waited two days off Alexandria; when, imagining its enemy might be in the Archipelago, or off Alexandretta, it left this station. On the thirty-first of July, it returned; but, in the interim, on the first, the French had arrived, and accomplished their purpose. Thirty days had elapsed since the troops and the greater part of their stores had been landed, and the conqueror was already in the chief city of the country, at leisure to cultivate the arts of peace; but admiral Brueys, though in momentary expectation of the British, was still, with his squadron, in the road of Abu-kir, at a few leagues from Alexandria. On commencing his march for Cairo, Bonaparte had sent him a letter, desiring him to enter, within twenty-four hours, the port of Alexandria; or, if, as was apprehended, his squadron, for want of sufficient water, could not enter, to land with the utmost expedition all the artillery and equipage of the army, and repair to Corfu‡. At the time of the general debarkation, it had been ordered by Bonaparte to form the fleet in line of battle before Marabu; but, two ships of war running foul of each other, had fallen on the admiral, and obliged him to anchor on the very spot where he then was§, and which happened to be among the rocks before Alexandria‖. Two vessels

---

Pieces Officielles † *Denon.* ‡ *Pieces Officiel'es.* § *Berthier.*
‖ *Pieces Officielles*

having

having lost their anchors at this station, he ran to Abu-kîr, which offered a better anchorage. Here, Bonaparte sent officers of the engineers and artillery, who convinced the admiral that he could receive no protection from the shore, that, if the British appeared during the two or three days that, as well to discharge the artillery, as to sound the entrance of the port of Alexandria, he must remain at Abu-kir, his only resource was in cutting his cables, and that it was of the first urgency for him to stay as short a time as possible. He left Alexandria in the firm belief that, within three days, the squadron would have entered the port, or sailed for Corfu. For twenty days, the Arabs cut off his communication with Alexandria. At length, he received a letter from the admiral, wherein the latter informed him that he had been reconnoitered by several british vessels, and that he had fortified himself, with the design of waiting for the enemy, embosomed in Abu-kîr. This extraordinary resolution filled the general with the most lively alarms, and the more as the letter, written on the nineteenth of July, had not reached him till the twenty-eighth. He sent one of his aides-de-camp, with orders not to return till he had seen the squadron under sail. On his way, the aid-de-camp was killed by a party of Arabs; but, leaving Caira on the twenty-ninth, had he arrived in safety his journey had yet been useless; for, on the afternoon of the thirty-first, rear-admiral Nelson entered the bay.

The scheme of fortification upon which admiral Brueys had placed his reliance, had been that of drawing up his ships as so many batteries, supported by the shore on the rear and by an islet and the castle of Abu-kir on the right of his line; but admiral Jervis had taught the british navy the bold and grand manœuvre of cutting

the

the line of battle, and sir Horatio Nelson, pursuing this principle almost to temerity, divided the French into two parts, stationed himself between them and the shore, and placed them between two fires. This was an enterprize worthy of success, and that because it was replete with danger. It did not insure victory; it braved defeat; the contest was long; and the laurels arduously won. The french line was doubled at half past six; at about half nine, the Orient caught fire, and at ten blew up. A long period of total silence ensued. Admiral Brueys, who had been wounded at eight, had been killed an hour before the destruction of the ship; and the loss of their commander encreased the confusion of the French. Admiral Nelson had received a wound in the head, and, for some time it was apprehended to have been mortal. The action recommenced. Its horrors were encreased by the serenity of nature; a clear sky, a full moon, resplendent stars, the stillness of night, and the calmness of the sea, contrasted with the murkiness of the smoke, the flashes and the roaring of the artillery. A second ship of the French was blown up. The sun rose on the war. Nine british vessels were dismasted, and two considerably battered; but, with the exception of two ships of the line, and two frigates, which had not been engaged, the whole of the french were either absolutely destroyed, or lying unmanageable on the water, the prizes of admiral Nelson. The four still in condition to fly, discovering at dawn the havoc made among their companions, cut their cables and escaped. Rear Admiral Nelson dispatched a seventy-four with the news of his victory, while himself remained in the bay, refitting his ships for sea*.

---

* *London Gazette, &c.*

" It

"It appears to me, says general Bonaparte, in his letter to the directory, that admiral Brueys was unwilling to retire to Corfu before he was absolutely certain that he could not enter the port of Alexandria, and before the army, of which he had long been without news, was secure from all necessity of retreat; but if, in this fatal event, he had his faults, he has expiated them by a glorious death*."

Though the capture of empty vessels, after their important cargo was withdrawn, may, comparatively, appear a barren triumph, this was far from being the fact. The naval power of France in the Mediterranean was annihilated; and were the resources of Egypt what they might, and its submission to the French troops how decided soever, these things were now matters unconnected with France. A wide sea separated the two countries; and, though Egypt might be wrested from the Porte, only the consent of Great Britain could unite it with France: besides, this victory gave a grace to the tone of dictation in which the former was now to speak to the Porte.

That the Porte was disposed to leave Egypt in the hands of the French is a fact which appears unquestionable. Though the embassador had not reached Constantinople, though the french ministers might use subterfuge in their explanations, the invasion was plain language; and yet the Porte required two months for circumlocution†. This extreme patience to tardy elucidation betrays an extraordinary willingness to hear; and, even without imagining this government very anxious to part with an important province, it may be easily believed that, yielding to the necessity of the case, it was not particularly displeased to part with it to France: certainly,

---

* *Pieces Officielles.* † See the manifesto of the Porte.

France,

France, deficient in maritime strength, and constantly checked in this important particular, would have been a less dangerous neighbour than Britain; and of the designs of Britain on Egypt, the Porte, with however little foundation, had long been jealous. Warned by the example of India*, she held it as a maxim of fundamental policy, to prevent Europeans, and most of all the British, from establishing themselves in the ports of Egypt. When that country was entered by the French, she had abundant reason to prefer a peaceable admission of this nation, or the adoption of domestic measures for its expulsion, to committing her cause to Britain and Russia; and, if a fair view of her interests be at all reconcileable with this reasoning, her conduct, both before and after she entered into a coalition with these powers, affords incontestable proof that it was that which she adopted. Of the manner in which this coalition was brought about, a french officer has related, as from the mouth of the vizir, that the Porte was forced into an immediate war against France, supported by Russia and Britain, under pain of immediate war with those two powers themselves †; and the conduct of the Porte will for ever corroborate the anecdote.

Allied, however, in what her partners called a *common cause*‡, she did come forward for the deliverance of her own dominions. A plan was arranged for an irruption of the russian and ottoman troops on the side of Syria, while the British and Russians acted in the Mediterranean, where the czar, passing the Dardanelles, joined with complacency in the blockade of Malta. Aware of the designs of his enemies,

---

* See a firman of the Porte, in the preface to *Political Recollections, &c.* by *George Baldwin, Esq. &c.* † *Pieces Officielles.* ‡ *State Papers,* vol. xi. p. 61.

Bonaparte

Bonaparte prepared to crush them in the bud, or at least to free himself at one point before he was attacked at the other. The Porte, in spite of every peaceful effort, was now his enemy; and it became incumbent on him to force it, if possible, into a change of sentiment. He resolved to enter Syria, the adjoining province of the empire.

When Ibrahim-bey had crossed the desert, he was flatteringly received by Ammed-el-Jezzar, the pasha of Syria. This pasha had long been the enemy of the french nation, and he eagerly seized the opportunity of gratifying his hatred. He had recently been appointed pasha of Egypt; and, designing to take possession of his pashalic by force of arms, he had possessed himself of the fort of Arish, the antient Larissa, which was even occupied by his advanced guard.

Under all these circumstances, Bonaparte prepared an expedition, of which, besides overpowering the pasha, there was reason to hope that, if successful, it might force the Porte to seek refuge in France from the alliance of Russia and Britain.

After a rapid march, the army arrived before Arish, in the middle of February, 1799. The village was presently forced with the bayonet, the inhabitants seeking security in the fort. In the evening, the fort was blockaded. The same day, a body of mamluks, escorting provisions for Arish, trusting to the superiority of their numbers, encamped behind a deep ravine, within half a league of the place. In the night, a part of Reynier's division turned the ravine, took the camels and baggage, and either killed or made prisoners all the mamluks who did not escape by speedy flight.

Hitherto, Bonaparte had remained at Caira. He learned that an english cruizer, with some other vessels, had commenced a bombardment of Alexandria; but, conceiving

ceiving that this could have no other object than of diverting him from his expedition, he left that city to an attack from which it could receive but little injury, and repaired, with his etat-major, to Arish, where he ordered a cannonade on one of the towers. The place had been repeatedly summoned; and, as soon as a breach began to be effected, this proceeding was renewed. The garrison, says general Bethier, was composed of Arnauts and Maugrabins, all barbarians, without chiefs, and ignorant of all the usages and principles of war among polished nations. They commenced a correspondence equally singular and curious, and which alone would paint their characters. Bonaparte, who had the strongest interest in avoiding waste of his army and ammunition, patiently waited the result of their whimsical proceedings, and deferred the assault. Parleys and fighting were successively renewed. At length, on the eleventh day of the siege, the garrison, to the number of six hundred, came out, and laid down its arms, on condition of being allowed to retire to Bagdad by the desert. A party of Maugrabins entered the french service.*

After the battle of Gaza, Bonaparte crossed an immense plain to Jaffa, a sea-port town, which he was compelled to take by assault. "Never," says this general, in his official dispatch, "did the horrors of war appear to me so hideous†." Without an idea of capitulation, the orientals truly fight for death or victory. On entering the place, the garrison defended itself from house to house, and it was only by killing four thousand ‡ of the pasha's troops, and a part of the inhabitants, that the enemy could be subdued. As soon as he was master of the city and forts, Bonaparte gave orders for sparing the inhabitants; and general

---

* *Relation des Campagnes, &c.* p. 55.
† *Pieces Officielles*, P. I. p. 147.
‡ *Ibid.*

Robin,

Robin, after some difficulty, stopped the disorders which usually follow an assault. Three hundred Egyptians, prisoners of the pasha, were restored to their houses. *

With a force somewhat short of thirteen thousand men, Bonaparte at length appeared before the town of Acca, the seat of the pasha el-Jezzar. The natural strength of this place consisted in its communication with the sea: for the rest, it was to be defended rather by men than by walls. The narrow limits of this memoir scarcely allow a line to the narrative of the siege of this place, a siege which will long be remembered to the glory of the defenders. A practicable breach was made; but the besieged repulsed repeated assaults. At length, Bonaparte retreated from the walls, and returned to Cairo.

Within a short period, a descent of the Turks occasioned a second battle at Abû-kir, in which the French were victorious.†

After this battle, four or five hundred wounded Turks remained in the hands of the French. Bonaparte sent them without exchange to the padrona-bey, vice-admiral of the squadron. The vessel in which they were carried brought back the London and Frankfort newspapers, from the tenth of June. In these, Bonaparte read the reverses of

---

* Berthier.

This affair, to the french generals, which appeared deplorable, supplied Sir Sydney Smith with a story of " the inhuman massacre at Jaffa," and Mr. Morier with that of the " four thousand five hundred prisoners of war" who were made to stand still while the soldiers murdered them by charge of bayonet, and which has this poetical ending: " To this day, their skeletons, and the sands steeped with gore, attest the barbarous act." It is lamentable to hear an embassador's secretary, a man who ought to know something of the calumnies to which public characters are exposed, bring all history into contempt by relating such things as these; but he goes on to say, that after the siege of Acca, Bonaparte poisoned his wounded.

† See *Denon's Travels*, vol. ii. p. 257.

the

the army of Italy, its retreat behind Tanaro, and its evacuation of a part of Switzerland. He resolved to return to Europe; but rear-admiral Gantaume, and others, represented to him that it was almost impossible to escape the british squadron, the badness of the french frigates, the season, and the blockade of the port, considered. He returned to Caira, leaving orders with the admiral to prepare two frigates, and inform him by a dromedary of any temporary absence of the British. On the twenty-fourth of August, at six in the morning, the admiral dispatched information that the british and turkish squadrons had sailed for Cyprus. At nine in the evening orders were sent to all who were to be of the voyage, to hold themselves in readiness at midnight to accompany the commander-in-chief in an excursion in lower Egypt. Bonaparte appointed general Kleber, who was at Damiatt, to meet him at Alexandria, and general Menou, who was at Rashid, to meet him on the beach of Abû-kir. He saw the latter at five o'clock on the 29th; but general Kleber did not arrive. He apprized general Menou of his design, and gave him the command of Alexandria. The rear-admiral, informed that Bonaparte had left Caira, had dropped into the road, a league from the shore. Bonaparte resolved to depart in the night, and waited only while every one could get on board. He gave all his instructions to general Menou, with orders to forward them to general Kleber, and he embarked from Egypt*.

Nine days after the departure of general Bonaparte, general Kleber published a proclamation to the army, in which he declared that imperious motives had determined the commander-in-chief to return to France; that, acting

---

* *Pieces Officielles*, P. I. p. 345.

for the welfare of the soldiery, neither the unfavourableness of the season nor a sea covered with enemies had been able to detain him; that powerful succours would arrive, or rather a peace worthy of their labours, and restoring them to their country; that their patience and bravery emboldened him to receive a burden which had been borne by Bonaparte; and that their pressing wants should be the objects of his earnest solicitude.

Towards the latter end of December 1799, the united Turks and British invested the fort of Arish. A great part of the french garrison was in a state of indiscipline; and, on the sixth day of the siege, some of the soldiers invited the besiegers from the walls, assisted them with ropes, and opened a postern for their admittance. The Turks entered; and cut off the heads of even those who had let them in.

Before he left Egypt, Bonaparte had commenced negotiations with the Porte, proposing the ultimate evacuation of that country, but stipulating to retain it during the war with Great Britain. These negotiations he had recommended it to general Kleber to continue. The difficulties of the latter's situation increased; and he entered with more earnestness than ever into a correspondence with the vizier.

In the course of this correspondence, which terminated in a convention entered into at the vizier's camp, near Arish, sir Sidney Smith, by whose valour the town of Acca had principally been defended, and who was known to the Turks and French for many other services in Egypt, took a very active share. When it was completed, he acceded to it on the part of Britain, and, in fulfilment of its terms, issued passports for the return of the French to Europe. The operations of these in Egypt appeared to be completed; and a part of the army was
even

even embarked, when admiral earl Keith, the british officer commanding in the Mediteranean, received the following secret order :

"WHEREAS the Right Honourable Lord Grenville, one of his Majesty's principal secretaries of state, has acquainted us, by his letter of this day's date, that a dispatch has been received from Lord Elgin, his Majesty's ambassador at Constantinople, stating, that the commander of the french army in Egypt had made proposals to the turkish government, offering to evacuate that country, upon condition of being suffered to return unmolested to France; that the turkish government appeared disposed to acquiesce in this offer; and that application had been made to his lordship, requesting him to grant passports for this purpose: and whereas, in consequence of this information, Lord Grenville has signified to us his Majesty's commands, that instructions should be given to the commander-in-chief of his Majesty's fleet in the Mediterranean, enjoining him not to consent, on any account, to the return of the french army to France, or to their capitulating in any other manner than jointly to the allied powers whose forces are employed against them, or upon any other terms than that of giving up their arms, and surrendering as prisoners of war to the allied forces so employed; your lordship is hereby required and directed, in pursuance of his Majesty's commands as above signified, to govern yourself accordingly, and on no account to consent to the return of the french army in Egypt to France, or to their capitulating, except on the conditions above specified.

"In case of the surrender of the army on those terms, your lordship is on no account to admit of the return to France of the officers, or any part of the army, on an engagement not to serve until exchanged, the fallacy of all such engagements, and the bad faith with which they have been observed by the enemy, having been proved by repeated instances, particularly in the case of the seamen taken in the battle of the Nile, and afterwards landed in Egypt; but in any such capitulation, to take care that a stipulation be made for the ac-

"tual

" tual detention of the officers and men, as prisoners of war,
" in some part of the territories of the allied powers, until
" they shall be exchanged; that the vessels of every descrip-
" tion, belonging to the enemy, in the port of Alexandria,
" shall also be surrendered, and be divided amongst the allies,
" in proportion to the naval force which each of them may
" have employed at that time in the blockade of Alexandria, or
" in any other operations against the enemy.

" If it should so happen, that his Majesty's ambassador at
" Constantinople should have granted passports, before his
" Majesty's pleasure in this respect can have been signified to
" him, your lordship is in such case to direct the commanders
" of his Majesty's ships of war under your orders, who may
" fall in with any other vessels having on board any of the ene-
" my's troops, and being furnished with such passports, to de-
" clare to the commanding officer of such troops, that the said
" passports are of no validity, not being given, as the laws of
" war require, by persons having any authority for that pur-
" pose; but that in this case they should not exercise any other
" act of hostility against such ships, or the troops therein em-
" barked, than what may be necessary in order to compel the
" vessels to return with the troops to Alexandria. .

" Your lordship is to communicate these determinations by a
" flag of truce, with as little delay as possible, to the french
" army in Egypt, unless you, or the officer employed by you
" for that purpose, shall have certain information that the
" whole negociation has been broken off, and that there is no
" longer any question of such separate and unauthorized capi-
" tulation*.

This order, issued by the lords of the admiralty on the
fifteenth of December 1799, was followed up by a cor-
responding communication from lord Keith to the french

---

* This paper was presented to the House of Commons by lord Hawkesbury. See *State Papers*, vol. xi. p. 53.

gene-

general, and a total rupture of the convention ensued. On the twenty-eight of March 1800 the same authority dispatched a second order to lord Keith, apprizing him of the willingness of the king his master, under the circumstances of the case, to allow of the return of the french army to France :

" The Right Hon. Lord Grenville, one of his Majesty's
" principal secretaries of state, having, in his letter of this
" day's date, acquainted us, that in consequence of the infor-
" mation contained in the dispatches lately received from your
" lordship, Lord Elgin, and Sir Sidney Smith, relative to the
" capitulation of the french army in Egypt, his Majesty had
" been pleased to signify his commands, that instructions
" should be transmitted to your lordship, expressing his Ma-
" jesty's disapprobation of the terms entered into by the said
" capitulation, those terms appearing to his Majesty to be
" more advantageous to the enemy than their situation entitled
" them to expect, and being likely to prejudice the interests of
" the allies; by restoring to the french government the services
" of a considerable and disciplined body of troops; that be-
" sides this objection to the terms, his Majesty does not con-
" sider Captain Sir Sidney Smith as having been authorized
" either to enter into or to sanction any such agreement in his
" Majesty's name, that officer having had no special authority
" for that purpose, and the case not being one in which the
" captain commanding his Majesty's ships on the coast of Egypt
" ought to have taken upon himself to enter into an agreement
" of this nature, without the sanction of his commanding offi-
" cer; but that, as the general commanding the enemy's troops
" appears to have treated him as a person whom he *bona fide*
" conceived to possess such authority, and as a part of the
" treaty was immediately to be executed by the enemy, so that
" by annulling this transaction (in as far as his Majesty's officer
" was a party thereto), the enemy could not be replaced in the
" same situation in which he before stood, his Majesty, from
" a scrupulous regard to the public faith, has judged it proper
" that his officers should abstain from any act inconsistent with

" the

" the engagements to which Captain Sir Sidney Smith has er-
" roneously given the sanction of his Majesty's name.

" And whereas Lord Grenville has at the same time ac-
" quainted us, that with this view he shall transmit to the Earl
" of Elgin his Majesty's commands to settle with the Porte the
" form of a passport to be given in the name of his Majesty,
" not as a party to the capitulation, but as an ally to the Porte;
" and that it is his Majesty's farther pleasure, the said pass-
" ports, as well as those which may have been in the interval
" (however informally) granted by Sir Sidney Smith, are to be
" respected by his Majesty's officers; but that although, from
" the consideration above-mentioned, his Majesty does not
" think proper to obstruct the execution of this treaty by the
" Porte in the manner therein stipulated, he does not feel him-
" self bound to authorize his officers to take any active part in
" it, or to furnish any convoy or transports for its execution, or
" to take any other share in carrying it into effect; yet, if any
" application should be made to your lordship, for liberty to
" send cartel ships from France to Egppt, for the transport of
" the army, under the capitulation, your lordship is to grant
" such passports accordingly, under such restrictions and pre-
" cautions as you may judge necessary, according to circum-
" stances:—to prevent this liberty being abused to any other
" purpose, we do, in pursuance of his Majesty's commands, as
" above signified, hereby require and direct your lordship to
" govern yourself accordingly, and to give the necessary or-
" ders in consequence to the commanders of his Majesty's ships
" and under your command, taking care at the same time to
" apprize Captain Sir Sidney Smith of his Majesty's pleasure on
" the subject of his proceedings herein; and in case your
" lordship should see any ground to apprehend any intention
" on the part of the Turks, or of the Russians, to prevent the
" execution of the capitulation, or to commit any act of hos-
" tility against the french army, either before or after its em-
" barkation, we do farther direct your lordship, in such case, to
" use your utmost endeavours to persuade them to all such mea-
                                                            " sures

" sures as may be the most consistent with the faithful obser-
" vance of the engagement contracted with the enemy*."

This order arrived too late. Lord Keith had said that the French should be permitted to leave Egypt only on laying down their arms, and surrendering themselves prisoners of war. These terms had inflamed the army; and, the grand-vizier having demanded to be put in possession of Caira, a battle ensued, which was fought near the site of the antient Heliopolis, and in which the turkish forces were wholly routed. On returning to Caira, general Kleber found himself obliged to besiege that city, which shortly submitted. The fortunes of the French were now wholly changed; and France, now governed by general Bonaparte, invested with the title of first-consul, resumed her hopes of maintaining the conquest.

The rupture of the treaty of Arish has been imputed to bad faith on the part of the british government, but this a charge wholly without foundation. Much importance has been thought to attach itself to the question whether Sir Sidney Smith was or was not a minister-plenipotentiary, the addition by which he described himself to the vizier and the french general, and in which quality he treated for the evacuation of Egypt; but, in truth, the question is wholly foreign to the subject. Sir Sidney Smith was a minister-plenipotentiary; but his powers extended to nothing more than the treating of and concluding a treaty of alliance between Great Britain and the Porte†. There was no falsehood; but there was a want of spirit of co-operation on the part of the Porte, a negligence in the framing of the treaty, and

---

* This paper was presented to the House of Commons by lord Hawkesbury. See *State Papers*, vol. xi. p. 53.

† See *State Papers*, vol. xi. p. 60.

a strange

a strange misapprehension of his proper functions in sir Sidney Smith.

From the battle of Heliopolis, a period of a year and an half, during which a peace was made with Murad-bey, and during which the French had the misfortune to lose general Kleber, by assassination, must be passed over, in order to arrive at the counter-invasion of the British, under the command of general sir Ralph Abercromby*.

On the second of March, 1801, the armament arrived before Abu-kir. The weather was now serene; but, it having been obliged to sail from Marmorice in a very imperfect state of preparation†, an immediate landing could not be made, and a severe gale of wind rendered this impracticable during the four following days. At length, on the seventh, the wind abating, the general reconnoitred the shore, and determined on the place of landing. The delay had afforded leisure to the French for assembling a large body of troops; but, in spite of a vigorous resistance, the British, on the morning of the eighth, gained possession of the peninsula‡. On the ninth, the remainder of the army was landed, and on the twelfth marched within two leagues of Alexandria,

---

* In this interval, also, several of the learned and scientific persons, who have been described as accompanying the expedition, and who had already traveled into upper Egypt, commenced a second journey: " I hope, says general Menou, " that they will now reach the oases, and penetrate an hundred or an hundred and fifty leagues above Assuan. We are assured that there are still existing ruins much more considerable than those of Thebes and Dendera: the same is said of the oases. Murad-bey offers to asist the research by every means in his power." " At this moment," he continues, " we are working hard at Saccara. I am about to cause new researches at the great pyramids. It is suspected, with much reason, that there exist other chambers above those already known." *Pieces Officielles*, P. II.

† London Gazette.   ‡ *Political Recollections, &c.*

and

and one of the enemy, who had posted himself advantageously on a ridge, with his right on the canal, and his left on the sea. The enemy attacked on the thirteenth, but was driven under the walls of Alexandria. On the twenty-first, he brought nearly his whole force into action, and the fortune of the day was with the British; but sir Ralph Abercromby received a wound, of which he died on the twenty-eighth: "I believe," says general Hutchinson, the officer second in command, "that he was wounded early in the action, but he concealed his situation from those about him, and continued in the field, giving his orders with that coolness and perspicuity which had ever marked his character, till long after the action was over, when he fainted with loss of blood. Here, if it were permitted for a soldier to regret any one who has fallen in the service of his country, I might be excused for lamenting him, more than any other person; but it is some consolation to those who tenderly loved him, that, as his life was honourable, so was his death glorious.*"

Under the orders of general Hutchinson, the enemy, now besieged in Alexandria, was cut off from all communication with the interior, by opening the canal into the lake Mareotis, which was entered by sir Sidney Smith, with seven gun-boats. The French cut the dyke in another place, to let the waters from lake Mareotis out upon the plain.

On the twenty-seventh of June, Caira was reduced; and, on the twenty-eight of August, Alexandria. Both Caira and Alexandria surrendered by capitulation; the principal article of which stipulated, that the French and auxiliary troops should be embarked and conveyed to the

---

* *London Gazette.*

french ports on the Mediterranean, with their arms, artillery, baggage, and effects, at the expense of the allied powers*.

On the ninth of October, preliminaries of peace were entered into between France and the Ottoman Porte†.

---

* *London Gazette.*   † *State Papers,* vol xi. p. 31.

THE AUTHOR'S PREFACE.*

AN Author's principal object, when he resolves to write a preface, is to give an idea of his work. I shall fulfil this species of duty by inserting the discourse which I had intended to deliver to the institute of Kaira, on my return from upper Egypt.

---

* M. Denon has prefixed to his book the following Dedication:

TO BONAPARTE:

To join the celebrity of your name with the splendour of the monuments of Egypt, is to link the glorious triumphs of our own age with the fabulous times of history; it is to re-kindle the ashes of Sesostris and of Mendes, like you conquerors, like you benefactors.

Europe, in learning that, in one of your most memorable expeditions, I accompanied you, will feel an eager interest in my work. I have neglected nothing to render it worthy of the hero to whom I desired to present it.

VIVANT DENON.

" You

"You have told me, citizens, that the institute expected me to give it an account of my travels in upper Egypt, by reading, in its several sittings, the journal that should accompany the drawings I have brought. The desire of gratifying the wish of the institute will hasten the arrangement of a crowd of notes, which I have taken without any other design than that of preserving the memory of all that dailily offered itself to my curiosity. I was taversing a country which Europe scarcely knows but by name; all it contained, therefore, was worthy of description; and I easily foresaw that, on my return, every one would interrogate me upon that which, according to his usual studies, or personal character, most excited his curiosity. I have drawn objects of all kinds; and if, in this country, because they represent only what they have under their eyes, I am fearful of fatiguing those to whom I show my numerous productions, arrived in France, I shall perhaps reproach myself for not having multiplied them still more; or, to speak more strictly, I shall lament that circumstances allowed me neither time nor opportunities. If my zeal has employed all that my means afforded, this

this have been powerfully seconded by the commander-in-chief, in whom the vastest conceptions produces no forgetfulness of details. As if he had known that the object of my journey was that of visiting the antiquities of upper Egypt, he sent me with the division that was to atchieve the conquest of that country. In general Desaix, I have found a scholar, a man of taste, a lover of the arts; and he has indulged me with every attention that circumstances allowed him to bestow. In general Belliard, I have found equanimity of character, friendship, and unabating kindness; in the officers, amenity; in all the soldiers of the twenty-first demi-brigade, an obliging cordiality; in a word, I was in some sort identified with the battalion they formed, and in the midst of which, if I may thus express myself, I had so establised my homestead, that, for the most part, I either forgot that I was making war, or that war was foreign to my occupations.

"As we had to pursue an enemy always on his saddle, the movements of the division were always sudden and numerous. I was obliged therefore sometimes rapidly to pass the most interesting antiquities, and some-

sometimes to stop where there was nothing to be observed : but, if I have experienced the fatigue of fruitless marches, I have experienced also that it is often advantageous to take a first glimpse of great objects before we proceed, to their parts ; that if at first they dazzle by their number, they afterwards class themselves in the mind by reflection ; that, if first impressions are to be carefully preserved, it is only in the absence of the object that gave them birth that they can be usefully examined and analyzed. I have also thought that an artist, on commencing his journey, should lay down all professional self-love ; that he should not occupy his attention with that which will or will not produce a fine picture, but with that general interest which the aspect of the scene he proposes to draw necessarily inspires. I have already been recompensed for the abandonment of this self-love that I have practised, by the complaisant curiosity which you, citizens, have manifested, in examining with eagerness the immense number of drawings I have brought; drawings which I have generally made on my knee, or standing, or even on horseback : I have never been able

to

to complete a single one to my wish, because during a whole year I have not once found a table sufficiently steady for using a ruler.

" It is to reply, then, to your questions that I have made this multitude of designs, often too small, because our marches were too precipitate for attacking the minutiæ of the objects of which I wished to bring away at the least the aspect and the effect. It was thus that I took in the mass the pyramids of Sakarah, over the site of which I galloped to fix myself for a month in the mud-houses of Benisuef. I have employed this time in comparing the characters, and in drawing the figures, and the costumes, the fabrics, and the landscape of the villages, of the people who now inhabit Egypt.

" At length, I saw the portico of Hermopolis; and the vast masses of its ruins gave me the first image of the colossal architecture of the Egyptians: on each rock that composed this edifice, there seemed to be engraved, POSTERITY, ETERNITY.

" Soon after, Denderah (Tintyris) taught me that it was not only in the doric, the ionic, and the corinthian orders, that the beauty

beauty of architecture was to be sought; that wherever there existed harmony of parts, there was beauty. The morning led me to these edifices, the evening tore me away, more agitated than satisfied. I had seen an hundred things; I had overlooked a thousand: I had entered for the first time into the archives of the sciences and arts. I had a presentiment that I could see nothing finer in Egypt; and twenty journeys that I afterwards made to *Denderah* have confirmed me in this opinion. The sciences and the arts, united by good taste, have decorated the temple of Isis: astronomy, morals, metaphysics, here have forms; and these forms adorn the cielings, the frises, and the sub-basements, with as much grace as our fribbling and insignificant arabesks our parlours.

" We continually advanced. I avow it, a thousand times I trembled, lest Murâd-bey, weary of flight, should return no more, nor try again the fortune of battle. I feared that that of Samanhut had been about to be the end of the drama: but, in the midst of the fight, he thought that the desert would be more fatal to us than his arms; and Desaix once more saw the opportunity for destroying him

him escape, and I, the hope of following him beyond the tropic re-vive.

" We marched towards Thebes; Thebes, of which the very name fills the imagination with sublime remembrances. As if it could have slipped from me, I drew it at the furthest distance at which I could perceive it; and, in making that sketch, I believed I felt that the sentiment by which I was actuated would be partaken by yourselves. We were obliged to cross it rapidly; scarcely had we descried an antiquity before we were obliged to leave it.

" There was a colossus which could be measured only by the eye, and by the sentiment of wonder which it occasioned; on the right, excavated and sculptured mountains; on the left, temples, which, at more than half a league, resembled still other rocks; palaces, other temples from which I was torn; and I turned mechanically to look for the hundred gates, a poetic expression, by which, in a single word, Homer intended to paint the superb city, extending to a width that Egypt but with difficulty contained, and overcharging the earth with the weight of its temples. Seven visits have not satisfied the

the curiosity excited by the first: it was only at the fourth that I could cross the river.

" Further on, Hermontis would have seemed magnificent had I not found it almost at the gates of Thebes. The temple of Esneh, the antient *Latopolis*, struck me as the perfection of the arts among the Egyptians, as one of the finest productions of antiquity; that of Edfu, or Apollinopolis-magna, as one of the grandest, the least injured, and the best situated of all the edifices of Egypt: in its present state, it still appeared to me a commanding fortress.

" It was here that the fate of my travels was decided, and that we set forward irrevocably on our march for Syené (Assuan); it was in this passage of the desert that for the first time I felt the weight of years, on which, in engaging in this expedition, I had not reckoned; my courage rather than my strength had sustained me to this point. Here, I quitted the army to remain with the demi-brigade that was to confine Murâd in the desert. Proud of finding the confines of my country the same with those of the Roman empire, I dwelt with glory in the quarters

quarters of the three cohorts by which they were formerly defended. During the two-and-twenty days that I remained on this celebrated spot, I took possession of all that lay around it. I pushed my conquests into Nubia itself, beyond Philoë, that delightful island, the treasures of which must yet be snatched from its wild inhabitants: six journeys, and five days of siege, at length gained me admittance to its temples. Feeling all the importance of making you acquainted with the place I had inhabited, and all the curiosities it contains, I drew even the rocks, even the granite-quarries whence have issued Egypt's colossal figures, her obelisks still more colossal, her rocks, overspread with hieroglyphics. With the outlines, I could have wished to have brought you the models of every interesting object. Unable to make a map of the country, I took a bird's-eye view of the entrance of the Nile into Egypt, and views of this river, rolling its waters among the sharp rocks of granite which seem to have marked the limits of burning Ethiopia and of a country more happy and more temperate. Leaving for ever those barren regions, I reposed in the verdant Elephan-

Elephantine, the garden of the tropics: I examined, I measured, all the antiquities it retains, and retired with regret from this peaceful abode, where gentle occupations had restored my health and strength.

" On the right bank of the Nile, I found Ombos, the city of the Crocodile, that of Iuno-Lucina, and Coptos, near which I had to defend my spoils against the atrocious fanaticism of the Meccans.

" Fixed at Keneh, I accompanied those who crossed the desert to place a barrier at Cosseir against new emigrations from Arabia. I saw what might be called the division of the chain of the Mokatam, the sterile borders of the Red-sea: I came to understand, to revere, that patient animal which nature seems to have placed in this region, to repair the error she had committed in making it a desert. I returned to Keneh, whence with each expedition of the detachment, and wherever it was sent, I successively set out to revisit Edfu, Esneh, Hermontis, Thebes, Denderah, Edfu, and Thebes again. If the love of antiquity often made me a soldier, complaisance for my researches often made the soldiers antiquarians. It was in these latter journies

journies that I visited the tombs of kings; that, in these mysterious repositories, I gained an idea of the art of painting among the Egyptians, of their arms, their houshold furniture, their utensils, their instruments of music, their ceremonies, and their triumphs: it was in these latter journies that I obtained conviction that the hieroglyphics sculptured on the walls were not only books of this learned people. After finding, in the low-reliefs, three persons in the act of writing, I further found that little roll of papyrus, that unique manuscript, which has already become the object of your curiosity; that frail rival of the pyramids, that precious pledge of a preserving climate, that monument which even time has reverenced, and which forty ages place in the rank of the most antient of all books.

" It was in these latter excursions that I endeavoured, by collecting similarities, to complete my collection of hieroglyphic pictures; it was in thinking of you, citizens, and of all the scholars of Europe, that I found courage to copy, with scrupulous exactitude the minute details of dull pictures, stripped of sense, and in which I could take

take no interest but with the assistance of your knowledge.

"On my return, citizens, laden with my works, the weight of which had grown with every day, I forgot the fatigue they cost me, in the thought that, completed under your eyes, and with the aid of your advice, I might one day render them to my country useful, and to you a worthy homage."

TRAVELS

TRAVELS

IN

UPPER AND LOWER EGYPT.

M. VIVANT DENON had long entertained an ardent desire to visit Egypt. A military expedition against that country was ordered by the directorial government of France, and general Bonaparte, who had been appointed commander in chief, invited him to make one among the men of learning and science who were to accompany the army, and by whose labours it was intended to adorn the triumph, secure the conquest, and multiply the benefits of this memorable enterprize. The possibility now presented, of gratifying the wish of his life, awakened it with new vigour; and, after providing for the comfort of those whose existence depended upon his own, M. Denon left Paris, together with his nephew, whom the brave and unfortunate Du Falga had done him the kindness to make his official companion.

M. Denon arrived at Toulon on the 13th of May, 1798;* and on the next day, embarked on board the Juno, one of the frigates destined to form the advanced-guard of the fleet. From the 14th to the 19th† the wind continued unfavourable, but on the latter day it changed to the northwest; and at dawn, the fleet and its convoy were in motion. By noon, the surrounding sea was covered with vessels. Thousands of men were leaving their country, their fortunes, their friends, their children, and their wives, almost all of whom knew nothing of the course they were about to steer, nor indeed of any thing that concerned their voyage, except that Bonaparte was the leader.

On the 20th of May,‡ the Orient, the admiral's ship, and on board of which was Bonaparte, left the harbour. Each vessel took her position in the order of sailing, and the voyage commenced, under a fair wind. The frigates were foremost; after these, followed the Orient, with the advice-boats, and the ships of the line: the convoy coasted between the islands of Hieres and the Levant. Two frigates were dispatched with orders for the convoy from Genoa to join. On the 22nd of May, the fleet was off St. Florence, in the island of Corsica.

The fleet steered for cape Corsica, keeping an

---

* 24 Floréal. An 6. French calendar.   † 30 Floréal

‡ 1 Prairial.

easterly course, and leaving Genoa and the ligurian shore on its left. Its military line was a league in extent; and the semicircle formed by the convoy, covered, at the least, the space of six. M. Denon counted a hundred and sixty sail of the latter, without being able to reckon the whole. After passing between cape Corsica and the island of Capraya, the light division of the fleet, at five o'clock on the 24th*, had the island of Pianosa on its east; but to the west of this island, the wind failed, and the heavy convoy lay motionless on the ocean. On the 26th, the frigates were before the mouths of the Bonifacio. The convoy had brought up, and the fleet might have made good progress, had it not been necessary to lay-to for the arrival of the divisions of Ajaccio and Civita-Veccia. On the morning of the 27th, land was entirely out of sight. At noon on the 29th, the frigates received orders to sail for Cagliari, and to return to Porto-Veccio, if an enemy of superior force were already there. On the evening of the 31st, M. Denon saw the point of Cagliari.

On the 5th of June,† orders were received for forming anew; an event which encouraged M. Denon and his companions to hope, that they were now to proceed in earnest, and make some advance toward the end of their voyage. The Diana led the van. The Juno passed the signals

---

* 5 Priarial.   † 17 Prairial.

to the Alcesta, by which they were in like manner passed to the Spartan, by her to the Aquilon, and finally, to the Admiral. In the case of the Diana giving chase to an enemy, the five other frigates were to stretch their sails to join her.

This evening, the crew of the Juno saw some small dolphins under the bows of the vessel; but while they were preparing to take them, the fish disappeared. M. Denon had an opportunity of observing them closely. He remarked, that they swam with an undulating motion resembling that of a ship; and that they curved their bodies in this manner when they sprang out of the water, which they sometimes did, to the distance of twenty feet. Their form was elegant; and their rapid movements conveyed to M. Denon, the idea rather of the gaiety of a tilt, than of the voracity of an animal hunting for prey.

On the 6th, a signal was made to the Juno, to pass the night in company with the fleet. M. Denon requested to be awakened at day-break, if land was then still in sight.

At half past three, on the morning of the 7th, he went upon deck, and the first beams of the sun discovered to him, that the whole fleet and convoy, making way, had sailed for the island of Malta. Sicily, with the cheerful and classic shores of which he had the day before feasted his eyes and his imagination, had disappeared. The weather was fair, but the wind was too still to allow

allow of fast sailing; and a chase made on a strange sail separated the Juno from the fleet, which she was not afterwards able to rejoin. A fish of eighty feet in length, passed within sight of the vessel.

At six, on the 8th of June,* the Juno discovered the island of Gozo, at the distance of seven leagues. This morning, all the ships of war passed under the admiral's stern. Since its leaving Toulon, this was the first time the Juno had approached the Orient; and the evolution appeared to the crew of the former, so sublime and awful, that except that they delivered, and this in a low tone of voice, the customary compliment, they preserved the most reverential silence.

On the 19th, the Juno weathered the northern extremity of Gozo; and a vessel being sent to reconnoitre several strange sail which were discovered a-head, it was found that general Desaix's division, the convoy from Civita-Veccia, of which they consisted, had kept along the coast of Italy, passed the straits of Messina, and got the start, by a few days, of the main fleet, on its way to Malta.

At five in the afternoon, the Juno passed Cumino and Cuminotto, two islands which lie between Gozo and Malta, and which, with These, compose the whole territory of the grand master. At six, Malta was in sight. Two wretched barks

---

* 20 Prairial.

came with tobacco, for sale. At night, not a single light appeared in the city. The Juno was off the entrance of the port, within cannon-shot of the fortress of St. Elmo. All the boats were ordered out. At nine o'clock, a signal was made for the frigates to form. There was scarcely any wind. In making the night-signals relative to these movements, both to the ships of war and the convoy, several muskets and guns were fired; and on their discharge, even the sole remaining light in the port was extinguished. The Juno's captain went on board the admiral, but the orders he received were not revealed.

On the 10th, at four in the morning, floating with tide, the Juno fell to leeward of the island. Taking advantage of a light breeze, a simicircular line was formed by the vessels, one extremity of which approached the point of St. Katharine, and the other, at a league's distance, the left of the city, completing a blockade of the port. The Juno was in the centre, off the forts St. Elmo and St. Angelo. The convoy was gone to anchor between the islands of Cumino and Gozo. A moment after, a cannon was discharged from fort St. Katharine, directed at the boats which approached the shore, and which comprized the debarkation of general Desaix. This was immediately followed by a second gun from the castle which commands the city, and on which the ecclesiastical standard was instantly displayed.

At

At the same time, at the other end of the circumvallation of vessels, the shallops landed the french soldiers and artillery. These were scarcely drawn up on the shore, before they marched against two posts, the defenders of which gave way, after a moment's resistance. Immediately, a fire was commenced on the boats and vessels, from the batteries of all the forts; and this fire was kept up till evening, with an imprudent precipitation which led to difficulties and confusion. At ten o'clock in the morning, the troops ascended the first eminence, and marched towards the rear of the city, in order to oppose a sortie of the besieged, whom they drove within their walls, and under their batteries. The firing was continued till the day had wholly withdrawn. This attempt, made by the knights, in conjunction with some of the country people, had a fatal issue: a commotion had arisen in the city, and on their return thither, many of the knights were massacred.

The wind fell; but the Juno availed herself of what remained of the breeze, to station herself nearer the other vessels, fearing lest, in the event of a calm, she should be at the mercy of two maltese galleys, which had anchored at the entrance of the harbour. M. Denon, who was constantly on deck, with a telescope in his hand, had an opportunity of observing whatever passed among the citizens. On the first day, every thing was warlike.

warlike. The knights in grand council; a perpetual communication between the city and the forts, to the latter of which all kinds of provisions and ammunition was sent. On the second day, the motion was merely that of agitation; only a part of the knights were in uniform; they disputed among themselves, and ceased to act.

On the 11th, at day-break, every thing remained the same as the evening before. A slow and insignificant fire was continued. A bark left the port, which was hailed, and conducted to the Orient: this bore the ecclesiastical standard; but at eleven o'clock, a second, bearing the parliamentary flag, brought the knights who chose to abandon Malta, and who were unwilling to be numbered among those by whom resistance was made to the French. Their communications manifested, that the resources of the Maltese were almost wholly exhausted. At four o'clock, the Juno was within half cannon-shot; and M. Denon, in surveying the forts, saw fewer men than guns.

The gates of the forts were closed, and all intercourse with the city had ceased; circumstances which betrayed a misunderstanding and want of confidence between the citizens and the knights. Aid-de-camp Junot was sent with the ultimatum of the general. Some minutes after, a deputation of twelve maltese commissioners went on board the Orient. The Juno was now perfectly

perfectly opposite the city, which, seen in this position, displayed the long streets which pierce its whole extent from north to south.

On the 12th, in the morning, M. Denon learned that the general's aid-de-camp had been received by the citizens with acclamations. By the assistance of his telescope, he discovered that the gate which closes the entrance of fort St. Elmo was assailed by a multitude of the populace, while those within sat on the batteries, silent, and in the attitudes of men in fearful expectation. At half past eleven, the parliamentary bark, which had remained with the Orient since the preceding evening, made towards the shore; the Juno received a signal to hoist the standard of her republic, and the next moment another, by which those on board were informed, that Malta belonged to France.

This island, says M. Denon, was to become a staple between our country, and that which we were going to possess. Its surrender had completed the conquest of the Mediterranean, and never had France arrived at so high a pitch of power. At five o'clock, the french troops entered the forts, under a salute from the fleet, of five hundred guns.

Geographers hesitate, remarks M. Denon, whether to join Malta with Europe or with Africa; but the figure, the moral character, the colour, and

and the language of the Maltese, ought to decide the question in favour of the latter.

The turkish and arabian slaves were released; and never was joy evinced in a more expressive manner than by these injured people. When they met a Frenchman, gratitude shone in their eyes, in the most interesting manner. To form an idea of the extent of their good fortune on this occasion, it must be known that their government would never have ransomed or exchanged them; that the burden of their chains was not lightened by a single hope; that they could not even entertain a thought of the end of their affliction.

On the 19th of June*, Bonaparte withdrew from Malta; leaving on the island, besides four thousand men, under the command of general Vaubois, an officer of the engineers, another of artillery, and a civil commissioner, all those who from any cause, wished to proceed no further on the voyage.

The aspect of Malta is barren; but M. Denon beheld with admiration, that every little rock, which has but the smallest portion of earth to cover it, forms, without exception, a delightful and abundant garden, in the medium climate of which all the plants of Asia and Africa might flourish. This first stove, as it were, he observes,

---

* 1 Messidor.

might

might be made to supply another at Toulon; and thus, by degrees, these productions might be brought to Paris. By this plan, they would be preserved from those destructive shocks which are occasioned by immediate removal into an extremely different climate; and, perhaps, a naturalization effected of a large number of those exotics which are now imported yearly, at great expense, and which in the second year languish, and in the third perish. The experiments already made on animals, adds M. Denon, seem to me to support this system of graduation.

The whole day of the 19th of June was employed in collecting the army, the light squadron, and the convoy. Towards six o'clock, the signal was given for sailing. The movement became general in every sense, and confusion ensued.

Obliged to yield a passage to the admiral, it was not perceived by the Juno, till too late, that the Leoben frigate was falling foul of her. The officer on deck insisted that the Leoben was in the wrong, and strictly persevered in his tactics. The captain, more anxious to save his frigate than convince the Leoben of her mistake, ordered a manœuvre. The officer ordered a different one; and the consequence was, a moment of inaction. There was, indeed, no time to act. The vessels approached each other, and the rigging of each was entangled and broken. A demi-manœuvre of the Leoben caused her to present her side only;
and

and the concussion was weakened by the tiers of guns which projected from either ship. The crash, however, was terrible; and the cries of four hundred men, whose arms were spread towards heaven, led M. Denon to believe that the Leoben had become the victim of the disaster. In endeavouring to clear the Leoben before she struck a second time, the Juno's starboard became exposed to the Artemisia, which was advancing in a contrary direction; and a seventy-two, which there had not been time to observe, ran her bowsprit over the forecastle. The alarm was now at its height. The second movement of the Leoben, presented her beams to the Juno, and laid her fore-yard on the deck of the latter. This incident, which might have been a very fatal one, was turned to advantage. The sailors of the Juno, and especially the Turks who had been released from the Maltese, ran to the yard, and made so effectual efforts to turn it away, that the blow, which did not receive any strength from the wind, was deadened; and the Juno escaped her danger for this time, at the trivial cost of a hole in her side-planks, made by the anchor of the Leoben. By this time, the Artemisia had glided under the stern of the Juno; the ship of the line also had passed; the efforts made to disembarrass the yard of the Leoben had repulsed her to a sufficient distance, and these several dangers, which had accumulated upon each other like clouds

clouds during a storm, had dissipated themselves as quickly.

On the 24th of June*, the Juno discovered the western coast of Candia†. On the 25th, at five in the morning, M. Denon found that the vessel had steered in a direction for the east of that island, without having advanced nearer than she was the evening before. During the night, the wind had been so violent that the whole convoy was dispersed; and the morning was passed in re-assembling it, and in shortening sail, to give it time to come up. It was during this manœuvre, that by means of a thick fog, chance concealed the french fleet from the english, which, at six leagues distance, steering westerly, went to seek it on the north of Candia.

On the evening of the 26th, the Juno received the signal to drop under the stern of the Orient. Her captain was ordered on board; and at his return, M. Denon was informed to his inexpressible joy, that this frigate was commanded to hasten forward to Alexandria, and there to learn of the french consul, whether the sailing of the fleet were known, and what were the dispositions of that city, in regard to the enterprize. In a word, that she was to be the first to anchor on the shore of Africa; and that she was charged with the duty of collecting together the Frenchmen

---

* 7 Messidor. † The ancient Crete.

resident

resident in Alexandria, and sheltering them from the first emotions of the inhabitants, on the approach of the fleet. From that moment, every sail was unfurled, to run with the utmost possible expedition the sixty leagues of water that were to be crossed; but there was scarcely any wind during the whole of the 26th and the following day.

After having put the Franks on their guard, the Juno was directed to return to the fleet, which she was to find cruizing at six leagues from cape Brulé. At noon, on the 27th, she was within thirty leagues of Alexandria; and at four o'clock, *land* was cried from the main-top. At six, it was seen from the deck. There was a breeze during the whole night; and at day-break, M. Denon saw the coast to the west, extending like a white ribband along the blue horizon of the sea. It was not variegated with a single tree, or a single house. He thought it wore the appearance, not of the melancholy of nature, but of her ruin, but of silence and of death. The prospect, however, did not lessen the cheerfulness of the soldiers: one of them, pointing to the desert with his finger, said to another, " There! look at the six acres that are decreed you!" The general laugh which this sally drew forth, may serve as a proof, adds M. Denon, that courage is disinterested, or at least that it has its source in noble sentiments.

This part of the Mediterranean is dangerous during

ring tempestuous weather, and in the fogs of winter, because on these occasions the low coast disappears, and can only be seen when it is too late; but the Juno had the good fortune to weather cape Durazzo in safety, steering east by south. At one o'clock in the afternoon, a lieutenant was sent ashore.

When the long shadows of evening, says M. Denon, had marked the outlines of the city, I distinguished the two ports; the lofty walls, flanked by numerous towers, no longer inclosing any thing but heaps of sand, and a few gardens, the pale green of whose palm-trees scarcely tempered the ardent whiteness of the soil; the turkish castle, the mosks*, their minarets; the celebrated pillar of Pompey; and my imagination went back to the past: I saw art triumph over nature; the genius of Alexandria employ the active hands of commerce, to lay, on a barren coast, the foundations of a magnificent city, and select that city as the depository of the trophies of the conquest of a world; the Ptolomies invite the arts and sciences, and collect that library which it took barbarism so many years to consume: it was there, said I, thinking of Cleopatra, of Cæsar, and of Anthony, that the empire of glory was sacrificed

---

* The word *mosk* comes from the french *mosque*, which is a coruption of the arabic *masged*, or *masjed*, or the turkish *misjid*, or *mesjed*.

to

to the empire of voluptuousness! After this, I saw ferocious ignorance establish itself on the ruins of the master-pieces of the arts, labouring to destroy them, and unable, notwithstanding, even yet to have disfigured those beautiful fragments which display the noble principles of their first design. I was awakened from this revery, this luxury of ruminating on grand objects, by the discharge of a cannon from our vessel, intended to bring-to a boat which made every use of the wind in order to enter Alexandria in spite of us, and carry, beyond a doubt, the news of our design. Night soon hid it from our view. Our uneasiness concerning it encreased every moment, and grew into alarm. At midnight, we were hailed by the voices of persons in fear; and presently our consul and his druggerman* were along our side, escaping from the vengeful sabre, and from the effects of the terror which had spread throughout the city.

By these persons, the Juno was informed, that an english fleet of forty ships of war had left Alexandria the evening before; that the English had declared they were looking for the french fleet, in order to fight it; that the English had been taken for French, and that the whole

---

* This word, which the French sometimes write *drogman*, and sometimes *truchement*, is a corruption of *torjmán* or *tarjamán*: it signifies, an *interpreter*.

country,

country, already warned of the french expedition, and of the capture of Malta, had risen on the instant, fortified the castle, added a militia to the regular troops, and assembled an army of Bedùins*.

The shereef had consented to the consul's coming on board the Juno, but in the actual custody of seamen of Alexandria, who were to take him back, and from whom M. Denon learned that the English had steered for Cyprus, where they thought the French were.

The Juno returned to meet the fleet. With the earliest dawn of day, she discovered the first division of the convoy, and at seven o'clock was along side the Orient.

M. Denon accompanied the consul into the presence of Bonaparte. The report they had to give was perplexing; the English had been seen, and might come up the next moment; the wind was strong; the convoy was mingled with the fleet, and in a degree of confusion that, in the event of the enemy's appearance, threatened the most disastrous defeat. Bonaparte caused the particulars he had heard to be repeated over again; and, after a silence of a few minutes, gave orders for debarkation.

Dispositions were made to bring the convoy as near to land as the danger of running ashore,

---

* The ù has the sound of *oo*, answering to the french *ou*.

during a high wind, would permit. The ships of war formed an outer circle of defence. All their sails were furled, and their anchors cast. Scarcely was this done, when the Juno was directed to cruise before the city, as near as the wind allowed, and to make false attacks, in order to effect a diversion.

The wind increased. The sea was so high, that the Juno vainly laboured, during all the rest of the day, to weigh her anchor. The night was too stormy to perform this operation, without risk of the vessel's being driven upon the boats and transports. These, however, effected a debarkation, though with unheard of difficulty and danger. The boats received one, by one, and at random, those who descended from the vessels; when they were filled, the waves appeared every instant on the point of swallowing them; or, at the mercy of the wind, they were forced upon others, or exposed to the same accident themselves; and, after escaping all this, on gaining the shore, they knew not where to touch, without bilging on the breakers. In the middle of the night, a boat without a tiller passed under the stern of the Juno, and called for help. A cable was thrown out; but scarcely was it caught by the unfortunate people when it became necessary to cut it; for, the waves dashing the boat against the Juno, it was on the point of being upset. The cries of the people in the boat, at the moment they found themselves

themselves abandoned, went to the souls of those on board the Juno; and the silence which succeeded gave birth to the most dismal apprehensions. The darkness redoubled the terrors of the night; and the debarkations were as slow as they were calamitous. On the next day, however, by six in the morning, a sufficient number of troops had gained the shore, to attack and take a little fort, called Marabût.

On the 2d of July*, the sea was calmer. At noon, the soldiers who had been carried by the Juno were under the center of the walls of Alexandria, near Pompey's pillar, and behind some hillocks, composed of the ruins of the antient city. These old walls presented nothing to the troops but a series of breaches; a single file shook them, and made a passage for the rest; but on approaching some bad fosses, they discovered more walls than they had at first perceived. A fire from the besieged, of extraordinary vivacity, here astonished them for a moment, but did not check their impetuosity. Under the fire of the enemy, they sought the most practicable breach. This they found at the west angle, where was the antique fort of Kibotos. They commenced an assault; and Kleber, Menou, and Lescale, were thrown down by the fire, and by the fall of part of the walls. Koraïm, shereef of Alexandria, who fought

---

* 14 Messidor.

at every point, seeing Menou fall, thought that the commander in chief was mortally wounded: a mistake which sustained for a moment the courage of the besieged. No one fled. Death on the breach was the only overthrow submitted to; and two hundred of the French actually fell.

The Juno was ordered to protect the entrance of the convoy into the old port; and M. Denon took this opportunity of going on shore. An old prejudice had said, that if ever a frankish vessel entered the old port, the empire of Alexandria was lost to the moslems; and, for the moment, the Juno's boat seemed to verify the prediction.

On reaching the city, there was no person to receive or repulse a stranger. With great difficulty, M. Denon and his companions persuaded some beggars, whom they found squatted on their heels, to show them the way to the headquarters. The houses were all shut up. Those who had been afraid to fight had fled; and those who had not been killed, concealed themselves lest, according to the oriental practice, they should be put to death by the victors. All was new to Europeans; the soil, the buildings, the persons, the costume, and the language of the inhabitants. The first scene that presented itself was a vast burying ground, covered with innumerable tombs, raised in white marble, upon white earth; and where a few meagre women, wrapt in long and ragged garments, looked like so many ghosts,

ghosts, wandering among the graves: the silence was interrupted only by the cries of the kites who hovered over this asylum of the dead. From the burying ground, they passed into narrow streets, equally solitary. In passing through Alexandria, M. Denon called to mind, or rather thought himself reading, the description given of that city by M. Volney; and he observes that form, colour, sensation, and every thing else is there painted with such a degree of truth, that if the same traveller had described all Egypt in that manner, no one would ever think it necessary to make another picture.

In his whole walk through this long city, M. Denon regarded it as a melancholy one, and found nothing that resembled Europe and its cheerfulness but the noise and activity of the sparrows. In its dogs, he could not recognize the friend of man, the faithful and generous companion, the gay and loyal courtier: they were here, morose egotists, strangers to the master under whose roof they were sheltered; independent, but still slaves, they mistrusted him whose abodes they nevertheless defended, but whose dead body they would without horror devour. M. Denon describes the number and ferociousness of these dogs as a subject of serious alarm to strangers.

On reaching the head-quarters, he found Bonaparte surrounded by the principal persons of the city, and the members of the old government, whose

whose oaths of fidelity he received: "I have taken you with arms in your hands," said Bonaparte to the shereef Koraim, "and I might treat you as a prisoner; but you have displayed courage, and as I believe courage inseparable from honour, I return you your arms, and believe that you will be as faithful to the republic as you have been to a bad government." M. Denon remarked in the physionomy of this man, whom he denominates shrewd, dissimulation shaken but not vanquished by the generous frankness of the commander-in-chief. He was not yet acquainted with their strength, nor sure that what had passed in the morning had not been the consequence of surprise; but when he saw thirty thousand men and trains of artillery, he endeavoured to win the favour of Bonaparte. He quitted the head-quarters no more: Bonaparte had retired to rest, before he left the anti-chamber; conduct worthy of remark, in a moslem.

On the 4th of June, M. Denon accompanied the general on a reconnoitring party. They visited all the forts, that is to say the ruins, and found them very indifferent edifices, or rather bad guns lying on a few stones that served to mount them. Bonaparte's orders were to pull down such as could be of no service, and to repair only such as might keep off the Bedúins. He gave all his attention to the batteries that might defend the ports,

They

They went close to Pompey's pillar. It fares with this monument, says M. Denon, as with that of almost every other celebrated object; it loses on being approached. It was named the pillar of Pompey in the fifteenth century, when learning began to revive from its lethargy. Learned men, rather than observers, were eager at that period to give names to all the remains of antiquity; these names have been handed down from age to age, without contradiction, and become consecrated by tradition. A monument had been erected in Alexandria to Pompey; this monument was lost; and it was believed to have been re-discovered in this pillar. It has since been made a trophy of Septimus Severus; but it stands upon the rubbish of the ancient city, and in the time of Septimus Severus the city of the Ptolemies was not in ruins. To make a solid foundation for the column, an obelisk was overturned, on the base of which has been placed a bad pedestal, which supports a beautiful shaft, surmounted by a corinthian capital, heavily chiseled.

If the shaft of this column, continues M. Denon, separate from its pedestal and capital, had made a part of an antique edifice, it would have attested its magnificence, and the purity of its execution: it must therefore be said, that this is a beautiful column, but not that it is a fine monument. It may be added, that a column is not a monument; that the column of *Sainte-Marie-Majeure*, though

one

one of the most beautiful existing, has no monumental character, is a mere fragment; and that if the columns of Trajan and Antoninus are exceptions to this doctrine, it is because they are rather colossal cylinders, on which is splendidly unrolled the history of the glorious expeditions of these emperors; and because, reduced to their mere forms and their dimensions, they would seem only heavy and melancholy monuments.

Digging round the column would doubtlessly be the means of making some discoveries respecting its origin. The earth which has been moved, and the manner in which it lies, have already proved that these researches would not be in vain: perhaps there might be discovered the foundations and *atrium* of the portico to which it belonged. Near this column are fragments of others, of the same material and diameter; the earth, on being dug, betrays the ruins and foundations of great buildings the outlines of which are still visible on the surface; as, a square of great magnitude, and a large circle, of which the principal dimensions, though covered with sand and rubbish, may even now be measured.

After observing that the column called of *Pompey* is of very chaste proportions, that the pedestal and capital are not of the same granite as the shaft, that the wormanship of the latter is heavy and seems no better than a botch, and that the foundation, formed of ruins, declares its erection

tion to be modern; it is natural to conclude that this monument is not antique, and that the period in which it was raised may with equal reason be referred to that of the greek emperors or that of the khalifs: since, if the pedestal and capital are sufficiently well executed to belong to the former of these eras, they have not so great perfection as to render it impossible that the art might be at that height in the latter.

Digging in this place might also ascertain the wall of the city in the time of the Ptolemies, when commerce and luxury had altered its first dimensions, and rendered them prodigious: that of the khalifs, which still exist, was a reduction, though at this day even this encloses fields and deserts. This circumvallation was constructed with ruins. The jambs and sommers of the gates which have been built for the walls and fortresses are formed only of columns of granite, with which even the pains to shape them for their new destinations has not been taken*.

Returning from the pillar towards the modern city, M. Denon crossed that of the Arabs, or rather that which is surrounded by their walls; this latter being at present only a desert over which is scattered a few inclosures, which during the

---

* The reader will find the subject of Pompey's pillar largely discussed in Dr. White's *Ægyptiaca,* and in M. Norry's *Report, Memoirs on Egypt, vol. 1.*

months of the inundation are gardens, and in which, during the remainder of the year, are preserved as many trees and vegetables as the ciftern each contains will supply. This cistern is the principle of their existence; if it dries up, the garden returns into heaps of rubbish and sand.

At the door of each of these gardens there are monuments of an amiable piety: these are reservoirs of water, with pumps by which they may be filled at pleasure, and which thus offer to the passenger the means of satisfying that want which, in this burning climate, ranks among the most urgent in nature.

M. Denon visited a ruin of a reddish hue, which is denominated, by the catholics, the house of St. Katharine the Learned, her who espoused the infant Jesus four hundred years after his death: this is a roman structure; and M. Denon supposes it to have been a hot-bath.

The obelisk called of Cleopatra was the next antiquity that presented itself. Another, which, having been overthrown, lies by the side of the former, demonstrates, says M. Denon that both decorated one of the entrances of the palace of the Ptolemies, of which, within a few paces from these, the ruins are still to be observed. These obelisks, as being covered with hieroglyphics, M. Denon regards as more interesting than the pillar called of Pompey, which is a mere column, of a height very little superior to that of many others.

On

On returning by the sea side to the bottom of the harbour, M. Denon remarked the ruins of buildings of all ages, equally injured by the ocean and by time. He distinguished the remains of baths, several chambers of which still exist, and which have been built in walls more antient than themselves. These fabrics appear to be arabian; and there have been raised around them, for their preservation, a sort of palisade of columns, the immense number of which proves the magnificence of the palace they decorated. After passing the bottom of the harbour, large saracenic buildings are met with, in which, with some magnificent particulars, there is a mixture of style that embarrasses the spectator: frises, ornamented with doric trygliphs, surmounted by vaults in ogives, ought to raise a belief, that these fabrics have been constructed with antique fragments which the Saracens mingled with their own architecture. The doors of these edifices may show the degree of indestructibility that belongs to the wood of the sycamore, which has remained entire, while, the iron with which it was garnished has yielded to the atmosphere, and wholly disappeared. Behind this species of fortress are the arabian hot baths, decorated with every kind of minute magnificence.

Near these baths is one of the principal mosks, formerly a primitive church, under the name of St. Anthanasia. This edifice, as much dilapidated as

it

it is superb, may convey a notion of the indolence of the Turks with regard to the objects of which they are most jealous. Before the arrival of the French, they would not suffer a christian to approach it;* but they preferred placing a guard at the gates, to giving them any repair. In the state in which the French found them, they would neither close nor turn on their hinges. This mosk has a covered portico, supported by arches on four ranks of columns, of various kinds of marble; and the walls and pavement of which are covered with mosaic work, in marble. The frise contains sentences of the koran, in large characters, executed in enamel. This portico opens into a square court, paved likewise with marble, and surrounded by a gallery, raised on columns similar to the others. The most wretched buildings are joined by the Turks to this and all the other monuments of saracenic magnificence. In the court, plants which have grown into trees, have forced up the marble pavement. In the center of this court, a little octagon temple incloses a cistern of Egyptian workmanship, and incomparable beauty,

---

* Besides the idea of religious pollution, which, as mohammedans, they entertain of the approach of a christian, the Turks had very good reason, as magistrates, for this precaution. Some years since, a christian merchant, laid a plan for stealing out of this mosk the antique sarcophagus contained in its court. What would the English say of an oriental agent that should attempt to carry away a monument from Westminster Abbey?

both

both on account of its form, and of the innumerable hieroglyphics with which it is covered, inside and out. This monument, which appears to be a sarcophagus of antient Egypt, may perhaps be illustrated by volumes of dissertations. It would require a month to draw all its parts.

Near this mosk are three columns of which no former traveler has spoken. Their present distance from each other render it probable that they have been re-set up; and digging round their scite would possibly prove that they are remnants of a large and magnificent edifice.

On advancing to the port of Rashid*, the horrors of war were found still existing in this quarter. On the arrival of the French, it had been defended by the Turks. Rashid is a sort of fortified suburb. It is composed of a groupe of houses, between which and Alexandria is a space of half a league.

On quitting their ships, the greatest part of the army had entered Alexandria only to pass through it to the desert. Bonaparte, who had possessed himself of this city with the rapidity that once did St. Lewis, avoided the error into which the latter fell. Without giving time for the enemy to reconnoitre, or for his troops to discover the penury of Alexandria, and its sterile territory, or gather information concerning the places they were

---

* Called by the Italians, *Rosetta*.

going

going to occupy, he caused the several divisions to march, immediately on their debarkation. One officer, among the rest, said to his troops at the moment of their landing: "My friends, you are going to sleep at Beda; you hear me: Beda; march;" and the soldiers marched. More inquisitive than astonished, they arrived at Beda, which they expected to find a village, built and peopled like those of Europe; but there was nothing but a well, covered with stones, through which distilled a little muddy and brackish water, which, collected in cups, was distributed among them in little rations, like brandy. Such, says M. Denon, was the first station taken by the french troops, in a distant part of the world, separated from their country by seas covered with enemies, and by desarts still more to be dreaded: yet this singular situation made no impression on their courage, or their gaiety.

On the second day of the march of the troops across the desert, from Alexandria, they met, near Beda, a young woman, whose face was smeared with blood. In one hand, she held a young infant, and with her other was vacantly stretched out to the object that might strike or guide it. Their curiosity was excited. They called their guide, who was at the same time their interpreter. They approached; and they heard the sighs of a being from whom the organs of tears had been torn away! Astonished, and desirous of an explanation,

nation, they questioned her. They learned that the dreadful spectacle before their eyes had been produced by a fit of jealousy. Its victim presumed to utter no murmurs, but only prayers in behalf of the innocent who partook her misfortune, and which was on the point of perishing with misery and hunger. The soldiers, struck with compassion, and forgetting their own wants in the presence of the more pressing ones of others, immediately gave her a part of their rations. They were bestowing part of the precious water with which they were threatened to be soon wholly without themselves, when they beheld the furious husband approach, who, feasting his eyes at a distance with the fruits of his vengeance, had kept its victims in sight. He sprang forward, snatched from the woman's hands the bread, the water (that last necessary of life!) which pity had given to misfortune: " Stop!" cried he: " she has lost her honour, she has wounded mine; this child is my shame, it is the son of guilt!" The soldiers resisted his attempt to deprive the woman of the food they had given her. His jealousy was irritated at seeing the object of his fury become that of the kindness of others. He drew a dagger, and gave the woman a mortal blow; then seized the child, threw it into the air, and destroyed it by its fall: afterwards, with stupid ferocity, he stood motionless, looking stedfastly at those who surrounded him, and defying their vengeance.

M. Denon

M. Denon inquired, whether there were no prohibitory laws against such an atrocious abuse of authority. He was answered, that the man had *done wrong* to stab the woman, because at the end of forty days, she might have been received into a house, and fed by charity.

Kleber's division, commanded by Dugua, had taken the route to Rashid*, for the purpose of protecting the fleet which had entered the Nile. On the 6th and 7th of June, the main army began its march, by the way of Birket and Demenhûr*. The Arabs attacked the advanced-guards, and harrassed the rest. Death was the forfeit paid by those who did not keep up with their columns. Desaix, having fallen fifty paces behind, was on the point of being taken; and Le Mireur, a distinguished officer, was assassinated at a hundred paces from the advanced-guard, in consequence of having failed to pay attention, through a melan-

---

* Rosetta.

† The name of this place is spelt Damanhur by General Reynier. The topographical names, in these countries, are usually set down from the pronunciation of the natives, and according to the judgment of the writer, as to the letters that, in his language, will produce a correspondent sound. To notice the synonyms thus produced, must be useful to the reader, since nothing produces so much confusion, and consequently so retards the acquisition of knowledge, as the use of several terms for the same thing.—English writers often increase the perplexity, by adopting the french orthography, which is proper only when they are originally french.

cholic

cholic abstraction of mind, to an invitation to keep with the rest. Adjutant Delanau, in crossing a ravin, was made a prisoner at the distance of a few paces from the army; a price was offered for his ransom; the Arabs quarreled about the sharing it; and, to settle the dispute, they burnt his brains.

The mamlûks were before the army. They were first seen in the neighbourhood of Demenhûr. There, they only reconnoitred; and this display of themselves, as well as the insignificant battle at Jibbrîsh, had rendered the soldiers acquainted with them, and removed that equivocal emotion, approaching to terror, which is always excited by an unknown enemy. On their part, seeing the french army composed only of infantry, a sort of soldiers for whom they had a sovereign contempt, they went away with an opinion of certain and easy victory; and no longer tormented a march already painful by its length, and the heat of the climate, and performed under the sufferings of hunger and thirst, and amidst the torments of hope continually disappointed and continually flattering anew. In a corn-country, the soldiers wanted bread; and with the image of a vast lake before their eyes, they raged with thirst. To explain this new species of calamity, it must be observed that it is the effect of an illusion which has not been found in any other region. This is produced by the *mirage* of projecting objects on the oblique rays of the sun, refracted by the whiteness of the burning earth; a phenomenon which offers so complete a resemblance of water, that the traveller is as much deceived the tenth time he sees it, as the first; and which thus tantalizes a thirst by so much the more ardent, as it occurs in precisely the hottest part of the day.*

The inhabitants deserted the villages as the army approached them, carrying away all the provisions they contained. Water-melons were the first refreshment which it received from the soil of Egypt; and the memory of this fruit lives in its gratitude. On reaching the Nile, the soldiers threw themselves into that river, clothed as they were, to drink, says M. Denon, at every pore.

After passing Rahmanieh, their marches, which were along the banks of the river, were infinitely less painful than before. On the 19th of July, they encamped for the night at Ammel-Dinar. They recommenced their march before day-break the next morning; and after twelve hours found themselves near Embabeh, where were the mamlûks in an entrenched camp, surrounded by a bad ditch, and defended by thirty-eight pieces of artillery. As soon as the enemy was discovered, the army prepared for battle. When Bonaparte had given his last orders, " Go," said he, pointing

---

* See a *Memoir on the optical phenomenon known by the name of mirage,* by M. Gaspard Monge.——*Memoirs on Egypt, vol. I.*

to

to the pyramids; "and think that from the heights of those monuments, forty ages survey our conduct!"

Desaix, who commanded the advanced guard, had passed the village; Reynier followed on his left; Dugua, Vial, and Bon, still on the left, formed a semicircle as they approached the Nile. Mûrat-bey, who had been to reconnoitre, and seen no cavalry, said he was going to cut down the French like *gourds*. On this, the most considerable body of the mamlûks which was before Embabeh, put itself in motion, and charged Dugua's division with a rapidity that scarcely gave it time to form. They were received with a discharge of field-pieces, which made them halt; and by an unskilful movement, they threw themselves on the bayonets of the division of Desaix. A continued and well-supported fire by files effected a second surprize. For a moment, they hesitated; then, suddenly attempting to turn the division, they passed between that of Reynier and that of Desaix, and thus received the cross-fire of both, which commenced their overthrow. Being now without a plan, one party returned towards Embabeh; the other sought to intrench itself within an inclosure surrounded by palm-trees, which lay to the west of the two divisions, and whence they were dislodged by the artillery: at length, they took the road to the desert of the pyramids. These were they who afterwards disputed Upper Egypt with the French.

During

During this time, the other divisions, on approaching the village, found themselves annoyed by the artillery of the intrenched camp. They resolved to attack it, and to avail themselves of a deep ditch, by which they would be defended from the cavalry. The divisions, preceded by their wings, marched in order of battle. The mamlùks attacked the wings in vain. They opened their thirty-eight pieces of artillery. The French precipitated themselves on the cannon, with so much impetuosity that they had no time to load again; and forced the trenches with the bayonet. Five hundred mamlùks on horseback, and as many fellahs, whose retreat, in turning Embabeh, and in taking an intrenched position behind a ditch that joined the Nile, generals Marmont and Rampon had cut off, performed prodigies of valour in vain. Not one of them would surrender, nor did one escape. Prevented from passing along the banks of the Nile, they threw themselves into the river, to rejoin the corps of Ibrahim-bey, who had stationed himself opposite, in order to cover Kaira*. From this moment, it was no longer a battle, but a massacre: the enemy seemed to defile, only to be shot; and to escape the fire of the battalions, only to be drowned. The whole of his artillery, four hun-

---

* Vulgarly, Cairo, or Kairo.

dred

dred camels, his baggage and his provisions, became the prize of the conqueror.

Mûrat-bey, seeing the village of Embabeh carried, no longer thought of any thing but securing his retreat. He was pursued to Jiza,* where he gave a signal to his followers to fly; and where the French took their station, after a march and battle of nine hours. Only ten soldiers were killed, and about thirty wounded.† General

---

* Djizeh, Gizeh, Gaza, or Gezah.

† Part of this relation is taken from the official narrative of general Berthier. The point of time at which the battle is represented on the plate, is that when two bodies of mamlûks made their attack at once: the first on the divisions of Dugua, Desaix, and Reynier; the second on the battalion commanded by general Rampon. M. Denon has here endeavoured to give an image of a mamlûk charge, of which he was often witness, and by the rapidity, disregard of danger, impetuosity, and chivalric valour of which he was always struck. He has also attempted to show the effect of the case-shot on this cavalry, which braved it to the very mouth of the cannon. He has introduced the foot-attendants of the combatants, their manner of carrying away the wounded, and leaving the field of battle; the camels bearing cartridges and warlike instruments; the palm-trees as they were at the season in which the battle took place, and the clefts in the earth produced by the inundation and the sun: in a word, whatever was characteristic of the country. The back-ground contains every interesting object comprehended within that vast horizon: on the right of the plate, is the road that leads through Suez into Asia, where is discovered the numerous body of Ibrahim-bey; the city of Kaira, at the foot of the Mokatam or Mokatan (the extremity of the arabic chain of mountains); the great aqueduct,
which

General Menou had remained at Alexandria, to recover of a wound he had received. He was charged with the organization of the government of Rashid, and was besides to take a survey of the Delta, or Lower Egypt. The general invited M. Denon to accompany him on his journey; and the latter consented the more willingly, that he was not only to enjoy the society of an amiable and intelligent man, whom he had long called his friend, but that he thought it would be interesting to visit this part of the country before he saw Upper Egypt.

They embarked in an advice-boat at the new port of Alexandria. They were scarcely a few leagues at sea, when general Menou was seized with a convulsive vomiting which, by occasioning him to fall head-foremost on the breach of a cannon, had nearly cost him his life. He was deprived of sense; and, alarmed by the largeness of

---

which reaches to Old Kaira, on the banks of the river Bûlak: near the front, is the Nile, with the islands of Räûdah, Bûlak, and Lazaret; the admiral's vessel of the fleet of Mûrat-bey, which he caused to be set on fire during the combat; on this side of the Nile is Jiza, the palace of Mûrat-bey, the plain and the pyramids of Saccara; the entire space between these and those of Jiza, whereon Memphis stood; and, on the extremest line, the lybian mountains, of which the chain lies north and south, as far as the pyramids of Jiza, and then, suddenly turning to the west, loses istself in the deserts of Barca.

wound,

the wound, of the degree of danger of which they could form no judgment, his companions debated among themselves whether to carry him on board the Orient, which was at anchor with the rest of the fleet at Abû-kîr, or to enter the Nile, which the sailors said could be done in a few hours, and where the sickness of the general would cease. The latter plan was adopted. Some hours afterwards, they found themselves, without previous knowledge, at one of the mouths of the Nile, when a scene of the most distressing nature ensued. The water of the Nile, repulsed by the wind, rose in waves of immense height, which were perpetually overwhelmed and broken by the current, with a frightful noise. A french vessel, which had been wrecked, and of which the waves were now completing the destruction, was the only sea-mark by which they could ascertain the coast. Several other vessels in the same situation, that is, in the same confusion with themselves, approached for the sake of mutual consultation, and were yet obliged to keep at a distance, for fear of falling upon each other; and nothing could be heard that was not uttered with a voice the loudness of which encreased the horror of the moment. There was no pilot of the coast; and none had any thing left to advise. General Menou continued to grow worse. It was resolved to reconnoitre the *bogaz*, or bar of the river; and for this purpose M. Denon and *chef-de-bataillon* Bonnicarrere got into

into the boat. Scarcely had they quitted their vessel, when they saw themselves surrounded by abysses, and could no longer behold any thing but the undulating summits of waves by which they were threatened to be buried. They were now a thousand fathoms from the aviso, to which it was out of their power to return. M. Denon grew sea-sick; and all that remained was to await the event with anxiety. He was covering himself with his mantle, in order prepare to pass the night in this situation, to hide from himself all further view of the scene, when their boat passed a felucca, on which he saw an unfortunate man who, in descending to a boat for debarkation, had remained suspended by a cord. Fatigued by the efforts he had made to maintain himself in this perilous condition, his arms were become elongated, and ready to let him drop into those of death. This sight gave M. Denon so great a fhock throughout his frame, that his sickness ceased. In indescribable agitation, he shouted rather than cried; and the seamen mingling their cries with his, they were at length heard on board the felucca. There, they could not, at first, make themselves understood. The men thought of every thing else before the wretched creature whose strength was expiring: at last, they discovered him, and in time to save his life.

The moments which this incident had occasioned to be lost, and the efforts that had been made

to

to keep on the wind-side, to be ready in case the man had fallen into the sea, had brought up the boat sufficiently to allow of her regaining the aviso. M. Denon and his companions boarded her in safety; and found themselves in exactly the same situation as that they had been in before they left her, without an idea of what further to attempt. The wind fell a little; but the sea continued high. The night, which turned out less tempestuous than the day, came on.

The general was too ill to take any share in the conduct to be pursued. The rest held a new council, and resolved to put themselves once more in the boat, hoping that by the help of the wreck as a beacon, they might be able to enter the Nile. In this they succeeded. After an hour's rowing, they gained the most pacific part of the most pacific of rivers, and in half an hour more, were surrounded by the freshest and most verdant of countries. General Menou had soon recovered sufficiently to maintain his seat, and had released his friends from all anxiety concerning his wound, which none of them had ventured to probe.

On their right, they observed a fort, and on their left, a battery, which were built for the defence of the mouth of the Nile, but which now stand at the distance of a league from the river. The construction of these forts, says M. Denon,
cannot

cannot be dated before the invention of gunpowder, which gives three hundred years for their utmost age; and from this may be inferred the rapidity with which the mud of the Nile has accumulated. The ruin of a battery stands before a mosk, and has a cannon of twenty-eight inches caliber, the only benefit expected from which is the procuration of favourable deliveries for those pregnant women by whom, with faith, it is bestrided.

An hour's journey beyond these, discovered to them Rashid, seated on the banks of the Nile, and embosomed by date-trees, banana-trees, and sycamores. Rashid is built on, and near the mouth of, the bobitinian branch of the Nile. According to Leo-Africanus, it owes its foundation to a governor of Egypt, under the khalifs, whom he does not name. Its old walls announce that it was once larger than at present. Like that of Alexandria, its population is daily decreasing. The few houses that continue to be built, are constructed of the old bricks that had belonged to edifices which became ruins in default of inhabitants and reparations. These houses are in general better built than those of Alexandria; but they are so slight, that were it not for the clemency of the climate, which destroys nothing, they could not stand. Each succeeding story projects farther into the street than that beneath it; so that the

two

two sides finish by almost touching each other. Hence the avenues are dark and melancholy. Many of the houses have been built by the Franks, and have more resemblance to the european architecture of the fourteenth century, than to the oriental manner, which prevails in the other towns in Egypt. The dwellings that lie on the Nile have not this inconvenience. These principally belong to foreign merchants; and their situation might be greatly embellished by the easy labour of building a quay along the shore. Besides a view of the navigation, these houses have also that of the delightful bank of the island called the Delta, which is a perfect garden, of a league in extent. When the government of this place was put into the hands of general Menou, many blows of the club were distributed among the populace. This was a remain of the oriental practice, the purpose of which seems to be, at once to drive away a mob, to ennoble a ceremony, and to make the weak sensible of the presence of the strong, and of the distance at which they ought to keep. The French never entered a village in which the shech did not command, for their honour, such a distribution, which ceased only at their intercession, and when he thought the due respect sufficiently manifested.

M. Denon remarked that the inhabitants of the left bank of the Nile, that is of the Delta,

Delta*, were more refined and sociable than those of the right; and he attributes this meliority to the abundance they enjoy, and the tranquility in which they are left by the Arabs, who never cross the river, and which tranquility is never known to the others, during a single moment of their lives.

In observing effects, says M. Denon, we are almost always led to complain of causes. Can the arab-husbandman be reproached with gloominess, mistrust, avarice, idleness, want of care for the future, while, besides the vexations of the barren soil he cultivates, the greedy bey, the shech, the mamlûk (a wandering enemy, always in arms), are taken into the account? when it is seen that he has constant reason to fear, from each of these, the pillage of whatever of superfluity he might venture to discover? The money, then, that he conceals, this money which is the representative of the enjoyments he denies himself, is all that he can call absolutely his own. His life is passed under the misfortune of possessing nothing, or that of expecting what he has to be torn away.

We, says M. Denon, had indeed driven away the mamlûks; but, being in want of every neces-

---

* The name *delta*, which was given by the greeks, on account of a resemblance in form to their letter Δ (D), is applied both to the whole of Lower Egypt, and to this Island in particular.

sary on our arrival, did we not ourselves, while we removed these, fill their place? and then for the bedûin-arabs, who are ill armed, and can make no resistance; whose ramparts are moving sands, whose lines are space, whose retreat is immensity; by whom could they be vanquished or confined? Shall we endeavour to win them by offers of land for cultivation? the husbandmen of Europe, once become hunters, cease to till the ground; and the bedûin is the primitive hunter: indolence and independance are the bases of his character; and to gratify and protect both the one and the other of these, he keeps himself in continual action, and endures the siege and tyranny of want. We have nothing, then, to offer to the bedûin that is equivalent to the advantage of robbing us; and this calculation is always the principle of the treaty into which he will be persuaded to enter.

Envy, that evil from which the abode of want is not exempt, hovers over even the burning sands of the desert. The bedûins, at war with all the universe, hate and envy only the bedûins who are not of their own horde. They enter into every war; they put themselves in motion the moment a domestic quarrel, or foreign enemy, troubles the repose of Egypt; and, without attaching themselves to either party, they make use of their hostilities to pillage both. Where is the booty, there

is

is the enemy of the bedûins. Their barbarity, meanwhile, has nothing in it atrocious. Those of the French who had been their prisoners, spoke of the evils they had suffered during their captivity, as the result rather of the manner of life than of the ferocity of this nation. Officers who had been taken, told M. Denon, that the labour required of them to perform was neither excessive nor cruel; it was only to be obedient to the women, and to load and lead the asses and camels. They were obliged, indeed, to encamp and decamp incessantly. All the tackle was packed up, and a march commenced in less than a quarter of an hour. This tackle consisted of a mill for corn and coffee, an iron-plate for dressing cakes, a large and a little coffee-pot, a few leathern bottles, a few sacks of corn, and the cloth of a tent, which covered the whole. A handful of roasted corn, and a dozen of dates, with a little water which, on account of its scarcity, had served every purpose before it was drank, was the common ration of a day spent in traveling: but these officers had not had their souls wounded by the least ill-treatment, nor did they retain any bitter recollection of an adverse condition of which it had been their lot but to partake.

Free from religious prejudices himself, the bedûin tolerates all. A few revered customs serve him for laws. His principles resemble the virtues

virtues which are sufficient for the partial association he forms, and for the patriarchal government under which he lives.

Of the hospitality of this people, continues M. Denon, I ought to cite the following instance: a french officer had been several months the prisoner of an arab chief. Surprized by our cavalry in his camp, at night, the latter had only time to fly; tents, flocks, provisions, all were taken. The next day, wandering, separated from his friends, without resource, he took from under his clothes a loaf; and, giving the half of it to his prisoner, " I know not," said he, " when we shall eat another; but I will never be accused of not having divided my last with the friend whom I had made." Can we hate such people, whatever may be the features of ferocity which they betray on other occasions? and what advantages over us do they not derive from this sobriety, so striking when compared with the wants that we have created for ourselves? can we seduce or reduce such men? will they not always reproach us with sowing rich harvests on the graves of their forefathers?

Before the French were masters of Kaira, the inhabitants of the banks of the Nile, believing their existence in Egypt very precarious, suffered the army to pass with every appearance of submission; but supposing that it must inevitably be destroyed by their invincible masters, and desirous that this submission should be pardoned, and moreover

moreover willing to indulge themselves in plundering, they made a practice of molesting and firing on the vessels which were sent up the river, for the use of the troops. In consequence, an aviso and a few troops were sent against them. Their instructions were pacific; and, accordingly, after receiving formal submissions and hostages they returned. Some days after, another vessel sailed for Kaira. She never reached that city; and it was only from the people of the country themselves, that it was learned she had been attacked above Fûëh*; that her people, after being all wounded, had thrown themselves into the water; that, hurried away by the current, they had been driven on shore; and that, seized and carried to Salmia, they were there shot. General Menou thought himself obliged to make an example of the offenders. Two hundred men, carried by a demi-zebeck, and other barks, landed within half a league of Salmia. A detachment turned the village; another followed the banks of the river; the third, which was to complete the circumvallation, remained fixed two leagues below. The enemy was drawn up, on horseback, before the village. He commenced the attack, and charged even to the points of the bayonets. The principal men being killed by the first fire of the French,

---

* Written, also, *Fûé* and *Fouah*; the latter is a french orthography.

and

and the rest seeing themselves surrounded, soon fell into disorder; but the third division, which was to have cut off their retreat, not coming up in time, the shech and those of his followers who still survived, made their escape. The village was given up to plunder during the day, and to fire as soon as night arrived. Its flames, and the discharge of several pieces of cannon, which continued till morning, warned the surrounding country, for ten leagues, that the vengeance taken had been complete and terrible.

The expedition returned to Fûëh, where all the shechs of the province, having been convoked, were assembled. These heard with respect and resignation the manifesto which was read to them concerning the late proceedings, and the principles upon which Salmia was to be restored. They named an aged shech to fill the place of him whom the French had dispossessed and proscribed, and sent him to collect the scattered inhabitants and bring back a deputation, which arrived on the third day. The detachment which had escorted the antient shech, had been received with acclamations. They declared that they had recognized paternal chastisement in the hand that had struck their village; that they had seen in the conduct of the French on that occasion the reverse of a disposition to do them harm, since only nine guilty persons had been killed, and only a quarter of the village burned. They added that the conflagration was extinguished, that the house of the former shech was destroyed, and that they had offered the remainder of their chickens and geese to the soldiers who had come to relieve the remorse with which, during three weeks, they had been tormented.

An ordinary post was established at Salmia, for the convenience of that town and its neighbourhood; and general Menou's expedition was finished by a tour of the department. He was welcomed in every village in a manner more than feodal; the principal personage of the place received him and his followers, and providing them with all and more than they could want, at the expense, as was afterwards found, of the inhabitants: this abuse, which served to develope to the French the customs of a country the manners of which they were about to change, they suffered, for that reason, to be continued for the time.

A large house, which had almost always belonged to a mamlûk formerly lord and master of the village, was suddenly furnished, according to the custom of the country, with mats, carpets, and cushions. A banquet commenced by the entrance of a number of servants, bringing cold and perfumed water, pipes, and coffee; half an hour afterwards, a carpet was spread, round which was formed a border of three or four kinds of loaves and cakes, while the center was covered with little plates of fruits, sweetmeats, creams, and other productions of the dairy, of which the greater part were exceedingly agreable, and in particular,

particular, highly perfumed. All this seemed to be but tasted, for in a few minutes the repast was finished; but, at the end of two hours more, the same carpet was covered again; other loaves were brought, and immense dishes of rice, dressed with fresh beef and with milk, half-sheep, badly roasted, large quarters of veal, boiled heads of sheep and calves, and sixty other dishes piled upon one another, and containing spiced ragouts, vegetables, jellies, confectionaries, and honey from the hive. Here were no chairs, no plates, no spoons or forks, no goblets or napkins. Squatted on their heels, with their knees bent towards their breasts, the company helped themselves to rice with their fingers, and divided the meat with their nails. They dipped the bread in the ragouts, and they used it to wipe their hands and mouths. They drank water from one pot. He that did the honours of the feast always drank first. He, also, tasted first of every dish; and this less to show that his guests need not entertain any suspicions, than to testify how careful he was of their safety, and what attention he paid to their persons. Napkins were not presented till after dinner, when water was brought to wash hands. After this, rose-water was sprinkled on every person present. The whole was concluded with pipes and coffee.

When the French had eaten, people of secondary rank came in, and supplied their places, and were themselves very quickly relieved by others: on a
principle

principle of religion, a poor beggar was next admitted; then came the servants, and then every one who would, till all was ate. If there was wanting to this dinner that convenience and elegance which would have given it zest to an European, it was impossible not to admire the plenty, the hospitable profusion, and at the same time the moderation of the guests, whom the number of dishes never kept above ten minutes at table.

On the morning of the 31st of July, 1798*, the French were masters of Egypt, Corfù, and Malta; thirty vessels of the line united these possessions with France, and rendered the whole one empire. England, meanwhile, was only cruizing in the Mediterranean with numerous fleets, for which she could not find even provisions but with much difficulty, and at a prodigious expense.

Bonaparte, feeling all the advantage of this situation, was desirous, in order to preserve it, that the fleet should enter the port of Alexandria: he offered a reward of two thousand zeckins† for the discovery of means of bringing this about, and a passage into the old-port was found. The evil genius of France, however, advised and persuaded the admiral to shut himself up at Abû-kîr, and thus, in one day, to change the result of a long series of successes.

On the afternoon of the 31st, chance led

---

* 14 Thermidor.
† *Shekins, sequins, chekins, zechins, zequins,* or *shereefs*: a turkish *zeckin* is worth about nine shillings sterling.

M. Denon

M. Denon and his companions to the convent of Abû-mandûr, which terminates a pleasant promenade from Rashid, along the borders of the Nile. A little further, there is a tower, of arabic construction. It stands in the middle of a large plain; and overlooks, on the one side, a yellow desert, of vast extent, terminated by the sea. When, however, the mind is saddened by this prospect, it can sooth itself by turning to all that nature has to display, of verdure, riches, and abundance; the plains of the Delta, covered with rice-fields and sugar-grounds, and intersected by innumerable canals, that terminate in the Nile, which river, at this part of its course, is always covered with barks, moving in every direction.

Arrived at this tower, they perceived, at the distance of seven leagues, twenty sail enter the bay of Abû-kîr. These vessels arrived, formed a line of battle, and attacked the fleet of the French, almost in the same moment. They heard the discharge of the first cannon at five o'clock. Soon after this, the smoke concealed the two fleets from their sight; but when it became dark, they were able to distinguish better, though they were too far off to understand what was passing. The danger they ran of being made prisoners by the smallest party of bedûins could not distract the anxious attention they paid to an event of so great interest. The rolling and redoubled noise of the cannon was continual: they saw that the battle was terrible; and that it was sustained on both sides

with

with equal obstinacy. On returning to Rashid, they went on the roofs of their houses: towards ten o'clock, a strong burst of light showed a fire to have taken place in the fleet; same minute, a dreadful explosion ensued, and then, as profound a silence. At eleven o'clock, a slow fire recommenced; at midnight, the battle was completely renewed; but at two o'clock in the morning it again ceased. At day-break, the cannonade began once more. At nine o'clock, a second vessel blew up. At ten, four ships, the only ones that remained entire, which they recognized to be french (and which at that moment they believed to be victors, because they were neither attacked nor followed), withdrew from the scene of action, under crowded sail.

M. Denon passed his time on the top of the tower of Abù-mandûr, incessantly examining the bay with his telescope. Three days passed before he learned the real event of the first and second of August. The bogaz shut up, and the communication with Alexandria intercepted, at length, however, made him fully aware, that circumstances had changed against the French; that, separated from the mother country, they were become colonists, who, till peace should arrive, were to exist by their own exertions, and by their own resources: in a word he learned that the english fleet had doubled the french line, not sufficiently supported by the island which should have defended it; that the enemy, taking the vessels of the

the latter one by one, by means of his double line, had rendered half its strength useless, leaving it only a spectator of the destruction of the other; that it was the Orient which had blown up at ten o'clock on the night of the thirty-first of July, and the Hercules which had followed the next morning; that the commanders of the ships the William-Tell and the Generous, and of the frigates the Diana and the Justice, seeing the rest in the power of the enemy, had taken advantage of his weariness, and escaped. He learned, in short, that the first of August had broken the fabric of the power and glory of France; that, destroying her fleet, it had bestowed the empire of the Mediterranean on her enemies.

The situation of the French was now entirely changed. Under the possibility of being attacked, it was become necessary to prepare for defence.

In one of the visits to the Nile which the fortifications carrying on for the security of its mouth rendered necessary, M. Denon had once more the bogaz or bar before his eyes. The Nile was now at its greatest height; and he had had an opportunity of witnessing the efforts of its weight of water against the waves of the sea, which at this season are driven against the stream for twelve hours of the day, by a wind from the north. This combat produces a bed of sand, which, gradually increased, becomes an island, and divides the river, forming two mouths, each having its shelves.

The

The agitation of these shelves carries to the banks a part of the sand which the current had deposited; and by means of this alluvion, the mouths close by degrees, till the one most obstructed becomes a part of the *terra-firma* of the island, while the other speedily forms a new bed, then an island, then two new mouths, and thus on continually. Now, may not these phenomena satisfactorily explain the antient geography of the mouths of the Nile, the voyage of Menelaus, in Homer, and the changes of the Delta; the space occupied by which was first a gulf, then a shallow, then cultivated ground, covered with fine cities and luxurious harvests, intersected with canals which, watering or draining the earth according to circumstances, carry plenty over the whole surface of the new-created country?

Since the loss of the fleet, the troops that were at Rashid* had been scattered among the castles and batteries in little-garrisons; it had become necessary, in order to maintain a communication between the two cities, to establish a caravan between Alexandria and Rashid, by the way of Abù-kîr, and soldiers were employed to protect these caravans from the Arabs: there remained, therefore, too small a number of troops at this latter place, to defend it in case of attack. Under these circumstances, it was proposed to form a militia of the travelers, the speculators, the useless, fickle, wandering and irresolute men who

---

* Rosetta.

had

had arrived at Alexandria, or already returned from Kaira: a large list, including amphibia who, corrupted by the campaigns of Italy, and having heard that the harvests of Egypt were the most abundant in the world, had thought that such a country must have fortunes ready made for the first possessors; epicures and debauchees who, with minds fascinated by Savary's account, had set out from Paris, in search of new pleasures at Kaira; speculators who came to supply the army, to feel the pulses of trade, and import and sell at high prices, whatever the colony could want: meanwhile, the beys had withdrawn all their money and magnificence from Kaira; the populace had pillaged the houses; Bonaparte did not want contractors; and the merchant-ships were blockaded by the English; misfortunes which, to the eyes of these travellers, threw a gloom over all Egypt. Confounded at finding themselves prisoners, disappointed in their projects, and obliged to concur in the defence and improvement of a place which they found would only promote the prosperity of the whole empire of France, they sent home the most melancholy recitals. These recitals, intercepted by the English, contributed to deceive that nation with respect to our condition. The English pleased themselves with believing that we were dying with hunger; sent back our prisoners, that they might hasten the period of our destruction; printed in their gazettes that half our army was in the hospitals;

that

that half the other half were employed in leading the blind remainder: and all this time, upper Egypt was supplying us with abundance of the best wheat, and the lower with the finest rice; the sugar of the country was sold at half the price of sugar in France; the numberless herds of buffaloes, oxen, sheep and goats, as well of the cultivators as of the Arab-pastors, sufficiently supplied the great increase of consumption at the very moment of the invasion, and promised abundance and superfluity for the future; and, for the luxury of the table, we could add every kind of poultry, fish, game, vegetables, and fruits. Such, then, were the objects of the first necessity which Egypt offered to her detractors; detractors who wanted gold to supply the illusions they had indulged, and who not finding gold, saw nothing around them but burning sands, fleas and gnats, dogs which disturbed their sleep, intractable husbands, and veiled women, who showed nothing but the eternal neck!

But let us abandon to the winds a cloud of butterflies who never fail to fly to the first blaze they see; let us turn to behold our triumphs and the peace re-open the port of Alexandria to sages, to industrious cultivators, to useful traders, to planters, in fine; who, without alarming themselves because Africa does not resemble Europe, will observe that in Egypt a man may obtain for three sous a day's subsistence of the best rice in the world; that a part of the lands which are no longer

longer inundated may be brought into tilth and pasture by canals; that wind-mills would raise the water to a greater height than the *pot-mills* at present employed, and by which so many oxen are exhausted, and so many hands occupied; that the islands of the Nile, and the greater part of the Delta, wait only for american planters, to produce fine sugar-canes from a soil that does not devour men in return: approaching Kaira, and proceeding beyond it, they will see that the ground only wants amelioration to make it the rival of every other, for plantations of indigo and cotton of every species; that, while they are making a prudent and certain fortune, they will breathe a pure and wholesome atmosphere, on the banks of a fertilizing and navigable river; they will see a new colony, with cities ready built, skilful workmen, accustomed to labour and to the climate, with whose assistance, and with that of canals which are traced to their hands, they will in a few years, create new provinces, the future abundance of which is not questionable, since modern industry will restore to them their antient splendour.

As for our thoughtless soldiers, continues M. Denon, they derided our beaten sailors: they imagined that Mûrat-bey had a white camel, laden with gold and diamonds; and nothing was talked of but Murat-bey and his white camel. As for myself, I had to see upper Egypt, and our situation led me to think that my travels were at an end.

The

The journey in the Delta being delayed by business which pressed on general Menou, M. Denon took the opportunity of returning by land over the country which, in coming from Alexandria, he had passed by sea. He joined a caravan, in order to seek the ruins of Canopus.

At midnight, the caravan reached the sea. The beach was scattered with the wrecks and the victims of the battle of Abû-kîr. The Arabs were burning the former, in order to procure the nails and pieces of iron they contained. The sight of the dead bodies of so many men who had fallen in the cause of their country, of so many men who, torn with difficulty from the arms of their friends and children, and on the expectation of whose return so many built their happiness, excited the strongest feelings of veneration and tenderness in the bosom of M. Denon. The rising of the sun dissipated the shades, but not so swiftly the darkened tint that overspread his thoughts. Meanwhile, the caravan stopped, and he learned that he was on the border of the lake Mahadieh, by which the plain of the desert is separated from the peninsula of Abû-kîr.

After crossing the mouth of the lake, and following two windings of the shore, bordered with little hills of sand, he arrived at the suburb of Abû-kîr. This bears considerable resemblance to the town itself, from which it is separated by a space

space of one hundred and fifty paces. The two together may be composed of forty or fifty indifferent and ruined cottages. At the end of the peninsula is a castle. This building makes a respectable appearance at a distance; but its bastions would tumble down at the third discharge of the demi-culverines that are on their ramparts. From observation of the ground on which it stands, M. Denon was convinced that this castle, which he thinks it advisable for a modern possessor to pull entirely down, could not be the castle in the sea belonging to Canopus or to Heraclea, which cities Strabo has spoken of as standing near the spot. About half a league before he reached Abû-kîr he had seen its springs. His companions praised the construction of the buildings by which they are enclosed. He returned, and found three square wells, of arabian fabric. They were surrounded by heaps that certainly contained ruins among which were mingled immense quantities of broken pottery, and sand, driven from the desert by the winds. He came away with a persuasion, that these were the ruins of Heraclea.

The next day, with a detachment of the caravan, he travelled along the coast, to the westward. On his way, he examined every little eminence; for, in lower Egypt, these are almost always the coverings of antiquities. After three quarters of an hour's march, he discovered, at the bottom of the bay, a little jut into the sea, composed of colossal

lossal ruins. With extraordinary pleasure, he instantly perceived a fragment of a hand, of which the first finger, fourteen inches in length, belonged to a statue of thirty-six feet in height. The granite, the workmanship, and the style of this morsel, left him no doubt that it was a remain of the remotest ages of egyptian history. By the attitude of this hand, by the fragments which lay near it, and by the mere habit of seeing egyptian figures, of which the design has little variety, he felt himself authorized to conclude that it had belonged to an Isis, holding a nilometer: it might have been easily brought away; but the change of place would have taken away almost all its value. Near this, several architectural members attested by their dimensions that they had belonged to a large and beautiful edifice of the doric order. The waves have covered and raged against these ruins for many ages, but they are still undefaced. More advanced into the sea, may be observed, among the fragments of the colossus, those of a sphinx, of which, as far as the madrepores and shell fish would permit a clear discernment, the head and fore legs are separated from the trunk. It is of the style and chisel of the Greeks; and the material is not granite, but a free-stone, resembling white marble, and of a transparency which M. Denon had never seen in this substance in any other country than Egypt. Its proportions showed it to have been from thirty to forty feet in length.

length. At a further distance, among architectural ruins, resembling those already mentioned, there is another figure of Isis, sufficiently perfect to show the attitude in which it stood. Its legs are broke, but the pieces lie at its side. This figure is in granite, and of the height of ten feet. This assemblage of fragments appear to have been thrown into the sea, in order to form a pier, for the preservation of an edifice now destroyed, but which, judging, from the traces it has left, must have been a bath, the ground-plan of which is cut in the rock. The parts which the sea does not cover, serve to protect some heads of water, which are built round with brick.

At something short of a mile from this spot, returning inland, and drawing towards Alexandria, several foundations of brick are discovered; and though the plan cannot be made out, some fragments of very elaborate workmanship give reason to conclude, that they have made parts of important buildings. Near these, are found many corinthian capitals, in marble, too much worn to be measured, but which must have belonged to bases of the same material, and shafts of apparently twenty inches diameter. Further on, a considerable number of fluted shafts of rose-coloured granite, all of the same proportions and material, and laboured with the same care, are indubitable ruins of a large and superb temple of the doric order. According to all that has been transmitted by
Strabo,

Strabo, concerning this part of Egypt, according to all that M. Denon had just seen and, as above, described, and especially the present fragments, he was convinced beyond a doubt, that these were the ruins of Canopus, and of its temple, built by the Greeks, of which the rites rivaled those of Lampsacus: that miraculous temple in which the old recovered their youth, and the sick their health. The bath adjoining was probably one of the means employed by the priests for the performance of these prodigies.

The soil retains nothing of the antient canopite luxuriance. Delicious as it formerly was, it now presents but a wild and cheerless aspect. Here M. Denon saw a shacal, which at first sight he mistook for a dog, and which animal bears more resemblance to the fox than to the wolf, though it is called the wolf of Africa. As it was necessary for his escort to return to the caravan, he went back to Abû-kîr: there, he found an express setting off, with dispatches which had arrived for the commander-in-chief. He took this opportunity of returning to Rashid.

The anniversary of the birth of Mohammed arrived. The French remarked that no preparations were made for celebrating this the most solemn festival of the hegirian year. Towards evening, general Menou sent for the mûfti, both whose dignities and whose emoluments had been increased by the arrival of the army. It was
found

found that this man had seized the opportunity of representing the French to the people as averse to the ceremonies of religion, insinuating that they had forbidden the rejoicings of the day. On his being desired to proclaim them immediately, he said the time was now too short for the preparations; but being answered in the oriental style, that if the time was too short to make preparations, it was yet long enough to put the mûfti in irons, the festival was proclaimed within a quarter of an hour, the town was illuminated, and the songs of devotion were united with those of joy and gratitude.

After supper, the French were invited to the residence of the principal civil magistrate, whom they found in the complete apparel of a turkish festival. The street was the assembly room, which admitted of being lengthened or contracted according to the number of assistants. An alcove, covered with carpets, was occupied by persons of distinction. Bonfires, with little lamps, and large torches, composed an illumination. On one side was warlike music, produced by small, short, and shrill hautboys, small kettle-drums, and large albanese tambourines; on the other, singers and violins, and in the midst, grecian dancers, and waiters with sweetmeats, coffee, syrups, rose-water, and pipes.

As soon as the French were seated, the warlike music commenced. A sort of coryphæus, or leader of the band, sung two words, which the chorus repeated in unison; but, whether it was the fault of the movement itself, or of the manner of performing it, the second measure immediately became a cacophony, as disagreeable to european ears as it was enchanting to arabian. It was remarkable, that the coryphæus, with the energy and enthusiasm of an improvisator, repeatedly took up again the same notes; and, when his nerves seemed no longer able to sustain the fire he wished to display, the chorus came to his assistance, and always with the same dissonance: the violins, with more harmony, then played the burdens, in which a little melody was lost amid superfluous ornament; and now the nasal voice of the inspired singer returned to increase the fastidious effeminacy of the semitones of the violin, which, constantly avoiding the key of the tune, went into the tenour, and always ended with the treble, in the manner of the seguidillas of the spaniards; a circumstance which proves that the stay of the Arabs in Spain naturalized this species of music in that country: after the couplet, the violin resumed the same time, with new variations, which the singer again disguised by an affected movement, so as wholly to lose it, and run into a mere delirium of expression, destitute of principle and measure: but by this very means, he ravished his auditors, and, at every return, wound up their ecstasy to a higher pitch. The dance which followed

lowed was of the same nature with the song; it represented neither joy nor gaiety, but a voluptuousness that soon became lascivious; and this so much the more disgusting, as the actors, all of whom were masculine, expressed, in the most indecent manner, scenes which love itself allows only beneath the shades of mystery.

Trivial affairs continually intervened to prevent general Menou's tour in the Delta, and M. Denon from atchieving the design of his voyage. Obliged to confine his observations to objects immediately around him, he noticed the facility with which, amid the variety of figures, the several races of people which inhabited Rashid might be distinguished from each other. He concluded that this town, a staple of commerce, must necessarily be a point of union between all the nations which are spread over the soil of Egypt, and must preserve them with more distinctness, and more originality of character than a large city, like Kaira, where they are mixed and corrupted by the relaxation of manners. He believed that he clearly recognized in the Copt, the old egyptian stock, a sort of tawny Nubian, resembling the antient sculpture of the country, with a flat face, and hair half woolly, eyes half open, and turned upward at the angles, high cheeks, a nose rather short than flat, a wide and flat mouth, at a distance from the nose, and bordered with large lips, a beard short and scanty, little

grace

grace in the person, bowed legs, without a flowing contour, and toes and fingers long and flat. He drew the heads of several of this race; among others, one of a drunken and ignorant priest, and another of an adroit acute subtle calculator. These are the moral qualities, he adds, which distinguish these earlier masters of Egypt. The first epoch of their degradation may be assigned to the conquest of Cambyses, who, a jealous and furious victor, governed by terror, changed the laws, persecuted the religious rites, mutilated what he could not destroy; and who, to enforce its obedience, debased his conquest. The second epoch was that of the persecution under Diocletian, when Egypt had received the christian faith; this persecution, which the egyptians met with martyrdom, naturally prepared the way to their subjugation by the mohammedans. Under the latter government, they were transformed into courtiers and agents of beys and kiashefs*. In this capacity, they rob their masters daily; but in doing so, they, in a measure, only reimburse themselves, since an act of oppression on the other part, takes from them in gross all that they have amassed in detail. To counteract this, they employ more art in concealing what they have acquired, than impudence in the acquisition.

After the Copts come the Arabs, the most nu-

---

* Or *cashefs*.

merous of the inhabitants of modern Egypt. Without having the more influence for their importance, they seem to be placed in Egypt to people the country, to cultivate the ground, to guard the flocks, to be its animals themselves: nevertheless, they are full of fire and expression. Their eyes, sunk and almost hid, glisten with activity and character; all their lines are angular; their beard short, with pointed locks; their lips small, open, and discovering fine teeth; their arms muscular; and all the rest more agile than beautiful, more nervous than well proportioned. It is in the fields, and still more in the Arabs of the desert, that these characteristic traits may be most decidedly perceived. Three very different classes of Arabs, however, must be distinguished: the pastor, or shepherd, who appears to be the original stock, and in whom the traits that have just been described are seen; the bedûin, or wanderer, on whom the state of warfare and lofty dependence in which he lives, bestows a wild haughtiness of character; and the cultivator, or husbandman, the most civilized, the most corrupted, the most subjugated, in consequence the most debased, the most varied in form and character, of the three; as may be seen in the shechs, or chiefs of villages, the fellahs, or farmers, the fakirs, or beggars, and, to conclude, in the manufacturers, who form the most abject class of the whole.

The

The Turks have beauties of a graver expression, united with forms of a softer contour. Their thick eye-lids leave less expression in their eyes; their noses are less acute, they have beautiful mouths and lips, long bushy beards, a less tawny complexion, and short necks. Their whole appearance is grave and dull; there is throughout an heaviness, which they consider noble, and which gives them an air of patronage, in spite of the nullity of their power: to speak like an artist, nothing can be made of their beauty, but the beauty of a Turk.

It is not the same with the Greeks, who must already be reckoned among the strangers that form a sort of body separate from the aborigines: their fine projections, their eyes full of acuteness and intelligence, the delicacy and pliancy of their traits and of their character, recals all that imagination can figure of their ancestors, and all that their monuments have transmitted of their elegance and taste. The abject condition to which they are reduced, on account of that fear which the superiority of their minds still inspires, has filled many of them with crafty roguery; but restored to themselves, they would probably soon become, as formerly, only skilfully ambitious. This is the nation of all others the most desirous of a revolution, come from what quarter it might. During the ceremony of taking possession of Rashid, a young Greek approached M. Denon, kissed his

his shoulder, and with his finger on his lips, and without venturing to utter a word, clandestinely gave him a bunch of flowers, which he had bought for that purpose; an action which seem to develope all his sensations, his political opinions, his fears, and his hopes.

After these, come the Jews, who, in Egypt, as every where else, are hated without being feared, despised and repulsed without ever being driven away. Whether or not it be attributed to the proximity of Egypt to their own country, the fact is that their physical character is more strikingly preserved there than any where else: those which are plain in features resemble the Jews of Europe; while the handsome and particularly the young, resemble the head which painting has preserved as that of Jesus. In the great cities of Egypt, the Jews are the rivals of the Copts, as placemen in the customs, intendants of pecuniary concerns, and in short in every thing belonging to calculation, and capable of giving the means of accumulating and concealing a fortune.

Another race of men, consisting of numerous individuals, is marked by very characteristic traits; and this is the people of Barabra, natives of the upper country, or Nubia, and the frontiers of the Habbesh, or Abyssinia. In these burning climates, frugal nature has bestowed nothing superfluous. The Barabrans have neither fat nor flesh; nothing but nerves, muscles, and tendons,

more

more elastic than strong: they do by activity and swiftness what others do by power. It would seem as if their arid soil had absorbed the portion of substance which nature owed them. Their glossy skin is of a deep transparent black. They bear most resemblance to the negroes, or natives of the west of Africa. Their eyes are sunk and brilliant, and surmounted by elliptic eyebrows; their nostrils are large; their nose pointed; their mouth wide, without thick lips; their hair and beards scanty, and in little curls. Wrinkled early in life, but agile to its latest period, age manifests itself only by the whiteness of their beards. Their bodies continue lank and nervous. Their physiognomy is chearful; they are active and well disposed. They are ordinarily employed as guards of magazines and timber-yards. They are clothed with a piece of white woollen cloth; they earn little; subsist on almost nothing; and serve their master with attachment and fidelity.

The pilgrimage to Mecca causes Egypt to be crossed by all the nations of Africa who are known by the name of Maugrabins,* or people of the west. It was now the period of the caravan's return. Bonaparte, who had made every exertion for its safe arrival at Kaira, had yet been unable to prevent Ibrahim-bey, who had fled into Syria, from arriving before him in the desert, and attacking it at Bel-

---

* Or Muggrebins.

beys.

beys. Ibrahim-bey suffered only the devout mendicants to reach Rashid, where they arrived in companies of two or three hundred each, formed of all the nations of Africa, from Fez to Tripoli. They were now in such a state of fatigue, that they all resembled each other; all as meagre as the country they had traversed was sterile, and emaciated like prisoners forgotten in their chains. It is impulse, it is the force of opinion, that renders man the undoubted superior of every other animal, in strength. When the space of which these pilgrims had overrun is recollected, and all they had suffered during their immense and dreadful journey, the mind becomes convinced that nothing but an intellectual object could have enabled them to face so many afflictions and fatigues; that the enthusiasm of a sentiment of piety, and the dignity attached to the title of *hadji* or pilgrim, proudly borne by those who have made the journey to Mecca, are the only levers that could move oriental indolence, and carry it through such an enterprize. To these motives, however, must be added the right arrogated by the hadjis for the rest of their lives of making every other moslem* believe the tales of all of which they have or have not been witnesses.

Of the women of Egypt, generally speaking, M. Denon remarks that he has deferred the description,

---

* Or *múslim:* vulgarly, *mussulman.*

scription, till the men shall no longer insist on their veils, and the aged of the sex, more scrupulous still, shall suffer the young to display those beauties which themselves had been forced to conceal. He observed, however, that the girls, on whom marriage had not laid the restraint of the veil, bore a general resemblance to the Egyptian statue of the goddess Isis; and that the women of the inferior rank, who were more careful to hide their noses and mouths* than any other part of their body, frequently discovered well formed limbs. They tatoo their eye-lids and chin; but this produces very little effect on the countenance. Their long drapery would not be destitute of nobleness were it not for a veil in the form of a ship's pendant, which falls from the eyes to the ground, and gives the whole costume a resemblance to the dismal habit of a penitent.

A gentleman of the country, who was under some obligations to M. Denon, testified his gratitude by inviting him to his house. In regard to his age, and the respect due to a stranger, he thought he could, for his better entertainment,

---

* M. Denon mentions a poor woman, who having but one morsel of cloth in the world, used it to cover mouth and nose. It might be questioned, whether the foundation of this custom were an excess of modesty, which forbade the lips to be seen, or a precaution against the receiving the infection of the plague by aspiration.

take

take him to breakfast with his wife. She was beautiful, but had an air of melancholy. Her husband, who was a merchant, understood a little italian, and served as an interpreter between them. His wife's complexion was dazlingly fair; and her hands of extraordinary delicacy and elegance. M. Denon admired them; she presented them to him. They had not much to say to each other. M. Denon kissed her hands; she, very much embarrassed as to what, with politeness, she could do next, left them in his; and he, fearful that he should seem weary of the favour, did not dare return them. How the embarrassment would otherwise have ended is uncertain, but happily some refreshments were brought in. These were set close to herself; and she offered them to M. Denon in a manner very peculiar, and which had in it a species of grace. He thought that he perceived her abstracted melancholy to be only an affectation of greatness, which, in her opinion, was to be shown by an indifference to all the magnificence by which she was surrounded and covered.

The lady represented in the plate, was a native of Egypt, but the wife of a Frank*. She was

---

* Frank is the name by which the orientals distinguish every native of Europe, which part of the world they call *Frankistan*, or the *country of the Franks*.

beautiful,

beautiful, says M. Denon, of amiable manners, and she loved her husband; but she was not amiable enough to love him alone: his jealousy was the cause of continual noisy quarrels; on her submission, she constantly promised to renounce the object of his jealousy; but the next day there was new affliction; she would weep, and repent again; still, her husband had always some fresh cause for scolding. She lived opposite my windows; the street was narrow; and this alone naturally rendered me the witness and confident of her sorrows. The plague appeared in the city: my fair neighbour was so sociable that she was sure to receive and give it; she actually did receive it from her last paramour; she honestly gave it to her husband; and all the three died. I regretted her: the singular goodness of her heart, the artlessness of her offences, the sincerity of her tears, had interested me; and this so much the more, as that, a simple confident, I had had no occasion to quarrel with her, either as her husband or as her lover, and that, happily, I was not at Rashid when the plague desolated this part of the country.

At length, the journey into the Delta commenced. On the afternoon of the 10th of September*, the party crossed the Nile. It consist-

---

* 24 Fructidor.

ed

1

Denon delin.t

J.Pass sculp.t

2

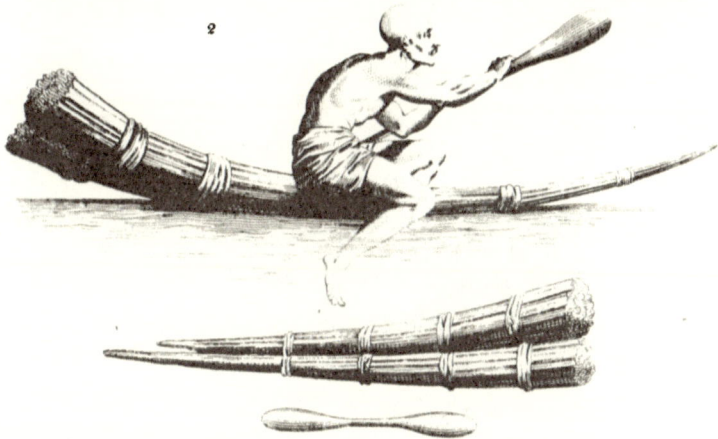

1. An Egyptian Lady. 2. The manner of passing the Nile.

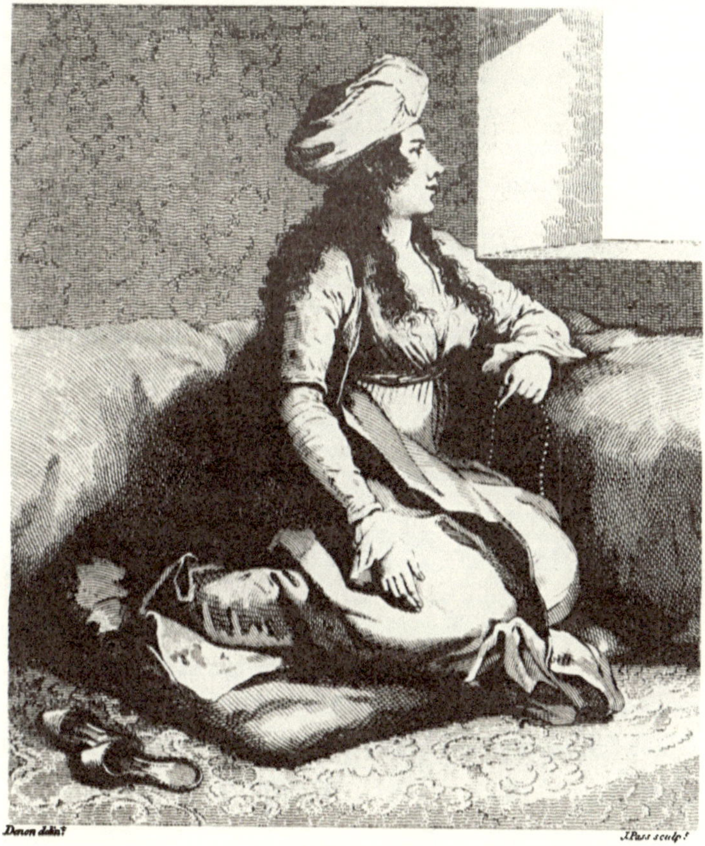

ed of generals Menou and Marmont, twelve artists and men of learning, and a detachment of two hundred soldiers. It passed through the thirteen villages of Mahadie, Elyeusera, Abûgeredi, Melahùeh, Abûserat, Ralaïcy, Bereda, Ekbet, Estaöna, Elbat, Elsezri, Sùffrano, and Elnegars; and arrived at night-fall at that of Mahadie-di-Berimbal. This nomenclature of villages, otherwise little interesting, will give an idea of the popularity of about eight miles of country, and of the abundance of the soil by which it is nourished. The next morning, the party reached Metubis*, in the province of Garbieh, after seeing the same proportion of villages as in the evening.

At Metubis*, general Menou had business with the shechs; on which account it was resolved not to proceed further till the morrow. Metubis, besides, is an object of learned curiosity. It is a question whether it have not been built on the scite of the antient Metelis; and, also, whether the known and tolerated licentiousness of its manners do not evince it to have succeeded Canopus, and enjoyed a similar reputation. The search after antiquities was fruitless. The people of the place spoke of some ruins at a league and an half to the south-east; but the evening was approaching, and the travelers, preferring

---

* Or Metabis.

their

their ease to the gratification of their curiosity, staid in the town. By way of pastime for the evening, they sent to the shechs, requesting the presence of a party of *almehs*, a sort of dancing-girls in Egypt, similar to the bayaders of Indostan. The government of the place, of which they, perhaps, may be said to make a part, raised difficulties against their attendance. Polluted by the eyes of infidels, their reputation might diminish; possibly, their station be lost: a specimen this, of the contempt in which a Frank is held by a moslem; since, here, the most corrupt of the community were to be defiled by his very looks! Some old offences, however, to be repaired, the presence of the general, and especially of two hundred soldiers, removed the obstacles. The almehs arrived, and did not appear to have any share of the political or religious scruples of the shechs. They denied, however, with a pleasing gracefulness, what the French thought the least of favours, such as that of discovering their eyes and lips, for all the rest was negligently free; and they soon seemed to forget concealment, clothed as they were with coloured gauzes, and ill-fastened girdles, which, every now and then, they carelessly tightened, with a playfulness that had something in it agreeable, and that reminded the French of their own countrywomen. They had brought two instruments, the one a bag-pipe, and the other a tambourine, made with an earthen pot, and which

was

was beat with their hands. They were seven in number. Two began to dance, while the others sung, accompanying themselves with castagnettes, in the form of little cymbals, of the size of a crown-piece: the motion by which these were rattled against each other, displayed the fingers and wrists of the almehs to great advantage. Their dance began voluptuously, and soon became lascivious. It was no longer any thing but a gross and indecent expression of the ecstasy of the senses; and, what rendered these pictures still the more disgusting, was that at the moment in which they kept the least bounds, the two musicians, with the bestiality of the lowest women in the streets of Europe disturbed with a coarse laugh the scene of intoxication that teminated the dance.

They drank brandy in large glaffes, like lemonade; and though young, and pretty, they were for the moft part, worn-out and faded.

The almehs, notwithftanding their diffoluteness, are received into the harems of the most respectable part of the community, as the tutors of young ladies, in every agreeable accomplifhment. They give lessons in dancing, singing, the graces, and every pleasurable art; nor is it surprizing that, where voluptuousness is the principal occupation of women, those of the sex who make a profeffion of gallantry fhould be the instructors of the rest. They are introduced at the entertainments given by the great among themselves; and when a husband
would

would spread festivity through his harem, the almehs are called upon to assist.* A scene of this description is the subject of the plate.

The next day the travelers visited the remains of antiquity of which they had been informed. They arrived at Koüm-êl-Hhamar, that is to say the *Red-Mountain*, a name doubtlessly taken from the little heap of brick, of a red colour, of which the ruin is composed. This ruin is without any thing characteristic. No vestige of antiquity was discovered, notwithstanding the solicitude of general Dolomieu and M. Denon to trace the antient Metelis, the capital of a nome, or province, of the same name. The country which they discerned to the north-east, beyond Komeh-Lachma, as far as the lake of Behrehlos,† was an uncultivated morass. They dined at Sindïon,‡ and slept at Fûëh. The next day, after passing El-Alàvi and Térâfa, they left the wood,

---

* The translator takes the liberty of observing, that there is much prejudice in the matter of the foregoing paragraph. It is common in Europe, as well as in Asia and Africa, to countenance, many persons, not for their virtues, but for their abilities. It appears that the almehs are mistresses of all the elegant accomplishments of civilized life. In this capacity, they are received into the harems or houses of the rich. On the whole, the character, as well as the situation, of women in the east is very much misunderstood in Europe. Not to enter into a discussion of the subject, let it be sufficient to suggest, that the same virtues are held in esteem in the one part of the world as in the other.

† Or Bûrlos.   ‡ Or Sandïon.

A Dance of Almehs in an Harem.

to survey some ruins which lie to the north-east. The mountain, or eminence, on which they stand is near Medyneh, and the ruins being, as the others, of a red colour, it is called Koüm-Hhamar-êl-Medyneh. Like the others, also, these ruins were only a heap of rubbish. From their scite the eye perceived about four square miles of uncultivated and arid soil; a sight which corrected the belief of the present universal fecundity of the Delta. The antiquaries had parted from the detachment, which they were to meet at Desuk,* and at which town they arrived, after traveling in a straight line from Koüm-Hhamar-êl-Medyneh, in the course of which they passed Gabrith, a village fortified with walls and towers, as is the practice of all lying beyond Fùëh, and not on the banks of the Nile. The land which they crossed in this journey, was less cultivated than that which they had been accustomed to see. The elevation above the river was too great to admit its being watered by means of the wheels. It was necessary to wait for the indundation before it could be sown with wheat and maize, and no after crops could be expected from it. In lands thus situated, the harvest is no sooner off the ground, than the earth, abandoned to the sun, cracks, and presents the appearance of a desert. The travelers passed through Salmia, where all the effects of the vengeance of the French

---

* Or Derûlh or Desûlh.

was still visible; but the countenances of the inhabitants of which did not manifest any resentment. The remark may be generally applied, that the people of the east do not preserve any rancour on account of the events of war. The Salmians, with cheerfulness and loyalty, furnished a guide to Mehâl-êl-Malek, and the canal of Ssa'idy.

The canal of Ssa'idy is of sufficient magnitude to carry the vessels of the Nile to the lake of Béréhlos. Desûk, a considerable village, which lies within two miles of the canal, contains a mosk highly revered throughout all the east. Twice a year, two hundred thousand souls are led thither by their devotion. The almehs come to it from all parts of Egypt, and the greatest miracle performed by Ibrahim, thus honoured at Desûk, is that of suspending the jealousy of the moslems, while they accord to their wives a state of freedom of which the latter are accused of availing themselves.

A palace, as it was called, had been prepared for the general, in which the whole party were lodged. This palace consisted of a court, an open gallery, on which was a room for luggage and, at the end, the principal chamber, without a door. In the center of the court was a sycamore. In Egypt, the shade of a sycamore must always be reckoned as affording a summer-chamber, or lodgings for the persons composing the household. General Menou gave audience from the windows,

in

in the manner of the beys, while the people were bringing a breakfast, supplied by the hospitality of the place.

On the following day, general Menou visited the remainder of the villages comprized within the province of Garbiëh. In this excursion Sanhûr-êl-Medyn was to be passed, and it was said that here were a considerable quantity of ruins. Here the travelers had hopes to find conviction that this town was the antient Saïs; once the metropolis, according to Strabo, of all this part of Lower Egypt. *El Medyn*, which signifies *the great*, encouraged their expectations. They crossed a thirsty plain, of considerable extent, which, though already watered, by a thousand trenches, cut from the Nile, waited for the inundation, to be rendered fertile.

The party returned to Desûk, without having been able to discover any thing in the devastations of Sanhûr-êl-Medyn.

The next day, a direction to the north-east, and the interior of the Delta, was taken. The travelers passed large navigable canals which, as they judged from the quality of the water, were supplied from the lake of Béhréhlos. Beyond these canals, the country, though its elevation was four feet above that on the other side, was already inundated. The banks of the canals served to communicate the villages, which rose above the water like so many islands, with each other. This situation of things detaching every object by itself, the travelers flattered themselves, that nothing interesting would escape them. They had promised themselves antiquities at Shahabas-Ammers, towards which village they approached by a narrow bank, which divided, by its meandring line, two seas of inundation. They gained two miles on the soldiery, in order to have the more time for observation. A guide on horseback, two guides on foot, a young man of Rashid, the generals Menou and Marmont, a medical man, who served as an interpreter, a draughtsman, and M. Denon, composed the foremost groupe; Dolomieu, leading a vicious horse by the bridle, and several servants, were at some distance behind. They were observing the favourable and picturesque situation of Kafr-Shahabas, a suburb before Shahabas, when the surgeon, riding up at full speed, exclaimed, " They are coming upon us with muskets!" The people cried, " *Erga!*" that is, " Go back!" The guides attempted to enter into explanation; but the reply was given by a discharge of muskets which, happily, though at a very small distance, did no injury. A second attempt to speak was made, but another discharge of muskets taught the travelers to save their horses legs from being broken, for these were their only resource. On turning to retreat, they perceived another troop of enemies, who were advancing along a road covered with water, to cut off the

only

only road they could follow. At this moment the draughtsman, struck with a fatal terror which took away all his faculties physical and moral, fell from his horse, on which he was no longer able to sit. It was vainly endeavoured to remount him, take him up behind another, or make him hold by the crupper. His hour was come; his head wholly forsook him; he cried out, without being master of any of his actions, or able to be prevailed upon to accept any assistance. Those who had fired were advancing; and, to avoid being surrounded, nothing was left but time to gallop through the balls which were flying on all sides. They reached the second groupe, in which was Dolomieu with his restive horse, and, now, a broken bridle. Denon had just time to tie it together for him; and this service was instantly repaid; for, while the latter remounted his horse, Dolomieu fell into a hole in which Denon would have been buried, but from which the former escaped because of his more than ordinary height. Denon took another road, and leaped a division which had been made in the bank by the enemy. The water already overflowed the ground by which they had come, running every where in torrents. After being entirely dispersed, every one reached the detachment in safety; and now the whole returned, resolved, in their anger, to carry Kafr-Shahabas by a *coup-de-main*. At four o'clock in the afternoon, they arrived before the village. They were fired upon

upon by forty men, entrenched behind a ditch. Their whole volley missed, as well as that returned by the French; but the former fell back on another party, which was drawn up under the walls: for the French now perceived, that this suburb was a little fortress, formed of four curtains, with towers at the angles, to one of which was added a castle. This outwork was separated from Shahabas by a canal, filled with water, and an esplanade of two thousand fathom. The chief place had hoisted a white flag; but the suburb continued to fire upon the French. The first attack of the latter was without success. The officer ordered to perform it, run away with by his horse, fell into the water; and his troop dispersed, to fall upon the inhabitants, who were carrying away their property. The two generals advanced, to stop the disorder and rally the troop. By this movement, the French were obliged to pass under the tower, and under the fire of the enemy, and several soldiers were, in consequence, killed. The fortress was turned. One of the towers was not manned. Of this, the gate was forced; and M. Denon, with the general, and thirty soldiers, entered. M. Denon and the general were the only persons on horseback; and the houses were so low, that they were within aim from three points of the works. At the instant that M. Denon warned general Menou of this circumstance, the horse of the latter fell under him, as by a thunder-a thunder-stroke. The general was thrown into a hole, where M. Denon, who thought him killed, afforded him the feeble assistance he was able, and whence, with the assistance of general Marmont and some volunteers, who had followed, he was withdrawn. The fire was violent on both sides; but the besieged were covered, well armed, and skilful shots, when they had once fixed their pieces. Several of the French being killed, and a dozen wounded, they were compelled to retreat. They attacked, in better order than before, the tower opposite to that of which they had possessed themselves. At first, the enemy lost several men. The houses were begun to be fired in order to uncover the castle. The position of the French became dangerous. Thirty men had been left to guard the baggage, and there were now but a small number with the general. At night-fall, the besieged raised terrible cries, which were answered by shouts from the circumjacent villages. In a short time, the reinforcements advanced. The French suffered them to draw near, and then, by a well-directed discharge of their fire-arms, speedily changed the cries of war into those of the wounded. The auxiliaries effected a retreat; and presently a deputation arrived from Shahabas, which was followed by the shech himself, bringing the flags. This latter informed the French, that the people with whom they were fighting were notorious robbers, with whom they must not hope to treat.

treat. A native, one of those released at Malta, acted as interpreter. The shech told them in confidence, that if they did not carry the place in the night, the party of the besieged would be too strong for them in the morning; that the people of the environs would cut off their retreat; and that they would all be killed. While he made these communications, his fine countenance was filled with an air of compassion.

The shech's advice was so much the better founded, as the carriage of a number of wounded along a narrow and broken causey would render it difficult to cover a retreat. While the French were consulting on the least disastrous means by which they might extricate themselves, before day-break, from the critical situation in which they were placed; the besieged, taking advantage of the darkness, pretended to call for and receive assistance; fired strongly on their flank-side, which they wished to preserve from attack; and, abandoning to the flames all their possessions, effected their retreat in the profoundest silence. The French did not hear them till they were obliged to take to the water. They fired on them at random; and a few of their camels which, in this emergency, they left behind, by retiring to the village, testified their flight. Masters of the field of battle, the military burnt every thing that would take fire. The soldiers, says M. Denon, indemnified themselves for the fatigue of the day and night,

night, by firing on two hundred asses, and two or three thousand chickens and pigeons*; and by bringing away seven or eight hundred sheep; but there remained nothing to indemnify amateurs of another cast for that of which this unfortunate event had deprived their curiosity; our hopes had been deceived, and our expedition rendered abortive; we had taken none but notes of little interest, and obtained only information of very uncertain truth, and amounting to almost nothing. At day-break, we began our return, without being impeded by any other obstacles than those which had been prepared the evening before. It is evident, that to have made such an excursion, we ought to have been accompanied by artillery; and that by delay, we had lost the season, which it was not in our power to drag after us.

On returning to Rashid, M. Denon found that those members of the institute which had remained at that place, were ordered by the commander-in-chief to join those at Kaira, for the purpose of completing the arrangement of the labours and sittings of that body. With his brethren, he embarked the next morning. In leaving the pro-

---

* In many of the villages of Egypt, the whole of the upper part of every house is laid out for the accommodation of pigeons, which are left to multiply, their dung being the whole object of this attention. This dung is principally employed as a manure for melons, and particularly water-melons, which are sown on the banks of the Nile, immediately after the inundation.

vince

vince of Rashid, they left the most fertile part of the Delta. Above Rahmaniëh, the sands of the desert approach, in several places, the very banks of the right of the Nile; the country grows naked; trees are scarce; and the horizon presents a line which it is almost impossible to describe. In the villages they passed, it was worthy of remark that the pyramidical talus of the antique-egyptian style, the ordonnance of the ground-plans, and the simplicity of the cymatiums still display themselves in the most modern huts of mud, and give an historic gravity to the landscape of Egypt, not to be found elsewhere.

At twenty miles on this side Kaira, they discovered the summits of the pyramids, piercing the horizon; and soon after, the Mokatam*, and, opposite to this, the chain which separate Egypt from Libya, and stops the sand of the desert from devouring the banks of the Nile: in the perpetual combat between the beneficent river and this destructive scourge, the arid wave often submerges the fields, changes their abundance into sterility, drives their inhabitant from his home, covers its walls, and leaves nothing visible but the tops of a few palm-trees, the last testimonies of their vegetable existence.

Night descended and equally hid the mountains, the pyramids, and the point of the Delta,

---

* Or *Mount-Kalam*.

where, among other extensive plans respecting Egypt, it had been proposed to build a new capital. At the return of day, M. Denon delighted himself with contemplating the surface of the Nile, now at its highest point of elevation, along which, at the feet, as it were, of the pyramids, glided, as they passed, innumerable villages, composing, every minute, new landscapes, of which those monuments were always the object and the interest. He wishes it had been possible for him to represent these on paper, with that delicate and transparent colouring which they derive from the immense volume of air by which they are surrounded. This is a peculiarity which they possess in preference to all other buildings, on account of the extraordinary superiority of their elevation. The immenseness of the atmospherical space through which they may be seen, gives them a diaphanous appearance, of the blue tint of the sky; and restores to them the unbroken lines of their angles, of which they have been robbed by time.

Towards nine o'clock, the noise of artillery announced the neighbourhood of Kaira, and the festival of the new year, which was being celebrated within that city. Innumerable minarets circled the Mokatam, and rose from the gardens which lay along the Nile. Old-Kaira, Bùlac, and Roda, grouping with the city, adding the charm of verdure, gave the city, under that aspect, a degree of grandeur, beauty, and even magnificence;

cence; but the illusion soon disappeared; each object returning, so to say, to its own place, nothing was left to be seen but a stack of villages, which have been placed, why it is not easy to discover, by just so much the more distant from a fine river, as they are the nearer to a barren rock.

On reaching the residence of the commander-in-chief, M. Denon learned that a detachment of two hundred men had just marched from Kaira, to protect a party of curious persons, who had not yet seen the pyramids. He lamented that he had not arrived a few hours before the departure of this expedition; but considered it as idle to visit objects of such importance without having provided the means of doing so with profit. He was, besides, so much fatigued with his two former journeys, that his worn-out muscles counseled him to be still. After dinner, however, the commander-in-chief observed, that it was impossible to go to the pyramids in safety without an escort; and that the attendance of a detachment of two hundred men was an advantage that could not be frequently expected. Impelled by this indirect persuasion from Bonaparte, M. Denon set off for Old-Kaira, joined the party, and crossed the Nile. It was dark when he arrived at Jiza. He knew not where he was to rest; but, determined to watch for a time, he suddenly found himself surrounded, through the enchantment of good fortune, by elegant divans of velvet, in a room where

where the perfume of the orange flower was
brought by the zephyr that had been loaded by
its spreading branches. He descended into the
garden, which, by the light of the moon, appeared
worthy of the descriptions of Savary. This was a
country-house belonging Mûrat-bey. He had
heard it depreciated, and he saw it only after the
march of a victorious army; yet he felt himself
unable to deny that, if nothing be destroyed by
useless comparisons, oriental enjoyments have
their zest; and that it is impossible to refuse the
senses the luxurious indulgence they offer. Here
were neither the long and pompous french ave-
nue, nor the twisted walk of the english gardens
(gardens where, in return for the exercise they
force, is obtained appetite and health); but, in
the east, unnecessary exercise is struck out of the
list of pleasures. From the midst of a group of
sycamores, the thick branches of which procure
a shade more than cool, enter kiosks, or tents,
opening at will, into copses of orange and jas-
mine: add to this enjoyments yet but imperfectly
known in Europe, but of which the deliciousness
may be conceived; as, for example, the charm of
being served by young slaves, the pliancy of whose
forms is always united to a countenance of mildness and affection. There, surrounded by beauty,
by all that nature has to gratify the senses, it is
doubtlessly permitted to the burning African to
taste as real and as intense pleasure as ourselves.

Yes:

Yes: this harmonious accordance, this divine gift, is every where, throughout the world; it is the property of nature, equally shared among all creatures that taste the fulness of their existence, whatever be the climate that has given them birth.

In the officer who commanded the escort, M. Denon found one of his friends. This gentleman made him one of the small number who, out of the three hundred persons that composed the company, were to enter the pyramids. In the morning, the journey was proceeded on, by means of the canals of irrigation. After landing several times on cultivated country, the barges were finally left behind, on the edge of the desert. M. Denon and his companions scarcely set foot on land before they found themselves in the sands, through which they waded to the plain on which the pyramids stand. On approaching these colossal monuments, their angular and inclined form takes from the appearance of their height and deceives the eye: besides, as every thing that is regular is small or great only by comparison, these masses, though they surpass every object that surrounds them, yet do not equal the extent of a mountain (the only great body with which the mind naturally compares them), the spectator is astonished to feel within himself an abatement of that impression which they had produced while at a distance; but as soon as he begins to measure

measure by a known scale these gigantic productions of art, they recover all their immensity: in fact, a hundred men who were at the door or opening of one of them when M. Denon came up, were so diminished by their situation, that they did not appear to be of human stature. I think, adds M. Denon, that in order to give, in picture, an idea of the dimensions of these edifices, it would be proper to represent, on the same painting or drawing, in its true proportion, a religious ceremony analogous to the antient usages. These monuments, stripped of their living scale, merely accompanied by a few figures in the front of the design, lose all the effect of their proportions and of the impression they ought to make. We have an example of comparison in Europe, in the church of St. Peter at Rome, of which the harmony of the proportions, or rather the graduation of the lines, conceals the height, the idea of which is not restored till, lowering the eyes on some priests going to say mass, followed by a troop of devotees, we imagine that we see a group of puppets about to play Athalia on the stage at Versailles.

Approaching the pyramids from Kaira, the first we meet with is that which is the only open one, and which is distinguished by the addition, *of Chæops*. At the elevation of sixty feet from the base of this pyramid there has been discovered an entrance which the architect had concealed under

under the third and outermost coating of the fabric. To this entrance the traveler ascends by a heap of rubbish and sand, part of which, possibly, has remained from the time of laying the foundation. It is the mouth of a gallery, sixty-five feet in length, which runs towards the center and the base of the building, without, however, extending to either. Rubbish, which at the time of building was perhaps but slovenly removed, or which, in consequence of the declivity, has fallen into it from the side of the edifice, added to the sand which a north wind blows into it daily from the desert, and which nothing removes, has rendered this gallery very incommodious for passing. At its extremity are two blocks of granite, which, stopping the progress of those who formerly investigated the pile, caused them to make an horizontal excavation of the mass itself, which turned out fruitless. Returning therefore to the blocks, and cutting an ascending passage round them, of twenty-two feet in length, they discovered a second gallery, also on an ascent, and an hundred and twenty feet in length. This gallery is very narrow, and so steep that, in order to ascend it, it was necessary to cut a sort of steps. At its top is what may be denominated a landing-place, of about fifteen feet square. Here three apertures present themselves. The first is sunk in a perpendicular direction; and this it is agreed to call *the well*. Time, light, and ropes, are necessary in order to ascertain its depth;

depth; but the noise made by a stone, on being dropped down, leads to a conclusion that its perpendicular direction is short. The width of its mouth is two feet by eighteen inches. To its right is an horizontal gallery of an hundred and seventy feet in length, and leading to the center of the pyramid. At its termination is a chamber, called *the queen's,* of a long-square form, eighteen feet two inches, by fifteen feet eight inches. Its original height is uncertain; because former visitants have dug up the flooring, and pulled in part of its sides, and left its bottom incumbered with the rubbish proceeding from these operations. The ceiling is in the form of an angle, almost equilateral. This chamber has no ornament, cornice, inscription, hieroglyphic, or sarcophagus; but it is formed of a fine calcareous stone, and the masonry is elaborate. If this chamber were designed to contain a corpse, then it is probable that the pyramid, destined for the tomb of two persons, was not finally closed at the time of depositing the body of the first; that this was really intended for the queen; and that the two blocks of granite which have been mentioned were reserved for that final inclosure of the whole.

Returning to the plat-form on which is *the well,* and from which, as has been said, apertures in three directions proceed, we commence a research into the third. After climbing a few feet, a large and magnificent gallery or slope is discovered, of an hundred and eighty feet in length, and proceeding like the former towards the center of the edifice. Its width is six feet six inches; in which must be comprehended two parapets of nineteen inches diameter, pierced, for the space of three feet six inches, in holes of twenty-two inches long and three wide. This slope was doubtlessly contrived for raising the sarcophagus; and the holes served to assist some machine in hoisting this mass up a place so rapidly inclined. The same machine would probably require the assistance of similar indentures above the lateral part of each of these holes, which, after being used, were repaired in the finishing. The width of the gallery is gradually less and less towards its top. This drawing-together of the sides is effected by eight projections of the height of six feet each; which, joined to twelve feet from the floor to the first plat-band, gives a total height of sixty feet to the key of this extraordinary vault. Arrived, with the assistance of some regular but modern indentures, at its top, we meet with a little plat-form or landing-place, and, after this, a sort of closet of granite, in the sides of which, large blocks of the same stone, filling the space between them, are dove-tailed. This barricade was intended to conceal and defend for ever the door of the principal sepulchre; a complication of construction which sets in the strongest light the importance attached by the Egyptians to the

inviolability

inviolability of their graves: but all that enthusiasm atchieved, avarice has rendered nugatory. With immense labour, a breach has been effected through thirty feet of granite, and a square door of three feet three inches discovered. This is the door of the royal chamber containing the sarcophagus; the little sanctuary which is the object of a building so monstrous, so colossal in comparison with every thing colossal that men have produced! The royal chamber is sixteen feet in depth by thirty-two in width, and eighteen in height. The door in this as in the queen's chamber, is in the angle of the longest side. Toward the bottom of the chamber, on the right of the door, is an insulated sarcophagus, of six feet eleven inches in length, three feet in width, and three feet one inch and six lines in height. When it is said that this tomb is a single block of granite, that the chamber is but a cabinet of the same material, half polished, and so exquisitely put together that no cement has been necessary in any part of its masonry, we shall have described this singular monument, and given an idea of the austerity of its magnificence.

The tomb is open and empty, nor does a single vestige of its lid remain. The only dilapidation in this chamber is that caused by an attempt to dig, at one of the angles of the floor, and two little holes, nearly round, at breast-height, and to which the curious have attached more importance
than

than they deserve. Here ends the research, as here appears to end the aim of this amazing undertaking, in which man seems to have tried his strength with nature.

M. Grosbert, an engineer, who has visited the pyramids, gives a base of seven hundred and and twenty feet, and a height of four hundred and forty eight*, to that of Chæops. He calculates the base by the mean proportion of the length of the stones; and the height by adding the measures of each of several gradations. According to the calculations of M. M. Grosbert and Maillet, the sepulchral chamber is a hundred and sixty feet above the plane on which the pyramid stands.

The base of the pyramid called *Chephrenes* is estimated by the same author at 655 feet, and its elevation at three hundred and ninety eight. Its coating, of which a portion still remains on the upper part, is a plaister composed of gypsum, sand, and pebbles. The *Miserinus*, or third pyramid, is said, also by M. Grosbert, to have a base of two hundred and eight feet, and an elevation of a hundred and sixty-two.

No more than two hours were allowed for the examination of the pyramids. M. Denon employed an hour and an half in visiting the interior of the only one that is open; and returned from

---

* The Paris-foot is to the London, as 1068 to 1000.

his

his journey wearied in body and in mind, and feeling his curiosity concerning the pyramids, rather than gratified, more irritated than before.

He had time only to take a general survey of the sphinx, a monument which deserves to be drawn with the most scrupulous care; a degree of attention which it has never received. Though its proportions are colossal, its contours are as delicate as correct. The expression of the head is soft, gracious, and tranquil. The character is african; but the mouth, the lips of which are thick, has a sweetness in its drawing and an elegance in its execution which are truly admirable: it is absolutely flesh and life. When a piece of sculpture like this was produced, the art must have been at a high degree of perfection. If it is without what it is agreed to call classic, that is to say, the straight and lofty lines which the Greeks gave to their divinities, justice has not, on the other hand, been done to the simplicity, nor to the grand and soft expression of nature, which demand admiration in this figure. On the whole, astonishment has been excited only by the dimensions of the sphinx, while the perfection of its execution, should awaken it still more.

We are almost as unacquainted with the epoch at which the pyramids were violated, as of that at which they were constructed: the latter, lost in the night of ages, opens an immense period in the annals of the arts: in this point of view, we cannot too warmly admire the masonry of the pyramids, the unalterability of their form and of their fabric; and, with regard to their vast dimensions, it may be said of these gigantic monuments, that they are the last link between the colossuses of art and those of nature.

Herodotus relates that he was informed the great pyramid was the tomb of Chæops; that the next was that of his brother Chephrénés, his successor; that that of Chæops alone had interior galleries; that a hundred thousand men had been employed during twenty years in building it; that the toil which the edifice cost rendered the prince odious to his subjects; and that, notwithstanding, the gratuitous labour which he forced from his people, the expences of feeding the workmen only were so great, that he was obliged to prostitute his daughter in order to complete the pile; and that, to conclude, out of the surplus of the profits of her prostitution, the princess had been able to build the little pyramid which stands opposite to this: now, either the egyptian princesses who prostituted themselves in those days must have charged high, or filial piety must have been carried a prodigious length by the daughter of Chæops; since, in her enthusiasm, she displayed even more devotion than her father required of her, having collected enough to erect a second pyramid on his account. But what exertion during a

man's

Pl. 1 to face p. 103 vol. I.

man's life to secure himself a secure asylum after his death! It must be added, that Chæops having shut up the temples during his reign, did not, when dead, find panegyrists among the sacerdotal historians of Egypt; and that Herodotus, the earliest author who throws light on this country, gave ear to many fables of these priests.

M. Denon was nearly a month at Kaira, during which he extended his researches throughout this superb city, this holy city, great among the great; this delight of the imagination, the splendours and opulence of which call forth the smile of the prophet: for such are the terms in which it is spoken of by the orientals. In point of fact, he saw an innumerable population, and extensive spaces for passengers; but not a single fine street, not a single beautiful building. There is a vast place, with the air of a field, called Lelbequier, wherein general Bonaparte resided: this, at the time of the inundation, had in it something agreeable, on account of its coolness, and the parties made on it at night, in barges. The palaces of Kaira, encircled with walls, sadden more than they embellish the streets. The habitations of the poor, still more neglected here than any where else, add to what is distressing in the sight of misery in all places, all the privations and negligence which the climate peculiarly permits. The observer is incessantly tempted to ask, where are the habitations

habitations of the four-and-twenty sovereigns?*
When, however, he has penetrated these species
of fortresses, he finds some conveniencies, some
refinement of luxury; fine marble baths; voluptuous stoves; mosaic chambers, in the midst of
which are basons of water and fountains; mattresses covered with rich stuffs and surrounded
with magnificent cushions: these divans commonly occupy the three sides of the room. The
windows, where there are any, never open;
and the light which they admit is dimmed by coloured glass, within very closely reticulated grates:
the principal light usually enters from a dome in
the center of the ceiling. The orientals, strangers
to all the uses we make of light, care very little
for procuring it. Generally speaking, every
thing they admire is favourable to repose; as, divans, on which one is rather laid than seated, on
which one is at ease, and from which it is troublesome to move; garments, of which the lower
parts are petticoats, by which the legs are confined; large sleeves which fall eight inches below
the fingers' ends; a turban with which it is impossible to bow the head; a habit of holding in
one hand a pipe with the vapour of which the
brain is intoxicated, and in the other a rosary of

---

* The beys are twenty-four in number.

which

which the beads are passed between the fingers; all this destroys activity, destroys imagination: they think without an object; without relish, do the same thing every day; and finish with having lived, without having endeavoured to vary the monotony of their existence.

The manners of such as are obliged to labour, are not very different from those of the rich. Accustomed to expect from their industry nothing beyond the ordinary routine, they never exert themselves with that hope. They never invent a method of doing better, nor seek for that which is invented; and they always reject any which they are obliged to stand, a position for which they have the greatest aversion. The joiner, the locksmith, the carpenter, the farrier, all work sitting; even the mason raises a minaret without being ever on his legs. Like savages, they seldom use more than one tool. One is quite astonished at what they are capable of doing; and one would be disposed to believe them ingenious if, adhering constantly to usage, they did not soon force one to think that, like the insect whose workmanship we admire, they are guided by an instinct from which they cannot stray.

But is it not despotism which, commanding always, recompensing never, is the source and permanent cause of this stagnation of industry? In upper Egypt, the arabian artificers, at a distance from their masters, sought the french military

tary manufacturers, worked with them, and, certain of adequate wages, laboured to give satisfaction, recommencing their toil when they had committed mistakes; they looked with enthusiasm at the operation of the wind-mill, and gazed on the effects of the rammer with transports of admiration: a secret sentiment of indolence inspired, perhaps, this admiration for two machines which assisted the heaviest labours necessity has imposed upon them; that of raising water, and forming banks to retain it. They build as little as they can help; they never repair any thing. If a wall threatens to tumble, it is left to do so. There are still some rooms in the house; and they lay the ruins on one side. At length, the whole building falls; and in this case they abandon the scite; or, if they are obliged to clear it, they carry the rubbish as short a distance as possible: it is this latter practice which has raised around every town in Egypt, and particularly Kaira, not eminences, but mountains, by which the eyes of the traveller is astonished, and for which he is at first unable to account.

 There are some considerable structures in Kaira, which should probably be attributed to the times of the khalifs, such as the palace of Joseph, the well of Joseph, and the granaries of Joseph, of which all travellers have spoken, and concerning which some have preserved the popular tradition which attributes them the to prudent care of the
Joseph

Joseph of Potiphar; but to confirm this, it would be necessary to show that Kaira is as old as Memphis*, and that in the age of this patriarch there were already ruins in the neighbourhood of the city, since these edifices have been built with the remains of others still more antient†. In a word, these buildings bear all the marks which distinguish every thing the moslems have erected in this country; that is to say, they are a mixture of magnificence, meanness, and ignorance. The aqueduct, which brings water from Old Kaira‡ to the castle over four thousand two hundred and forty yards of ground, would be a structure wor-

---

* According to the arabian MSS. Kaira was built by Jeuhar, a Greek, who, in the year 968, was sent by Abû-Tammim to siege Egypt, in which enterprize he succeeded. The founder had desired the buildings to be begun under the horoscope or ascendant of the planet Mars, called, by the Arabs, *Kahir*, or the conqueror: whence it was styled *Kahira*, or *Kaira*. See *Travels in Africa by W. G. Browne*, p. 100.

† " The mint is fixed in the castle, built by the celebrated *Yussuf* [Joseph] *Abû Moddafar-ibin-Aiûb*, whose title of honour was *Salah-eddin* [or *Selah-el-din*, the *Saladin* of the crusaders], in the sixth century of Mohammedism. The people of the country, who are in the habit of confounding all history and chronology, attribute it to Joseph the son of Isaac, whose palace they say it was; but it is unnecessary to confute an opinion wholly unsupported by facts." *Browne's Travels in Africa,* p. 78.

‡ Or *Misr-el-Attiké.*

thy

thy of remark, if, in the course of its extent, it did not exhibit the same incongruous assemblage.

The castle, irregularly built, and without any real means of defense, has nevertheless some parts advantageously disposed. In it is lodged, or rather confined, the pasha. The only chamber remarkable in his apartments is that of the divan, where the beys are assembled, and which has often witnessed the bloody scenes of this tempestuous government. Here, also, is seen the well of Joseph, cut in a rock, of nearly three hundred feet in depth, and of which all the particulars have been given by Norden. In its plan, the palace of Joseph is a fine conception : the admiration of the observer is commanded by the application made by the arabian architects of the antique fragments which they have employed in its construction, and the address with which they have often mingled ornaments after their own taste.

Now that the moslems have exhausted the columns of antient Egypt, and continue to raise mosks without demolishing those which are in ruins, they employ the Franks to bring them new ones by the dozen. The latter purchase them at Carara, of all sizes. The moslems surround their astragals with circles of iron, and set them under the arches of the porticoes of their mosks. The saracenic ornaments which rise above those columns, the style of which is a paltry grecian, compose a mixture of architecture the most detestable
that

that can be imagined. The minarets and the tombs are the only fabrics in which the arabian style is preserved with integrity; and if in this there be not found that which ought to be the beauty of architecture, an assuring solidity; there is at least observed with pleasure ornaments which produce richness without heaviness, and an elegance so complete in all its parts, that it never excites the idea of insipidity or meanness. The cemetery of the mamlùks affords examples: on leaving the masses of Kaira, we are perfectly surprized at beholding another city, built entirely of white marble, in which the edifices, composed of columns surmounted by domes, or painted palankîns, sculptured and gilt, form an elegant and cheerful assemblage. There wants nothing but trees, to render this funereal retreat a scene of delight.

M. Denon was making a draught of this sanctuary of the dead, when his ears were assailed by outcries. At first, he imagined this to proceed from the assistants at a burial procession, according to the custom of Egypt; but he soon saw that the women were flying instead of weeping, and that they made signs that he should follow. The idea of the scourge of the country rushed into his mind; but having an open space before his eyes, and seeing no Arabs approaching, he returned to his draught. He was scarcely seated, however, before he saw men flying also; and being at some distance

tance from the soldiery, he thought it prudent to retire. He found some agitation in the streets, and in the eyes of those he met. On reaching his home, he learned that there had been a disturbance in the city, and that the commandant had been assassinated. Muskets were firing. The palace of the institute, which adjoined the fields, and was situated in the midst of large gardens, where a delicious tranquility was enjoyed in times of quiet, became an abandoned spot under troublesome circumstances, and the first to be attacked by the Arabs, if called in by the people of the place, or if they came of their own accord. On the side of the city, also, it was in the neighbourhood of the poorest class of the people, and consequently that the most to be feared. M. Denon learned that the house of general Caffarelli had been pillaged, and that several persons of the commission of arts had perished. The members of the institute called over the muster-roll of their body, and found four absent: an hour afterwards, they learned that they had been massacred. No information was received from Bonaparte. Night arrived. The firing was partial; but cries on all sides announced a general insurrection. General Dumas, on his return from a pursuit of the Arabs, had made great carnage among the rebels on his entering the city. He had cut off the head of the leader of the sedition, while he was harranguing the people. Meanwhile, full an half of the city,

and

and that the more populous, was kept in a state of blockade by the insurgents. More than four thousand citizens had entrenched themselves within a mosk. Two companies of grenadiers had been repulsed; and the artillery was unable to act in the narrow and winding streets. Stone and lances destroyed their victims, while the hands by which they were sent remained undiscovered. The commander-in-chief sent a detachment for the protection of the institute; but was obliged to withdraw it at midnight. The night was quiet; for the Turks do not like to fight when it is dark, and make it a scruple of conscience to kill their enemies after sun-set. M. Denon, on his part, upon the principle that forethought, as soon as it is useless, becomes an idle inquietude, and trusting to the care of others, whose terror kept them on the alert, went to bed. The next morning, the war recommenced with the first appearance of light. Muskets were brought to the institute, and all the members put themselves in arms. They named commanders; but every one had his own plan of operations, and no one thought it his duty to obey. Dolomieu, Cordier, Delisle, Saint-Surion, and Denon had apartments at some distance from the rest. The house was liable to be pillaged by whoever would take the trouble. Sixty men came to the assistance of their brethren; and thus set at ease respecting them, they determined on putting themselves into a situation that might enable

enable them to hold out if attacked by ordinary strength, four hours at least; and thus to wait for the assistance which their fire would doubtlessly bring. At one moment, they believed themselves invested. They saw all the peaceable inhabitants in flight; and heard outcries on the walls, and the whistling of balls over their terraces. These they demolished, in order that they might crush with their materials those who should attempt to force their doors. In case of extremity, the staircase, by which they might be reached, was to be made a machine of war, by which all their enemies were to be overwhelmed at once. At length, the heavy artillery of the castle produced a diversion in their favour. Consternation succeeded to fury. The French could not batter the mosk; but this became the only refuge of their enemies; all who could not avail themselves of this begged for clemency. The mosk itself was turned; a battery taught the moslems that with the French the fight would not cease with the day. The former removed their barricades, and attempted a sortie; but, on being repulsed, they surrendered. The rest of the night was quiet; and the next day the members of the institute were released from their intrenchments.

The French had now conquered Kaira, which on their entrance only submitted to the vanquishers of the mamlûks. The apathetic and timid Egyptians smiled at the flight of those who had vexed

vexed them with innumerable acts of injustice and oppression; but they regretted their tyrants when they were called upon to repay their liberators: returned to their first alarms, they had listened to the representations of the mùfti; and, animated by a fanatic enthusiasm, they had formed a conspiracy in silence. Death ought, perhaps, to have been inflicted on all whose eyes had seen the french companies retreat; but in the conduct pursued, forgiveness out-ran repentance; and the spirit of revenge was not stifled by terror. A few traitors were arrested and punished; but the mosks, which had been the asylum of guilt, were restored; and the pride of the guilty was exalted by this condescension: fanaticism was not overcome by fear; and no danger that surrounded Bonaparte could shake those sentiments of goodness by which he governed himself on this occasion: he was desirous to be as merciful as he might have been rigid; and the passed was overlooked, while the French bewailed numerous and important losses among their countrymen.

General Dupuis, an excellent commander, who, during two years spent in the brilliant campaigns of Italy, had braved all the dangers with which the career of glory is beset, was assassinated while on a reconnoitring party, by a random weapon: a knife fastened in the end of a stick, and thrown from a window, cut the artery of his arm; and he died within a few instants. The young and brave

brave Sulkowsky, scarcely recovered from the wounds which he had received in the chivalric affray of Salayer, went to reconnoitre the enemy. Discovering him, he commenced an attack, notwithstanding the disproportion of the numbers. He overthrew him, pursued, and fell into an ambuscade. His horse, pierced with a lance, fell upon him; and he was trodden down by those who came to his assistance. Thus fell one of the most distinguished officers of the army: an observer on its marches, a knight in its battles, the pen relaxed his hands during its fatigues. He had written an account of the march to Belbeys with all the grace and interest which another ought to give to that of the combats he sustained, and the glorious wounds he received. Ambitious of glory, this young stranger had sought it in the warfare of the French; checking the vivacity of his character, he had restrained his conduct within the bounds prescribed by him whom he had chosen for his master; desirous of distinction, he pushed this passion even to jealousy; and the task he proposed for himself manifested the extent of what was to have been expected from him. M. Denon was the confident of the passion of his youth, of his noble ambition; this was laudable and great: it was by study, and by real merit, that he sought its gratification. Only a few hours had passed since, in a friendly conversation, he had interested his friend by his energy, when the news of of his death arrived to shake and freeze his soul.

If the populace, a few of the great, and all the devotees, betrayed fanaticism and cruelty in the revolt of Kaira, the moderate class, that in which, in all countries, reside reason and the virtues, was perfectly humane and liberal, notwithstanding the manners, the religious system, and the language, which made strangers of the French: while the galleries of the minarets holily excited to murder, while carnage and death scowered the streets, all those in whose houses the French resided were eager to conceal, to save them, and to prevent their wants: an old lady of the quarter in which the institute stood, told them that the wall only was between them and her, and that if they were attacked they had only to beat it in, and find an asylum in her harem: a neighbour, without having been asked, brought them provisions at his own expense; at a time when nothing was to be bought in the city, and every thing threatened a famine: the same man took away all exterior marks by which their abode might have been rendered distinguishable to the populace, and sat down to smoke before their door, in order to make the assailants believe the house his own: two young people, being pursued in the street, were seized by strangers, and carried into a house; they regarded themselves as victims reserved for a more deliberate cruelty; they grew desperate; and

and their gaolers, unable to make them understand their design, gave them their own children, as sincere hostages of the mildness and benevolence of their intentions. Many anecdotes of sensibility delicate like this, which assured the being of humanity at a moment when all its bonds seemed to be being broke, might equally be related. If the grave moslem represses the expression of sensibility where others glory in manifesting it, it is only because he would maintain the lofty rigour of his character. But let us pass to other subjects.

The caverns of Ssakkarah had been opened, and a sepulchral chamber, containing more than five hundred ibis-mummies, discovered. Two of these were given to M. Denon, and he could not resist the desire of opening one.

The pots which enclose these birds, and serve for their sarcophaguses*, are of a red and common earth, of from fourteen to eighteen inches in height; their form bears a general resemblance to a sugar-pot; they are found in great numbers at Ssakkarah, in subterranean chambers; these chambers are so dry, that the pots on being taken out appears still new, and that their antiquity

---

* The term *sarcophagus* is a very improper one when used in speaking of egyptian burial; the great object of this was the preservation of the body, while the *sarcophagus* was a tomb made of a kind of stone which *ate* or *destroyed* it.

might

might be doubted if the art of embalment were not lost, and if the bird whose mummy is found had not left the soil of Egypt: it is said that a few are sometimes seen in the lake Menzaleh, between Damiatt and the ruins of Pelusium: but M. Denon, in spite of reiterated inquiries of native sportsmen, and of those who made researches in natural history their peculiar object, found no person who could assure him of his having seen one.

On proceeding to open the pot and the mummy it contained, the solder which fastened its lid, and which was made only of a kind of chalk, gave way with a slight effort. The enswathed bird was loose in the pot; and this explains the state of pulverization in which mummies of this kind arrive in Europe, after the justlings of their journey. At first sight, the mummy of an ibis appears like that of a new-born infant; a fine cloth, of a bister-tint, and which appears to have been soaked in an aromatic fluid, after being crossed over the lower part of the body, covers the whole of one side; under this envelope, a double thread binds the mummy, horizontally and transversally, in the manner of a net, in all its parts; under this thread, the second envelope resembles the first, swathing the body in a similar manner; below this are little bandages, of an inch and an half in width, which, like the thread, are wound round the bird in every direction. The bandages
re-

removed, a third swathing is discovered, under which are little pellets of cloth, adapted to the inferior part, and so placed as to maintain the form of the mummy, and increase its consistence; all this taken away, the mummy assumes the figure of a pupa or chrysalis, ready to expand its wings; this last envelope, much coarser than the former, and dipped in a thicker balm, had received a colour of a deeper brown, and a substance less pliant; the form is here somewhat visible: this envelope was opened; but, as if the material employed had been applied in too hot a state, or that it had had some corrosive quality, it had carbonized every thing to which it had penetrated, and the bones fell into powder as soon as they were uncovered, or as soon as it was attempted to detach them from their adherence to the cloth, or to the embalming matter. The wish to render the research complete, induced M. Denon to open his second pot; in this was found a larger, compacter, and heavier, mummy: there was this difference in the envelopes of the second, that, instead of a swathing for its innermost covering, it had bands of two colours, alternately crossed by threads symetrically enveloping the little bundle as before. M. Denon also observed a little cockade, fastened on the side, near the top, and which at first appeared a fanciful ornament, but which was found to be a little bandage, wound up, and fastened to the bundle by the gluten

gluten of the balm: he has since had opportunities of observing that it was in this manner the embalmer, perhaps after finishing his operation, scrupulously enveloped and attached to the general mass the little fragments of feathers which had been separated under his hands, so that no part of the animal should be lost. This minute care manifests that the Egyptians joined religious ideas with their embalments; and it helped to explain to him, in the sequel, the meaning of the little mummies that he found in company with embalmed human bodies which he opened. All the other envelopes of the second mummy were the same as those of the first; the last did not adhere, and under it was found a skeleton, without a fragment of any one of the most delicate bones. The feathers of the head and beard were preserved; it might be seen, notwithstanding the alteration of their colour by the balsamic liquor, that the upper part had been white, and the extremities of a red-brown; the tail short, with feathers of little strength.

By means of the two-fold developements which M. Denon and his companions had performed, they were enabled to judge of the method of effecting this species of embalment. The operator took away all the interior parts of the bird, boiled them in the balm, and replaced them; after this, he doubled the wing against the body of the bird, the length of the wings making the whole height

height of the mummy; he bent back his legs, laying along the sides of the breast, put the head between the thighs, in such a manner that the extremity of the beak reached that of the tail; and, holding the bird, thus trussed, by the inferior end, he fitted the first cloth, fully saturated with the balsamic and glutenous matter, finishing the envelopement at the lower part, and applying two pellets to give consistence to the place which contained nothing but the tail, the wing-feathers, and the beak; after this he applied the greater cloth, of a finer weft, dipped in a thinner fluid, five inches wide, and three feet long; this he first wrapped from the top to the bottom, fixing it by winding a thread irregularly round; fastening this underneath, he adapted bandages three inches in width, the extremities of which were kept together by the gluten of a black and thick matter.

There is a very visible variety in the degree of care which was bestowed upon the embalments of these birds; the earthern pot alone is the same for all. This inequality in the formation of mummies found in the same cave, proves that there was for these, as for those of men, a variety of price; by consequence that it was done at the expense of private persons; and thus that it is to be presumed that the embalmed birds have not been nourished in common at certain temples or at certain colleges, in gratitude for the services rendered

dered by the species. If it had been with these birds as with the god Apis, single individuals would have sufficed, and these pots would not be found by thousands. It ought then to be believed, that the ibis, the destroyer of all reptiles, must have been held in veneration in a country where they abound at a certain season of the year; and, that like the stork in Holland, this bird being domesticated by the attentions paid him, each house had its own faithful attendant, to whom after its death the master, according to his means, gave the honours of sepulture. Herodotus tells us that he was informed, that in the earliest times remembered, they were numerous; that in proportion as the morasses of upper Egypt became dry, they had come down to the lower, to follow their prey; assertions that agree very well with what is reported by those travelers who have seen them occasionally on the lake Menzaleh. If the species had diminished in the days of Herodotus, it is not astonishing that in ours its existence should have become problematical. Herodotus relates, that the priests of Heliopolis informed him that, on the retreat of the waters of the Nile, there arrived, by the way of the valleys which separate Egypt from Arabia, clouds of winged-serpents; that the ibis met these serpents and devoured them: he adds that he had never seen the winged-serpents, but that he had gone into the valleys, and found multitudes of the skeletons of these monsters. With deference to the father of history, the ibis had

had no need of the creation of arabian dragons to render it interesting to Egypt, which herself produces so many mischievous reptiles; but the venerable Herodotus was a Greek, and he loved the marvelous.

Serpents with wings are no longer thought of in Egypt; but this animal is still an occasion of delusion. Psylluses were one day introduced at the palace of the commander-in-chief; several questions were put to them relative to the mysteries of their sect, and their connection with the serpents whom they appeared to command; they displayed more audacity than intelligence in their replies: resort was had to experiment: " Can you discover," said the commander-in-chief, "whether there be any serpents within this palace? and, if there are, can you oblige them to come out of their retreat?" They replied in the affirmative to both questions: they were put to the proof; they went through the apartments; a moment after they declared that there was a serpent; they re-commenced their research to discover where it was, fell into a few convulsions on passing a jar placed in one of the chambers of the palace, and pointed that the animal was there; in fact, it came forth. This was a true Comus's trick; the French watched them, and were convinced that they were very skilful.

Always curious to observe the means which men employ to influence opinion, M. Denon had regretted his not having been at Rashid at the time of of the procession of the feast of Ibrahim, wherein the convulsions of the psylluses is the part of the ceremony which interests the public the most: to obtain an equivalent for his loss, he addressed himself to the head of the sect, who was keeper of the okal or warehouse of the Franks: he flattered him: the psyllus promised to make him a spectator of the ecstasies of a psyllus into whom, according to his expression, he was to *breathe the spirit.* In his curiosity, he imagined, he discovered an inclination to proselytism, and proposed initiation: M. Denon accepted it; but having learned that in the ceremony of reception the grand-master spat into the mouth of the neöphyte, the idea of this circumstance cooled his desire, and he felt that it would not be firm enough to stand the trial; so, giving some money to the keeper of the okal, the grand-master promised to let him see an inspiration. In a word, the moment arrived; the chief of the psyllusses came to him in all the gravity of his supremacy: he was clothed in a long robe, of which the magnificence was relieved by the indifferent raiment of three of the initiated who accompanied him, and who had only a few rags on their bodies.

They had brought some serpents; they put them out of a leathern bag in which they had them confined, and, by irritation, caused them to rise and hiss. M. Denon remarked that they were

were principally irritated by the light, for as soon as their anger ceased, and they no longer attempted to bite; they had this peculiarity, that below their heads, for the length of six inches, anger dilated their skin to the width of a hand. He clearly saw that he should for the future be as little fearful of the bite of a serpent as a psyllus; for, having carefully remarked that in attacking them with one hand they seized them close to the head with the other, he, to their great scandal, did all that they had done, and without danger. From this juggle they went to the grand mystery: a psyllus took one of the serpents, the lower jaw of which he had previously broken, and of which he further scraped the gums till the whole palate was gone; this done, he laid hold of it with an affectation of transport, approached the chief, who, with that of gravity bestowed on him the breath, that is to say that, after some mysterious words, he breathed in his mouth; instantly the other, seized with a holy convulsion, his arms and legs distorted, his eyes staring from his head, began to tear the animal with his teeth; and his two supporters, who held him with difficulty, moved by what he seemed to suffer, tore from his hand the serpent, while he resisted the attempt; as soon as he was separated from it, he remained as if in stupor: the chief approached him, muttered a few words, resumed the spirit by aspiration, and he returned to his natural state; but he

who

who had obtained possession of the serpent, tormented with eagerness to consummate the mystery, demanded the breath likewise; and, as he was more vigorous than the former, his cries and convulsions were still stronger and more ridiculous. M. Denon believed himself initiated, and the jugglery ceased*.

The sect of the psylluses has existed in these countries from the remotest antiquity†: they were particularly celebrated in the Cyrenaic; the god Knuphis, or the architect of the universe, according to Strabo and Eusebius, was adored at Elephantis under the figure of a serpent.

The camels are the waggons of Kaira; they bring all the provisions, and they carry away the filth: the saddle-horses hold the place of chaises, the asses of coaches; they are to be found in every street, ready bridled, and always ready for a journey. The ass, melancholy in Europe, and always the more sad the nearer he is to the north, is in Egypt in his most favourable climate: there,

---

* The serpents are neither mischievous nor dangerous.

† Pliny represents the tomb of their king Psyllus as still subsisting; and adds that the psylluses cured the bite of the serpent with their simple saliva or by a mere touch, or at least that they said they did. According to the same author, these people were cut to pieces by the Nasamons, their neighbours, who took possession of their dwellings; but a few escaped the general destruction; and in his time there subsisted some of the descendants of these ancient psylluses.

in

in consequence, he seems to enjoy the fulness of his existence: spirited, active, and willing, he is the gentlest and surest animal that can be mounted; his natural paces are the amble and the gallop, and, without fatiguing his rider, he goes over the great extent of ground which it is necessary to cross in passing from one part of Kaira to another.

An arabian caravan arrived from mount Sinaï; it brought charcoal, gum, and almonds; it was composed of five hundred men, and seven hundred camels; this was a very expensive manner of bringing merchandize which was to produce but very little money: but the merchants were in want of articles which they could not procure elsewhere, and they had only charcoal to give in exchange.

The commander-in-chief desired that some one would profit by their return to obtain acquaintance with the road to Tor: M. Denon was tempted to penetrate that of Sinaï; he offered to the commander-in-chief to undertake the journey, provided he would secure his return: he replied that he would keep the head of the caravan as an hostage: he smiled at M. Denon's idea of reconnoitring, and drawing the scites in twelve days, of the miraculous part of the progress of Moses, from his departure from Memphis to his arrival in the desert of Pharan; that, without wandering for forty years, he was to see Sinaï, and traverse one of the parts of the earth of which the
annals

annals go the highest; the cradle of three religious systems, the country of three legislators who have swayed the opinions of mankind, and all three the offspring of the family of Abraham.

On his first proposition of his wish to the chief of the Arabs, the latter declared that for all the gold in the world he would not charge himself with M. Denon; that it would be to risk the life of that gentleman, the lives of the monks of mount Sinaï, and those of all the individuals of the caravan; because two powerful tribes, the Ovatis and the Ayaidis, had vengeance to wreak on the French. At the same juncture that he gave an account to the commander-in-chief of his unsuccessful mission, the latter was giving orders respecting the departure of a convoy for general Desaix. He had wished to go to the east, but he now requested a passport for the south; and within a few hours he had begun his expedition.

The next morning, at day break, he was at the distance of two miles of Ssakkarah, the vessel having made, for want of wind, only eight during the night. He had now a distant but comprehensive view of the pyramids of Ssakkarah. Though they were at some distance from the river, he could perceive that the nearest, of a middling size, was composed of steps, or graduated platforms, making so many terraces; after these came other little pyramids, almost levelled with the ground: at half a mile from these, there was one

one which appeared to have as extensive a base as the largest of those of Jiza, but less elevation; this was in very good preservation: at another mile from the last was one which was the largest of all those of Ssakkarah; its form was irregular, that is to say that its outline was waved like that of a reversed bracket: very near to this, there was a little one; and nearer the Nile, another, absolutely in ruins, and which had no other form than that of a gray-brown rock; its colour resulted from its material, which appeared to be unburnt brick: M. Denon thought that the banks of the river concealed other still smaller pyramids. This multitude of pyramids, the plain of the mummies, the caverns of the ibises, all prove that the territory of Ssakkarah was the *necropolis* to the south of Memphis, and the opposite suburb of that where stand the pyramids of Jiza, another *city of the dead,* which terminated Memphis to the north, and which to this day marks the boundaries of its extent.

In the afternoon, opposite Missenda, another pyramid came within sight very large, but so ruinous that in any of the other parts of Egypt, and at the great distance which it was seen from the Nile, it might have been taken for a little hill: two miles further, was another, still larger, and still more deformed.

The little islands that lay thus far up the Nile were covered with mallards, herons, and pelicans.
  Towards

Towards evening, M. Denon saw the pyramid of Medûn, between the villages of Rigga and Kafr-êl-Risk. In the night, he arrived at Saoyeh. Here, though the French were accommodated with the most showy and the best house in the village, they were indebted to their philosophy for the tranquillity with which they resigned themselves to many inconveniencies. In this part of Egypt, all the buildings are formed of mud and cut straw, dried in the sun; the stairs, the windows, the ovens, the utensils, and the furniture, are all of the same materials; so that, were it possible for a momentaneous change to take place in the order of things which nature has fixed imperturvably in Egypt, if it were to happen, for example, that extraordinary winds should stop and produce a dissolution of one of the groupes of clouds which the north-wind drives in summer against the mountains of Abyssinia, the villages and towns might be washed away and liquefied in a few hours, and a crop of corn sown in their places: but, thanks to the climate, a house built in this frail manner lasts a man's life; and this is enough for him whose son must buy of his sovereign the soil for which himself has already paid.

On the morning of M. Denon's arrival at Ssakkarah a column of three hundred men was ordered out to levy the *miri* or territorial tax, and a requisition of horses and buffaloes: in this, the French followed the custom of the mamlûks who, for the same

same purpose, severally made military excursion, through their peculiar departments, encamping before the towns and villages, and living at their expense till, what they had to receive was paid; and which calls to mind what Diodorus-Siculus has said of the Egyptians, that they thought themselves dupes if they paid without being forced by blows. M. Denon remarked that, without ever refusing, they made use of various ingenious methods to delay for a few hours the moment of parting with their money.

The movements of this column assisted M. Denon in examining the country and its monuments. He had a nearer view of the pyramid of Medûn, the total height of what remained of which he estimated at two hundred feet.

All the country over which he passed was abundant, producing wheat, sainfoin, barley, beans, lentils, and dûra or sorgo, which is a species of millet, very generally cultivated in upper Egypt. While the grain of this plant is green, the country people broil it like maïz: they mash the green cane like that of sugar; the leaves feed the cattle, the pith serves for tinder; the cane for firewood; the grain is made into flour, and the flour into cakes; but none of all these productions are good.

Between Medûn and Sapht were the ruins of a mosk, among which were some large columns of cipoline marble. These may be the remains
of

of the ancient Nicopolis, but no evidence of the fact is to be found.

The second route of the column was to Meimùnd, a very rich village, containing ten thousand inhabitants; it is surrounded, like all the others, with heaps of filth and rubbish which, in a flat country, form so many mountains from which all the circumjacent land may be surveyed: these little hills, therefore, are the favourite retreats of the inhabitants, a part of whom ascend them every evening, and, squatting in their manner, take the air, smoke their pipes, and observe whether the plain is tranquil. The inconvenience of these piles of filth is that they spread a stench through the villages, render them unwholesome by confining the air, and glue together the eyes of the inhabitants with a dusty powder mingled with imperceptible atoms of straw, and thus become one of the numerous causes of the disorders of the eyes with which Egypt is afflicted.

From Meimùnd the road was taken to El-Ehaffer, a pretty village, seated in an excellent country: the inhabitants collect a gum, known by the name of gum-arabic, drawn by incision from a mimosa, called egyptian thorn, or cassia, which bears small yellow and very odoriferous flowers. From El-Ehaffer, the eye discovered Abù-sir, Benni-âly, Dallasta, Basher, Ta-bùsh, Bùsh, Leitùn, and Eshmend-êl-Arab. Without El-Ehaffer, were encamped a dozen Arabs. The tent of the chief was

was composed of an old woollen cloth, supported by nine stakes; under it was all the furniture of the household, consisting of a mat, a carpet of the same material as the tent, two sacks (one of wheat for the master and one of barley for his mare), a large jar to contain clothes, a hand-mill for grinding corn, a cage of chickens, a vessel for the hens to lay their eggs in, pots, coffee-pots, and cups.

On arriving at Shendaûyëh, those who first entered the village found the inhabitants in arms. A misunderstanding ensued, in consequence of which some muskets were fired, and several of the people killed; but an explanation took place, and all was amicably settled. A moment after, however, a violent outcry arose, such as bespoke some terrible catastrophe happened or to happen. The case was, the pioneers had been about to chop some dry branches off a rotten tree which the soldiers had thought very well adapted for boiling their soup; and this was a more serious vexation than the former.

The belief in a supreme Being, certain principles in morals, in a word, the whole that reason teaches, suffices for a man of sense; but, to satisfy the passions of the ignorant man, there must be intermediate divinities, gross divinities adapted to a gross imagination, vicious divinities, so to say, with which he may enter into treaty concerning his vicious habits. The religion of Mohammed,

med, which reduces itself to precepts, is not sufficient, therefore, for the fantastic ignorance of the Arabs; in consequence, notwithstanding their implicit respect for the koran, and their unqualified reverence for whatever has fallen from their prophet, notwithstanding the anathema pronounced on all who wander from this, they have been unable to resist the inroads of heresy and the charms of idolatry: they have, then, their saints, to whom they assign no peculiar place in paradise, where every thing is common, but for whom they raise tombs, and whose ashes they revere; and, what is strangely stupid, these saints never become the objects of their devotion till after they have served for laughing-stocks during their lives. To the *poor in spirit,* when dead, they attribute power and influence: one is the father of light, and he cures disorders in the eyes; another is the father of generation, and he presides over labours, &c. The greater part of these saints, squatted at the corner of a wall, have passed their lives in continually repeating the word *allah,** and receiving without gratitude the means of subsistence; others have beat their heads with stones; others, covered with rosaries, have chanted hymns; others, in fine, as the fakirs, have remained motionless and entirely naked, never betraying the least sensa-

---

* A name of the Deity.

tion, and waiting for alms which they did not ask, and for which they returned no thanks. Besides this idolatry, there are other species which have connection with magic: such, for example, is the veneration for stones and trees which contain a good or a bad genius, from which, without profanation, nothing can be taken, to which domestic secrets are confided, and projects communicated, and of which the rites are mysterious and private, though the reverence is public. There was a tree of this description at Shendäûyëh, and the danger with which it had been threatened was the cause of the disturbance. This tree was remarkably aged. It had but one branch which bore leaves. All the rest, dead and broken were scrupulously preserved on the spot where, on leaving the trunk, they had fallen. On examining it closely, M. Denon found locks of hair fastened to it with nails, teeth, little leathern bags, and little flags; and, close at hand, tombs, insulated stones, and a seat in the form of a saddle, above which was placed a large lamp. The locks of hair had been nailed by wives to restrain the inconstancy of their husbands; the teeth had belonged to those who were growing, and been consecrated on imploring the appearance of the second; miracles of the most ordinary kind, for all the people of the place had the whitest and the best of teeth: the stones were votive, and their object, that a house which was about to be built
might

might always be inhabited by those who were going to build it; the seat was that on which the votary placed himself while addressing his nightly devotions, after it the lamp above it.

At Shendäüyëh the French spent the night in a wood of palm-trees, where, for the first time, they saw turf in Egypt. The next morning, they proceeded to Benésûëf. Desaix had been ordered to pursue Mûrat-bey, and complete the conquest of upper Egypt, in which the latter had taken refuge after the battle of the pyramids. On the 25th of August*, he struck his camp before Kaira, and set out together with a flotilla which was to convoy his march.

Informed that some barks with provisions and ammunition for the mamlûks, were at Reshqäseh, Desaix, in spite of the inundation, marched to surprize them; and the twenty-first light, after crossing eight canals and the lake Bâten†, where the water was up to their arm-pits, came up with the convoy at Benaseh, drove away the mamlûks who were to defend it, and made it their prize. Mûrat had fled into the valley of Faïûm ‡; Desaix rejoined his division at Abû-jairjeh, marched to Tarût-êl-shereef, where he took his position at the entrance of the canal of Joseph‖,

---

* 8 Fructidor. † Or *Bathen* or *Batûn*. ‡ *Feiûm*, or *Faïoum*; the latter is the french orthography. ‖ Or *Bahr-êl-yussuf*.

to

to insure a communication with Kaira. Arrived at Siût, whence the mamlûks had fled, he endeavoured to overtake them at Beneädy, whither they had retired with their women and baggage; but these having finally joined Mûrat-bey in Faiùm, he returned to Siût*, in order to redescend to Tarût-êl-shereef, where he embarked his army on the canal of Joseph. Arrived off Mansûra, on the borders of the desert, he, at last, met Mûrat-bey: unable to effect his debarkation under the fire of the enemy, he ordered those who had landed to return on board, intending to fall down to Minkia; the mamlûks, encouraged by this counter-march, harrassed the barks; some companies of grenadiers chased and dispersed them; the debarkation effected, the troops formed into square battalions, and resumed the road to the desert, accompanied by the barks, as far as Mansûra itself Mûrat-bey was at four miles distance; while his rear-guard harrassed the French, he gained the heights, where they saw his army open with all the magnificence of the east. With telescopes, they discerned his person, blazing with gold and gems; he was surrounded by all the beys and kiashefs under his command. The French marched directly forward; and the splendid cavalry which they had to oppose, always irresolute in it operations, and cannonaded by the only two

---

* Or *Osiot*; in the french, *Sioulh*.

pieces

pieces which could follow it, stopped, turned, and fled to Elalamon. In following it, the French left their barks; they wanted food, and were obliged to return to them for biscuit: the enemy thought they fled; he attacked them with cries resembling howlings: the artillery drove away the mass; but the most determined advanced to brave the musketry with their sabres; they actually carried away two prisoners from the very points of the bayonets, and night alone delivered the French from their valour. On regaining the barks, the army loaded itself with biscuit and, after taking a little repose, recommenced its march.

During this time, Mùrat-bey had caused a stranger to arrive in his army with news that the English had destroyed those of the French who were at Alexandria, that the inhabitants of Kaira had massacred those who had occupied that city, in a word that there remained in Egypt only the handful of soldiers whom they had put to flight the evening before, and whom they should presently annihilate: in consequence, a festival was given, and in this festival there was a sham battle, in which the French were represented by Arabs, who had orders to suffer themselves to be beaten. The feast concluded with the murder of the two prisoners who had been taken two days before.

Desaix learned that Mùrat was at Sediman, where he was preparing to meet and give battle
to

to the French: Desaix resolved to commence the attack: as soon as he had left the open and cultivated country, and entered on an uninterrupted surface where the eye could ascertain his number, he was assaulted by cries of ferocious joy; but the enemy deferred till the morrow the victory of which he believed himself secure. The night was passed by the mamlûks in carousals within their camp; in the dark, their patrols insulted the french pickets, by mimicking their language. At the dawn of day, they formed into a hollow square, flanked by two lesser bodies: soon after, the French saw Mûrat-bey, at the head of his mamlûks, and eight or ten thousand Arabs, lining the horizon for two miles. A valley lay between the two armies, which must be passed before the French could attack their enemy. Scarcely did Mûrat see them in this disadvantageous position before he surrounded them on all sides, charging them with a bravery which approached to fury. The closeness of the french body rendered the number of his men of no ad-advantage to him. Their musquetry did great execution, and repulsed him for the time. The mamlûks stopped, wheeled as if to take to flight, and suddenly fell on one of the squadrons, which they completely levelled with the ground; all who were not killed, by a spontaneous movement, fell down: this movement uncovered the enemy to the center of the French; it made use of the
instant

instant to give a heavy fire: the mamlûks stopped and wheeled once more. Those of the squadron who were not killed came into the ranks. The French were attacked by the whole body again, no longer with the cries of victory but with those of rage: valour was equally manifested on either side: the barrels of the french muskets were hacked by the sabres of the mamlûks; their horses were precipitated on their ranks, without shaking them; the animals fell back at the sight of the bayonets; their riders turned them, hoping to force the ranks by their kicks: the French, who knew that their safety depended upon their union, pressed together without disorder, and attacked without engaging; the carnage was every where, but there was no battle: ill-success of the attempts of the mamlûks had driven them wild with fury; they threw their arms which could not otherwise have reached the French; as if this battle were to have been the last, the troops were assailed with firelocks, warlike instruments, pistols, battle-axes, and showers of sabres. Those who were dismounted crept under the bayonets, endeavouring to cut the legs of the soldiers; the dying collected their strength and still struggled with the dying, and their blood, which mingled while it drank the dust, did not appease their animosity. One of the French, prostrate, had closed with an expiring mamlûk, whom he held by the throat: "How," said an officer,

officer, " in your situation, can you be guilty of any thing so shocking?"—" You," replied he, " talk very well, at your ease; but I have but a moment to live, and I wish to enjoy it a little."

The enemy had suspended his attack; he had committed great slaughter among the French; in falling back he did not fly; and the situation of the latter was not improved: scarcely had he retired, when he opened a battery which had hitherto been concealed, and which, at each discharge, carried off six or eight soldiers. For a moment, the French were lost in consternation and stupor; the number of the wounded increased every instant. To give the word to march was to bend to the courage of the enemy, and to expose themselves to every species of danger; not to do so, was to give useless extent to the evil, and to expose the whole army to destruction: to march was to abandon the wounded, and to abandon them was to give them up to certain death; a dreadful circumstance in all wars, and more especially in the barbarian war they were carrying on. Desaix, distracted with the alternative, remained motionless a moment; at length, the general interest commanded him to act, the voice of necessity drowned that of the unfortunate wounded, and the army began its march. The only choice was between victory and total destruction; the extremity of this situation so united the interests of all, that the army was
only

only as one individual, and that, to speak of the brave, every man of which it was composed ought to be mentioned: the light artillery, commanded by the ardent Tournerie, did prodigies of address and celerity; and while this dismounted some of the guns of the mamlûks, the grenadiers came up; the battery was abandoned; the cavalry, panic-struck, fell back, wheeled, fled, disappeared like a vapour, and left the French without an enemy to oppose.

Never was there a battle more terrible, a victory more brilliant, or a catastrophe more unexpected. The actual advantage gained by the battle of Sediman was that of detaching the Arabs from the mamlûks; but much was to be added on the score of the impression of the French tactics on the fears of the latter. Mûrat-bey, no longer hoping to break the lines of the infantry, to repulse, or even to resist them, reduced the french army to the occupation of following a light and rapid enemy, who, in his ceaseless precaution, left it neither repose nor security. The war carried on by the French became the same as that of Anthony among the Parthians: the roman legions putting to flight battalions without obtaining successes, found resistance only in the space the enemy left before them; but, exhausted with daily losses, fatigued with victories, they gladly left the country of a people who, always conquered but never subjugated, came on the

morrow

morrow of a defeat to harrass, with increased audacity, those to whom, on the preceding evening, they had abandoned a field of battle by which the victor never gained an advantage*.

The heat of the days, and the coolness of the nights at this season, afflicted the army with numerous opthalmies: this disorder is unavoidable when long marches or great fatigues are followed by nightly watchings, during which the humidity

---

* Among the anecdotes that might be related of the conduct of individuals in this battle, the following deserves to be particularized: A wounded soldier, whom his comrade would have carried off the field, pointed out the desperateness of his condition, and the inutility of attempting to deliver him from death: the other made him observe that the enemy was approaching; be replied, that to tarry would be to make both his victims, while his friend, disencumbered might effect his escape: " Leave me," said he, " you may escape, I must perish." The recital comes from a friend who, with tears, reproached himself for having yielded to the love of life. Another, wounded, covered his head to avoid the sight of the death that was coming upon him, begging his comrades to dispatch him, that he might not fall under the hands of the barbarians. Valour has the same language in every age, and in every rank : " Do not weep on my account," said the dying Anthony to Cleopatra; " after a glorious life, I could be conquered only by a Roman." Does not the generosity of the soldier who persuaded his comrade to abandon him resemble that of the chevalier de Lorda, who got off the back of the sailor that could not carry him to the beach? If the french soldiers betray some of the brutal passions in a moment of pillage, they manifest all the virtues in the day of battle.

of the air repels perspiration: these contrasts produce fluxions that attack either the eyes or the bowels.

Dessaix, in haste to collect the miri and levy horses, in the province of which he had become possessed, left three hundred and fifty men at Faiûm, and set out to reduce the villages which Mûrat-bey had excited to arms. While he was overrunning the province, a thousand mamlûks, accompanied by many fellahs, or husbandmen, entered the town and attacked the wounded who remained there; but they were repulsed. Desaix returned, and the whole army moved to Benêsûëf, to dispute with Mûrat-bey the miri of that rich province.

Arrived at Benêsûëf, Desaix, in order to provide himself with the means of taking the field again, repaired to Kaira. On the right bank of the Nile, opposite Benêsûëf, the arabic chain lowers, retires, and forms the valley of Araba, or of Chariots, terminated by mount Kolsun, famous for the grottoes of the two fathers of the cenobites, saint Anthony and saint Paul, the founders of the contemplative system, a system as useless to human society as pertinaciously respected by misled nations. On the ground that covers the two grottoes, in which lived these holy hermits, there still exist two monasteries, from one of which, it is said, is discovered mount Sinaï, which lies on the opposite side of the Red-Sea. The opening

opening of this valley, towards the Nile, presents only a melancholy plain, of which but a narrow border, lying along the river, is cultivated; beyond this ribband there are perceived a few remains of villages overwhelmed by the sand, presenting an affecting view of the destruction daily taking place, through a continual incroachment of the desert on the inundated soil.

Nothing is so melancholy as to walk over these villages, to push away with the feet the sand from off their roofs, to stumble against the points of their minarets; to think that there lay cultivated fields; that, here, trees spread their shade; that, here, again, were the dwellings of men, and that all is gone: around their walls, within their walls, every where is silence: these mute villages are like the dead, whose remains inspire terror.

The antient Egyptians have designated this encroachment of the sands, by the clandestine entrance of Typhon into the bed of Isis, his half-sister, an incest which would change Egypt into a desert as frightful as that by which it is bounded; and this great event must happen if ever the Nile should find a more rapid declivity in one of the valleys by which it is bordered than in the bed on which it at present flows, and which it is daily filling up. This idea, which, at first sight, is an extraordinary one, will assume an air of probability if local circumstances be considered. The

rising

rising of the Nile, and the destruction of its banks, have already made an artificial canal which would already have covered the Faïûm with water, had not the khalif Yussuf raised new banks above the antient ones, and dug a canal of communication below Benésûëf to restore to the river what its annual overflux pours into that vast bason. Without causeys, raised to stop the inundation, the deep hollows would soon transform this province into one vast lake: this was what actually happened about twenty-five years ago, through an extraordinary inundation, in which, the river having risen above the banks of Hilahön*, it was feared that the Faïûm would have remained under water, or the Nile returned to a channel which it is almost evident it used in very remote ages. It was to remedy this inconvenience, that a sluice was constructed at Hilhaön, by means of which a discharge is effected of all the water more than sufficient to water without submerging the province. If then a system might be hazarded, it should be said that, more antiently than the most antique times of which we have any knowledge, all the Delta was but one great gulf, through which flowed the waters of the Mediterranean; that the Nile passed through the valley of Faïûm; that, by the way of what is now called the Waterless-River, it fell into the

---

* Or Illäûn, or Ellahûn.

lake Mareötis, which was one of its openings into the sea, as the lake Mahadieh was that of the canopite mouth, and as the lakes of Behrehlos and Menzaleh still are of the sebenitic, mendaisian, tanitic, and pelusiac; that the Bahr-Belamáëh*, or Waterless-River, is the remain of the bed of the antient course of the river, in which are found, in a state of petrifaction, unquestionable testimonies of the former presence of water, as the relics of vegetation and of human labours; that the Nile, at a certain epoch, finding a greater declivity to the north than to the north-west, precipitated itself into the gulf the existence of which we have supposed; that at first it formed marshes, and afterwards the Delta. It results from this, that the earliest labours of the Egyptians, as the lake Mœris, now lake Bàten, and the first dike, were originally designed only to retain a part of the waters of the inundation, to water the province of Arsinoë, which threatened to become sterile, and that, in times posterior to this, the lake Mœris, or Bàten, no longer receiving sufficient to water the valley of Faïûm, it became necessary to draw a supply by means of an opening higher up the river, and to dig the canal of Yussuf, which doubtlessly bears the name of the khalif who performed this noble work; but, fear-

---

* The term *bahr* is used to denote, indifferently, the sea, a river, or a canal; but not a lake or pool.

ing,

ing, at the same time, that, in great inundations, the valley would become permanently inundated, this prince raised new banks above the antient, as they exist at present, and caused the canals of Bûsh and Zaöyëh to be dug, to carry back to the Nile its superfluous waters.

Observations on the levels and on the works of the antient Egyptians at various epochs, together with accurate plans and charts, will possibly, at some future time, be the result of a tranquil possession of the country: these will establish certainties in the place of systems; they will show to what extent the Egyptians have been occupied through all ages in the management of the waters of the Nile, and how largely, even in times of ignorance, they have still preserved their intelligence on this subject. According to what has now been advanced, if the Nile continue to press on its right, to enlarge, as it has already, the branch of Damiatt at the expense of that of Rashid; if it abandon this latter as it formerly did the Bahr-Belamáëh, and afterwards the mouth of Canopus; if, in short, it leave the lake of Behrehlos to cast itself entire into that of Menzaleh, or form new branches and new lakes to the east of Pelusium; if nature, to conclude, always stronger than any thing that can be opposed to her, has doomed the Delta to become a barren soil, the inhabitants will follow the Nile in its progress, and always find upon its banks that
abun-

abundance which, wherever they come, its beneficent waters spread around them.

After the departure of general Desaix, excursions were made to reconnoitre, and to levy contributions. Visiting the entrance of the valley of Faïùm, about two miles to the west of Benésûëf, after a march of two hours, the French arrived at Davalta, a beautiful village, that is to say, a beautiful landscape; for, in Egypt, nature, when she is beautiful, is admirable, in spite of all with which men disfigure her, and in spite of those detractors of Savary who are angry with his delightful descriptions. With all deference to such, it must yet be allowed that here nature herself, unassisted by human industry, plants groves of palms, under which she unites the orange, the sycamore, the oponcia, the banana, the acacia, and the pomegranate; that these trees form groupes of the sweetest variety of verdure; that when these thickets are surrounded, as far as the eye can see, by fields covered with ripe dùra, of sugar-canes ready for the harvest, with wheat, with flax, and with trefoil which covers with velvet the cracks in the earth, as fast as the inundation retires; when, during the winter-months of Europe, there are beneath the eyes this brilliant picture of the riches of spring, assuring the abundance of summer, it must be said, with the traveler mentioned, that Egypt is the country most wonderfully organized by nature, and that it wants
nothing

nothing but shady hills with rivulets flowing from the sides, a government that would render its population industrious, and the repulsion of the bedûins, to become the finest and the best of regions.

After crossing the rich country of which we are more immediately speaking, the French arrived at Dindyra, where they halted for the night. Seated at its entrance, the pyramid of Hilhäon, resembles a fortress placed to command the valley. Is it to be believed that this is the pyramid of Mendes? Is the canal of Bâten, which abuts it, the Mœris, hollowed by the hands of man, as Herodotus and Diodorus have believed? Accustomed as we are to the gigantic labours of the Egyptians, we cannot persuade ourselves that a lake like that of Geneva has been their work.

All that the antient historiographers and geometricians have said concerning the lake Mœris is equivocal and obscure: we clearly see that what they have written was dictated to them by the colleges of priests, who were always jealous of what respected their country, and who could with peculiar ease throw a mysterious veil on this province, which lay out of the ordinary track; and hence have originated a lake dug to the depth of three hundred feet, the pyramid elevated in the midst, the famous labyrinth, the palace of an hundred chambers, the palace for the nourishment of crocodiles, in a word all that is fabulous in the history

history of man, and all that remains incredible in that of Egypt. But, from the aspect of what exists, there certainly has been a canal, which is that of Bâten, and which was still under water when the French approached it; the pyramid may be that of Mendes, who may have built it at the extremity of the canal, which may be the Mœris; the birket, or lake, of Kerùn is an assemblage of water which has been supplied and renewed by the excess of the inundation of the valley, and always existing, of which the bason was formed by the soil; its water became salt at the epoch in which the Nile ceased to flow through the Bahr-Bela-maëh. The evidences of this system are the local forms, the existence of a bed of a river extending to the sea, its disposition and incrustations, the depth of the lake, its extent, the support of its mass to the north by a broken chain of rocks which rise east and west, and turn to the north-west, lowering their heights, and following the Bahr-Bela-maëh; add to these the natrôn-lakes, and, more than all, the chain to the north of the pyramid, which, cut into a peak, like all the mountains which at this day the current approaches, closes the valley, presenting to the eyes a dry river, and the ravages of its course.

The ruins which are found near the town of Faiùm are doublessly those of Arsinoë. M. Denon did not visit either these or those which stand at the western extremity of the lake, near the

the village of Kasr-Kerun; but he was shown a plan, which contained only a few chambers, and a portico decorated with hieroglyphics.

The pyramid of Hilahön is more injured by time than the others which he had seen, and it appears to have been built with less magnificence; its fabric is composed of masses of calcareous stone, which are covered with unburnt bricks; this frail edifice, more antient perhaps than the pyramids of Memphis*, is still, under the favourable climate of Egypt, in existence; while a few northern winters would have accomplished its destruction.

On the ninth of December†, general Desaix returned from Kaira, bringing with him two hundred cavalry, six pieces of artillery, six armed *djermas*, and two or three hundred infantry, by which additions the strength of his division was raised to three thousand infantry, two hundred horse, and eight pieces of light artillery. On the sixteenth, the army left Benésùëf; its column was two miles in length; all breathed joy and hope. At one in the morning it reached El-Be-. ranka, and breakfasted the next morning at Babeh, a village remarkable only for possessing the wrist of saint George, a relic to be earnestly recommended to every pious knight: here, the

---

* At Jiza. † 19 Frimaire.

arabic chain borders so closely on the Nile, that it leaves only a green edge on its banks.

At Miniél-Guidi, the march was delayed by accidents which happened to the artillery in passing the canals; at this place, also, it received information that the mamlûks were at Féshneh. While the French waited in the shade for the coming up of the artillery, a criminal was brought before general Desaix: " Here is a robber," was the cry; " he stole two muskets belonging to the volunteers; he was taken in the fact;" and a beautiful boy of twelve years old was brought forward. His arm had received a large wound from a sabre; he looked at the wound without emotion; he presented himself with an artless and assured air to the general, whom he immediately knew for his judge. So powerful is the grace of artlessness, that not an individual present retained an angry sentiment against him. He was asked, who had told him to steal the muskets: *Nobody;* what had induced him to commit the robbery: *He knew not, the strong,— God;* whether he had any parents: *Only a mother, very poor, and blind;* the general told him that if he would acknowledge who had sent him, nothing should be done to him; but that if he persisted in concealing this, he should immediately suffer the punishment he deserved: *I have told you, nobody sent me,—God alone inspired me;* then, laying his cap at the general's feet; *Here is my my head, cut it off:* " Poor little wretch," said the general, " let him be dismissed." He saw that his sentence was pronounced; he looked at the general, at those who were to take him away, and guessing what he could not understand, he departed with a smile of confidence.

To this moving scene succeeded a very uncommon event, that of a shower of rain: it recalled Europe and the first odours of spring on the seventeenth of December. Some moments after, news arrived that the mamlùks were within two leagues, with an army of fellahs. On approaching Féshneh, a detachment of mamlùks was discovered, which waited till the French were within half cannon-shot, and then disappeared: it was said that the main body was at Sasta-Elsayeneh two miles from them; but notwithstanding the general's eagerness to join the enemy, the army could not reach Sasta before night, and till two hours after the mamlùks had retired. At Sasta, it was found that the news of their march had arrived at noon, at the moment in which the inhabitants were consulting on an extraordinary imposition which they were commanded to raise; and that from that time, the mamlùks had thought of nothing but loading their camels, calling the French the *scourge of God,* sent to punish them for their faults: and truly, adds M. Denon, they might have used less pious expressions.

On the eighteenth, at day-break, the French left Sasta. The mamlùks were by this time six
miles

miles off, taking a route between the canal of Yussef and the desert. On crossing the canal a third time, M. Denon did not find its course correspond with that represented in all the charts: only a general leveling of the whole country can explain the system and management of its irrigation, and ascertain what it is belongs to nature and what to man in this interesting part of Egypt. Towards evening, the French forded the canal, at a place where it seemed to be only the lowest part of the valley, a natural receptacle of water, and not the work of art, which no where manifested itself.

On a simple view of the levels, M. Denon feels himself disposed to believe, that this part of Egypt is become lower than the banks of the Nile, raised as they are by the mud annually deposited, and that after the general inundation, the ebbing of the waters causes it to assemble in this canal. He afterwards observed in upper Egypt the effect of the filtration which they perform: having, in that region, neither valleys or canals in which to empty themselves, the great mass of the waters penetrate the vegetable soil, after which, meeting with a bed of clay, they return, by veins, to the river, when its decrease has reduced it below the surface of that bed. May it not be to a similar operation of nature that we owe the oäses?*

---

* *Oäsis* is a term applied to an insulated extent of fertile ground, seated in the desert.

The

The French saw some bustards; as is the case with all the animals common to the two continents, they were smaller than those of Europe. News being brought to the army that the mamlûks had attacked the advanced-guard, the army quickened its march. Not finding the enemy, however, it halted for the night near the village of Benashieh, in a pretty wood of palms.

On the nineteenth the French were obliged, by the delays attending the artillery, to stop at Benesech; a circumstance in which, though it was vexatious to general Desaix, who was impatient to come up with the mamlûks, M. Denon, for his personal gratification, rejoiced.

Benesech was built on the ruins of the antient Oxyrinchus, the capital of the thirty-third nome of Egypt: there remain nothing of its former existence but a few stone trunks of columns, marble columns in the mosks, and a column still standing, with its capital and a part of its entablature, which indicate that it formed the angle of a portico of the composite order. Oxyrinchus, formerly a metropolis, surrounded by a fertile plain, at the distance of about four miles from the libyan chain, has disappeared beneath the sand; the antient Benesech, beyond Oxyrinchus, has also disappeared beneath the sand; the new city is obliged to retreat from this scourge with the daily loss of some of its houses, and will finish by intrenching itself beyond the canal of Joseph, on the banks of of which it will still be threatened. This beautiful canal seems to present its flowery banks as a consolation for the horrors of the desert: of the *desert*, that word terrible to him who has once seen the object it denotes! an horizon without bounds, where the eye is oppressed by space, on the surface of which, if it be uniform, it is painful to gaze, where the hill only conceals or discovers decrepitude and dissolution, where the silence of non-existence reigns in solitude over immensity. It is because of this, doubtless, that the Turks here place their tombs: tombs in a desert are death and annihilation.

Fatigued with drawing, continues M. Denon, and believing myself alone, I had given myself up to all the melancholy which the scene inspired, when I perceived Desaix in the same attitude with myself, and afflicted with the same sensations.

" My friend," said he, " is not this an error of nature? nothing receives life; all seems to exist for the purpose of saddening and terrifying: it seems as if Providence, after having provided abundantly for the other parts of the world, had been suddenly deficient in an element when she wished to fabricate this, and that, not knowing how to proceed, she had left it unfinished."—" Is it not rather," said I, " the decrepitude of the part of the world the most antiently inhabited? may it not have been the abuses of human industry that have reduced it to this state? In this desert there are

are valleys, and petrified wood, consequently, there have been rivers, and forests; these latter have been destroyed; and from that epoch there has been no more dew, no more mists, no more rain, no more rivers, no more of life, no more of any thing."

Within the mosks of Benesech, the French found a large number of columns of different kinds of marble, which are doubtlessly the spoils of the antient Oxyrinchus, but which have not belonged to the times of the Egyptians.

The army recommenced its march, following the canal, which, in this part, resembles the Marne.* It had advanced about a mile, when it saw a considerable explosion, of which it did not hear the noise. It was conjectured to be a signal, and it was not till the next day they found that it had been caused by an accidental firing of a quantity of powder of the mamlûks. A quarter of an hour after the explosion, a convoy of eight hundred sheep was seized. The village of Elsack was reached too late to save it from being pillaged. In the strictest sense of the word, *nothing* was left in the houses. The French invited the arabian inhabitants, who had fled into the fields, to return to their houses; but the latter replied coldly: " What should we go home for? do not these deserts resemble our houses?"

---

* A river in France.

On

On the twenty-first of December,* after leaving Tata, a large village, inhabited by Copts and an arab chief, by whom the French officers had been accommodated with a fine house and mats, they crossed a field of peas, then in seed, and of barley in flower.

At noon, they arrived at Mynyëh, a large and pretty town, where there was formerly a temple of Anubis: there, M. Denon discovered no ruins. He saw some fine columns in the great mosk. These may have belonged to the temple of Anubis; but they are certainly the work of an age posterior to that of the temples of high egyptian antiquity which M. Denon beheld in the sequel of his travels.

The mamlûks had left the town of Mynyëh, and escaped being surprized by the french cavalry, which entered within two hours after their retreat; they had been obliged to abandon five vessels, armed with ten cannon, a mortar, and a bomb; they had buried two other pieces, which were discovered to the French by several greek deserters, by whom they were joined.

From Mynyeh to Komeh-êl-Kasr, at which latter place they slept, the country was more abundant and more rich than any they had previously passed; and the villages were so numerous and so contiguous to each other that, standing in the

---

* 1 Nivose.

midst

midst of the plain, M. Denon counted twenty-four by which he was encircled. They were not disfigured by hills of rubbish, but so planted with spreading trees, that they seemed to present the pictures which travelers have given of the habitations in the islands of the Pacific sea.

The next day, at eleven o'clock, the French were between Antinoë and Hermopolis. M. Denon was not very anxious to visit Antinoë; he had previously examined monuments of the age of Adrian, and he did not imagine that what that emperor had built in Egypt could have any thing novel; but he burnt with desire to see Hermopolis, where he knew there was a celebrated portico; his satisfaction, therefore, was extreme, when Desaix proposed taking three hundred horse to Ashmûnin, while the infantry proceeded to Meloï.

On approaching the eminence on which the portico has been built, he saw it rise above the horizon, and display its gigantic forms: he crossed the canal of Abû-Assi, and climbing over mountains of ruins, he reached this beautiful remain of the highest antiquity.

I sighed, says M. Denon, with happiness: this, so to say, was the first fruit of all the labour I had performed; with the exceptions of the pyramids, it was the first monument that presented me with a model of the antique-egyptian architecture, the first stones that had preserved their primitive order, which, without mixture or alteration, had
remained

remained four thousand years to give me an immense idea of the arts and of their perfection in this country. A peasant, brought from the cottages of his hamlet, and suddenly placed before an edifice like his, would believe that there was a wide interval between himself and the creatures by whom it was constructed: without an idea of architecture, he would say: This is the house of a god; a man would not dare to inhabit it. Was it the Egyptians who invented and perfected this fine, this noble art? this is a question to which it is difficult to reply; but what I have never doubted of from the moment I beheld the portico of Hermopolis is this, that the Greeks never invented or performed any thing of a grander character.

There are in this architecture parts which, considered by themselves, or reduced into drawings, appear somewhat uncouth; but, in their mass, they awe criticism: here, we dare neither adopt nor reject; but what we cannot but admire is the beauty of the principal lines, the perfection of the workmanship, and the disposition of the ornaments, which produce a richness when near, without taking from the simplicity that produces the great. The immense number of hieroglyphics which cover all the parts of this edifice not only have no relief, but they do not cut a single line; they disappear at the distance of twenty paces, and leave the architecture all its gravity. Half buried

buried, among the eminences, at two hundred toises from the portico, are enormous masses of stone, and substructions, which appear to have been those belonging to an edifice of which some columns of granite, buried, and scarcely distinguishable above the surface, made a part: further off, but still among the ruins of the great Hermopolis, is built a mosk, adorned with many columns of cipoline marble, of middling height, and all retouched by the Arabs; beyond this is the large village of Ashmûnin, peopled with nearly five thousand inhabitants, to whom we were a curiosity as extraordinary as their temple had been to us.

We slept at Mynyeh, at half a league from Ashmûnin.

Hermopolis, or the great city of Mercury, the capital of the thirty-fifth nome, was built by Ishmûn, the son of Misraim. To give some idea of the colossal proportions of the portico of its temple, it will be sufficient to say that the diameter of its columns is eight feet ten inches; their distances the same; that of the two columns of the center, within which the door is comprized, is twelve feet; which, together, give a hundred and twenty feet for the facade of the portico: its height is sixty feet. The architrave is composed of five stones of twenty-two feet each in length; the frize the same; the only stone which remains of the cornice is thirty-four feet: these details may convey an idea at once of the skill possessed by the

the Egyptians in raising these enormous masses, and of the magnificence of the materials they employed. The stones are of a free-stone of the fineness of marble: they are joined only by the exactness of their laying. With respect to the plan of the temple, nothing can be discovered of its outward walls or of its nave. The second rank of columns was inclosed to the height of the door; the the rest were intirely open: it appears probable that the part immediately behind these was not the nave or sacred part of the temple, but a border or kind of court by which this was preceded. What authorizes this opinion is, that the frize and cornice have on this side the same ornaments and projections as on the side of the entrance-front. The shafts of the columns resemble fasces, or bundles of sticks, and the base, the foot of the plant *lotus*, at its rising from the root. The capitals have no analogy with any known capital; but they hold the same station, the gravity of the egyptian architecture allowed for, as the capital of the doric, in the architecture of the Greeks, and it may be said that the former is richer than the latter. All the other members have their correspondents in the grecian architecture: on the astragal of either side of the portico, and under the roof between the two columns of the center, are winged globes, emblems repeated in the same place in all egyptian temples. The hieroglyphics which are on the crowns of the capitals are all similar, and all the cielings are decorated

rated with a meander composed of stars, painted of the aurora-colour, on a blue ground.

Meloï is still a larger and prettier town than Mynyëh: its bason is well built, and it has a spacious house belonging to the mamlûks, which might easily be fortified.

Though general Desaix, on account of the number of hours which the cavalry had been under arms, took M. Denon, himself worn with fatigues, from the portico of Hermopolis before he had had time to examine it with the minuteness he wished, it was late when they reached Meloï. M. Denon was lodged without the walls; and, after losing some time in discovering his way, he found himself before a pretty house, apparently comfortable. The owner, contentedly seated at the door, showed him that he had put general Belliard to sleep in a chamber, and signified that he would find room in the same. He had slept so long in the fields, that he was tempted to accept this sort of accommodation. Scarcely had he fallen asleep before he awaked in an agitation which made him think himself in an high fever. Overcome both with fever and sleep, alternately under the alarm of a serious disease and of the drowsiness of lassitude, he heard his companion mutter, also half asleep, " I am very ill;" " I am no better," replied he: this dialogue awakened both; they arose, left their chamber, and, by the light of the moon, respectively found each other red, bloated

bloated, and scarcely to be known: at first, they knew not what to think of their condition; but, when thoroughly awoke, they perceived that they had been the prey of all sorts of vermin.

The houses of upper Egypt are vast dove-cots, in which the owner reserves only a single chamber for himself, in which he lodges with the hens, chickens, and all the devouring insects which beset those animals. The chase of these insects occupies his day; and the texture of his skin, braves their bite at night: under these impressions, their host, who really thought he had amply provided for their ease, was unable to enter into the motives of their flight. They delivered themselves from the most hungry of their guests, promising themselves to partake again of a similar hospitality.

On the twenty-fourth of December the French continued their marches in pursuit of the mamlûks; these were always eight miles before them, destroying the country between them, and constantly alluding the pursuit of the army. Towards evening, there came a deputation, with flags in sign of alliance: these were christians from whom the mamlûks had demanded a contribution of one hundred camels; and of whose camels, the poor people not being able to give those demanded, they had killed sixty: this procedure having irritated the christians, they, on their part, had killed eight mamlûks, whose heads they
proposed

proposed to present to the French: they all spoke at once, repeating the same expressions an hundred times; but, happily for the ears of their audience, the assembly was held in a field of luzern which, at the same time, provided the deputation with refreshment; the persons composing it eating the herb with the avidity of one who had found a delicious food of which he was fearful not to have time enough to satisfy himself.

The French slept at El-Gansanieh, where they were very well accommodated in the tomb of a santon.

On the twenty-fifth, they were marching to mount Falut, where they obtained news that the mamlûks were at Béneädy, to which place they hastened. Agitated by every thing around me, says M. Denon, my heart beat with joy whenever the mamlûks were mentioned. I did not reflect that I had no cause of animosity or rancour against them; that, since they had never injured the remains of antiquity, I had nothing to reproach them with; that if they had wrongfully acquired the soil we were treading, it was not for us to find fault; and that, at least, a possession of many ages had established their right: but the preparations for a battle is a scene of so much activity, presenting so fine a picture, and producing results so important for those who are engaged in it, that it leaves little room for moral reflections; success is the only object of thought:

thought: the game is so interesting, that those who play must be anxious to win.

The French arrived at Bénéady, where their hopes were again disappointed: they found only Arabs, whom their cavalry drove into the desert. Bénéady is a rich village of a mile in length, advantageously situated for the commerce of the caravans of the kingdom of Fùr; possessing an abundant territory, its population is always sufficiently numerous to enable it to compromise with the mamlûks, and resist their extortions. It appeared necessary for the French, also, to temporize with Bénéady. The amicable advances of the people were made in such a manner as to resemble conditions; and it was judged proper to conceal the sense of the insolence of these proceedings under the mask of cordiality. Surrounded by Arabs from whom they fear nothing, whose wants they supply, and of whom, in consequence, they can dispose, the inhabitants of Bénéady have a degree of influence in the province that would embarrass every government that might be established in Egypt: they came to meet the French, and they conducted them out of their territory; and neither party wished to pass the night with the other. The French slept at Benisanet.

On the twenty-sixth, before they entered Siùt, they found a large bridge, a sluice, and a bank to restrain the waters of the Nile. These arabian

arabian works, doubtlessly copied from the antique, are as useful as they are extensive : throughout, it appears that the distribution of the water has been effected with more intelligence, and by more simple means, in upper Egypt than in the lower.

Siût is a large well-peopled city, built, according to appearances, on the scite of Licopolis or the *city of the wolf.* Why a *city of the wolf* in a country where there are no wolves, for the wolf is an animal of the north? Was this a worship borrowed from the Greeks? or have the Latins, who set down this denomination in an age when they applied themselves but little to natural history, omitted to make any distinction between the wolf and the shacal? There are no antiquities in this city; but the libyan chain, at the foot of which it is built, contains so large a number of tombs, that the fact of its occupying the place of a large antient city cannot be doubted.

M. Denon was eager to examine an egyptian mountain. He had seen two chains from Kaira, without daring to run the hazard of approaching either. He found this part of the libyan chain a ruin of nature, formed of horizontal beds, and layers of calcareous stone, more or less soft, more or less white, intersected with large nipple-shaped and concentrated flints, which appeared to be the kernels or bones of this long chain, to maintain its existence, and suspend its total destruction: this dissolution

dissolution is daily taking place, through the impression of the saline atmosphere, which penetrates every part of the surface of the calcareous stone, decomposes it, causes it to descend, so to to say, in rivulets of sand, which are first accumulated below the rock, then rolled away by the winds, and lastly, wave by wave, driven on the villages and fields, which they change into mournful deserts. The rocks are at about half a mile from Siût; in the intervening space is a pretty house, occupied by the kiashef who governed for Soliman-bey. The rocks are hollowed into innumerable tombs, more or less great, and decorated with more or less magnificence: this magnificence testifies the antient proximity of a great city. All the inner porches of these caverns are covered with hieroglyphics, which, if the language were understood, it would require a month to read, and which, merely to copy, would employ years. With the little light which enters by the outer door, M. Denon perceived that all the ornaments employed by the Greeks in their architecture, and which are vulgarly called grecian, are there executed with exquisite taste and delicacy. If these excavations were severally the product of one and the same operation, as the regularity of their plans appears to indicate, the fabrication of a tomb was a great undertaking: but it is to be believed that, when completed, it served a whole family, a whole race, for ever; it would also appear that the living
entered

entered it, to perform certain rites in favour of the dead: for, if it had never been intended to visit these monuments, what end could be served by elaborate decorations, inscriptions never to be read, and pomp concealed and lost? At various epochs or festivals of the year, or at a new interment, there were doubtlessly celebrated some funereal *functions* wherein the magnificence of the ceremonies was supported by the splendour of the place; and this is the more probable because the decorations of the interior present a striking contrast with the simplicity of the exterior, which is the natural rock, such as it has just been described. There is one consisting of a single chamber, which contains innumerable sepulchres regularly cut in the rocks; these have all been opened, for the sake of carrying off the mummies: M. Denon found some fragments, as cloth, hands, heads, and broken bones. A description of one of the most considerable and least dilapidated of these tombs will convey a more particular account of their general fabrication. This consists of a sort of porch, a hall which opens into two chambers and a gallery, which gallery conducts to three other chambers. The porch, like the rest, is an excavation of the rock; the parts wanting to the symetry of its sides being supplied by a clothing of stucco, still in high preservation. At the most exterior part, there is no other ornament than a torus, which borders an elliptic arch; but from this to the end

of

of the last chamber, the whole is lined with hieroglyphics, and the cielings are ornamented with painting and sculpture: on the sides of the entrance are large figures which are repeated on the jambs. There did not appear to be any traces of hinges or fastenings: the upper part of the aperture is wider than the lower. The third door leads to the great chamber, in which was the sarcophagus. The floor has been every where dug up.

Beside these larger grottoes, there are small ones in such number that the whole mountain is become hollow and sonorous. Farther on, to the south, are the remains of large quarries, the cavities of which are sustained by pilasters: one part of these quarries has been inhabited by pious solitaries; across the rocks, in these boundless retreats, they joined the austere prospect of the desert to that of a flood which in its majestic course spreads abundance on its banks. This was an emblem of their lives. Before their retreat, perplexed with cares, riches, and anxieties; and, afterwards, enjoying serenity and contemplative pleasures: the muteness of nature imitated the silence to which they were condemned; the constant and august splendor of the sky of Egypt irresistibly commanded eternal admiration; the awaking of day was not hailed by cries of joy, or the gambols of animals; nature, grave and superb, seemed to inspire only the profoundest sentiment of humble gratitude: in a word, the
grotto

grotto of the cenobite might seem to have been placed here by the order and the choice of God himself; all that could animate nature shared with him in his melancholy and lethargic meditation on that Providence which is the eternal distributor of eternal blessings.

Little niches, plaisterings in stucco, and a few paintings in a red colour, representing the cross, and inscriptions which M. Denon believes to be in the coptic language, are the only evidences and relics of the habitation of these austere cells by their no less austere cenobites. In the season in which the French arrived, nothing could be comparable to the verdure of all tints that covered the banks of the Nile as far as the sight could discover.

The next morning, the French followed all the sinuosities of the canal of Abû-Assi, which is the furthermost of upper Egypt, and considerable enough to be an arm of the Nile: it shares with that flood the width of the valley which, during that day's march did not appear to be more than two miles across, but cultivated with more industry and skill than other parts of Egypt the French had previously witnessed: roads were traced which demonstrated that with little expense there might be constructed better, and which would last almost for ever in a climate where it neither rains nor freezes. At every mile, they found a cistern,

cistern, with a little hospitable construction to supply the traveler and his horse with water: philanthropic establishments, which characterize arabian charity. Towards the middle of the day, the French approached the desert, where M. Denon saw three objects which he had not met with before: the dûm-palm, the leaf of which resembles that of the racket-palm, and which has not, like the date-tree, a single stem, but from eight to fifteen; its ligneous fruit is attached in bunches to the extremities of its principal branches, from which spring tufts which compose the foliage of the tree; it is of a triangular form, and the bigness of an egg; its first envelope is spungy, and eats like the carob; its savour is sweet, approaching the taste of gingerbread; under this envelope is a hard and filamentary corticel, like that of the cocoa, to which fruit the whole has more resemblance than to any other; but it is wholly without the fine woody shell. Its pulp is without savour. It becomes exceedingly hard, and is then made into beads for rosaries, which take a dye and polish.

The second novelty was a beautiful little bird which, from its form and habits, should be ranked among the fly-birds. It caught insects momentarily, and with admirable address. Its colour is a green, clear and brilliant; its head and the upper part of its wings are gold-coloured; its beak is long,

long, sharp, and pointed; in its tail, one feather is half an inch longer than the rest: its size is that of the lesser titmouse.

A little farther on, M. Denon observed several swallows, the colour of which was exactly that of the sand over which they flew*: these swallows do not emigrate, for none of their colour are seen in Europe: they are of the species of the white-tail.

After a march of thirteen hours, the army reached Gamerissiem. The excesses of the soldiers rendered its arrival unfortunate for the village: robbed, dishonoured, and driven to extremities, the inhabitants fell upon the patrols who were sent for their succour; and the patrols, attacked by the furious inhabitants, killed several of them, for want of mutual explanation.

On the twenty-eighth, the army followed the desert, which is bordered by a series of villages. Notwithstanding the coolness of the night, the heat of the day, and the productions of the earth

---

* A few pages back, the desert is represented as *wholly destitute of life*. Here is full evidence of a fact, the reverse of which would contradict all analogy: the desert is not wholly destitute of life. These swallows would not fly over the sands unless there were insects to be caught; nor would they be masked under the colour of those sands unless there were enemies against which they were to be protected. Here, then, the existence of three descriptions of animals is ascertained. That these swallows do not emigrate, is a proof that the desert produces food throughout the year.

announced

announced the neighbourhood of the tropic; the barley was ripe, the wheat in grain, and the melons, planted in the open fields were in flower. The army spent the night in a wood near Narcetta.

In the night-watchings of the army in Egypt, groups of palm-trees, enlightened from below by a multitude of fires, other groups of persons still more varied by their several occupations, frequently presented the most striking pictures, to which the pompous and elegant forms of the palm-trees gave an air of festivity, which would have been delightful in this fine country if the excess of lassitude produced by the fatigues of the day had not compelled an attention to undeniable wants, in preference to superfluous enjoyments. In the degree that a palm-tree has a melancholy appearance when in a waterless region, it presents only a meagre tuft above its dry and slender trunk, so does it give pomp, elegance, and lightness, to a clump of trees of low stems and abundant foliage, or when only young plantations of its own kind are mingled with the old. But it is one of the inconveniences of the vegetables of Egypt, that is it difficult to inhabit them; nineteen of its trees and plants being armed with merciless thorns, which forbid the enjoyment, unaccompanied with disturbing precaution, of that shade which is the constant object of desire.

On

On the twenty-ninth the French crossed the desert. In their way, they found a coptic convent, which the mamlûks had fired the preceding evening and which was still consuming. Its state prevented M. Denon from entering it; it wholly resembled the white convent, which had also been set on fire at the same time, but the monks of which, on their flight, had left the door open, and a few servants to save the wrecks. The red convent is so called because built of brick, and because this epithet distinguishes it from the other, which is within twenty minutes march, and which, for similar reasons, is called the white convent.

The erection of this edifice is attributed to saint Helena, an origin that the plan upon which it is built renders probable. There was doubtlessly a convent adjoining this church: some blocks of granite, and traces of a wall, attest its antient existence. The sight of these buildings would lead us to suppose that if it was saint Helena who caused them to be constructed, the emperor, her husband, placed large sums of money at her disposal. The convent, not being built, like the church, in such a manner that it could be shut and defended, has certainly been burnt or destroyed under circumstances of the same kind as those which had now taken place. The structure of this church is such that, with portcullises at the doors, and a few pieces of cannon on the walls, it would still be very capable of defense against the

Arabs

Arabs, and even against the mamlûks; but, destitute of arms, the poor monks who inhabit it have nothing with which to oppose their enemies but patience, resignation, sanctity, and, more than all, their poverty, which, in all other situations, would be their safeguard: in the actual one, however, the mamlûks had to avenge on catholics the evils they were receiving from catholics.

Since the antient destruction of the convent, the monks had lodged in the lateral gallery of the church; if they could be said to be lodged in the little huts which were built under its pompous porticoes: it was the picture of poverty in the palace of pride.

The fathers had fled: the French found only the brothers, and these covered with rags, and scarcely restored from the agonies of the preceding evening. To form an idea of the life, character, and means of subsistence of these monks, the reader must consult general Andreossy's excellent memoir on the lakes of natrôn, and the convents of El-Baramùs, Saint-Ephraim, and Saint-Macarius: this accurate and judicious observer has described their necessities, their perpetual warfare with the Arabs, the misfortunes of their existence, and the moral causes which enable them to support and perpetuate their establishments.*

---

* Memoirs on Egypt, Vol. I.

The French returned to the Nile, and crossed the field of battle on which, in the preceding war between the Turks and the mamlûks, Hassein-pasha was beaten by Mûrat-bey, and where the latter, with five thousand mamlûks, put to flight eighteen thousand Turks and three thousand mamlûks. Malem-Jacob, the Copt, who accompanied them as intendant of the finances, a spectator and actor in this battle, described all the particulars. He showed with what superiority of talent Mûrat had taken advantages, and profited by those which fell in his way: the same Mûrat must have reddened with rage to fly over the same ground before five thousand infantry. While the French were commenting on the vicissitudes of fortune, carried away by the interest of the conversation, they had very imprudently, as frequently happened, advanced a mile before the army. M. Denon said jestingly to Desaix, that it would be very ridiculous for an historian to have to tell that he had had his head cut off in a rencontre with five or six mamlûks; and that for himself he should be sorry to leave his own behind a bush, where it would be utterly forgot: at this moment they were passing Minshieh; and adjutant Clement came up to the general with intelligence that there were mamlûks in this village: in a word, there appeared two, then six, then ten, then four more, then two others, and then attendants: they advanced within musket-shot to observe

serve the French: for these to have turned their backs would have been to render themselves prisoners at once; the country was enclosed: Desaix resolved to put the best appearance on his situation, and dispose his small party for resistance; he had four fusileers whom he stationed alternately in all points, so as to multiply them by their movements: he placed some ditches between himself and the mamlûks; he gained time; the advanced-guard at length appeared, the mamlûks retired. Intelligence was received that Mùrat was waiting for the French before Djirjieh: before them, they heard violent outcries, and saw clouds of dust arise; and Desaix flattered himself that he was about to obtain the battle after which he had been running for fourteen days. M. Denon was sent to hasten the infantry; passing at full gallop, he saw an antique quay on the banks of the Nile, with stairs descending into two basons, and was inclined to think these the remains of Ptolémaïs. A cannon was discharged, to bring up the cavalry, which had slept at half a league from the infantry; and, within half an hour the French were prepared to fight: they marched in order of battle; but the mamlûks had disappeared, and they arrived at Djirjieh without having joined their enemies.

Seated at his table, says M. Denon, with his map before him, the unpitying reader says to the poor traveler, harrassed, pursued, famished, the
butt

butt of all the miseries of war, here are Aphroditópolis, Crocodilópolis, Ptolémaïs; what have you done with these cities? if you can give no account of them, what have you been doing there? had you not a horse to carry you, an army to protect you, an interpreter to make inquiries? —Certainly; but have the goodness, reader, to recollect that we were surrounded by Arabs and mamlûks, and that most probably they would have seized, robbed, and killed me if I had ventured to go an hundred paces from the army, to gather you a few bricks at Aphroditópolis.

This lined quay, which I passed in galloping to Minishiëh, was Ptolémäis; it could be nothing else.

A little patience, and we shall examine together a soil new to research, and see that of which Herodotus himself has only spoken upon the authority of lying information; that which modern travelers have dared to design and measure only in the midst of every species of anxiety: in truth, these unfortunate travelers, momentarily pillaged, upon endless pretences, by raïs, by their interpreters, by all the shechs, kiashefs, and pashas, abandoned by these, robbed by others, suspected for sorcerers, persecuted for the treasures which they have been supposed to find, or that they sought to discover, and who have always been threatened with the loss of their drawings and notes, if not with attempts upon their persons; these

these travelers, I say, are not to be condemned for having omitted to transmit all the particulars which might be wished respecting a country so curious, but so dangerous.

Thanks to the courageous obstinacy of Mûrat-bey, which prompted him to try the fate of war, we still continued our pursuit, and we shall at last enter the promised land.

Djirjïeh, at which the French arrived at two o'clock in the afternoon, is the capital of upper Egypt; it is as large as Mynyëh, and as Meloï, smaller than Siùt, and less handsome than either of the three: the name of Djirjieh or Girgeh is derived to it from a large monastery, more antient than the city, dedicated to saint George, which name, in the pronunciation of the country, is rendered *Djairge*; the convent still exists, and it contains some european monks. The Nile washes the buildings of Djirjieh, and daily demolishes a part; it could not be accommodated with even a bad harbour for small vessels, without considerable expense: this city is interesting, therefore, only on account of its situation, which is equi-distant from Kaira and Syeneh, and on that of the richness of its territory. The French found a supply of provisions, at very low prices; bread at one sous the pound, twelve eggs for two sous, two pigeons for three sous, a goose of five pounds weight for twelve sous: and this was the result, not of poverty, but of abundance; for, after,

after, during a stay of three weeks, the wants of five thousand persons had increased the consumption and the money in circulation, the prices of every thing remained the same.

The barks of the French did not rejoin them; and they were in want of biscuit and shoes: they pitched their camp, built ovens, and even prepared a barrack for five hundred men: the army rested, and M. Denon received the personal advantage of easing his eyes, with the total loss of which he was threatened. He had not the assistance of a single officinal drug; but a pot of honey, which he found in the house of a shech with whom he lodged, and a jar of vinegar, supplied the place: he ate of the honey to indigestion; and cooled his blood by drinking the vinegar, diluted with water, and sweetened with sugar.

On the second of January*, the French learned that the country-people, seduced by the mamlùks, had assembled in the rear, to attack them on the back, while the latter had promised to attack them on their front. It was only a month since they had robbed a caravan of two hundred merchants from India, by the way of the Red-sea, Kosseir, and Kûss, and they thought themselves valiant. Forty insurgent villages had raised six

---

* 13 Nivose.

or seven thousand men; but a charge of the French cavalry cut off twelve hundred, and convinced the rest, that their project was futile.

At Djirjieh, the French met with a nubian prince, a brother of the sovereign of Fûr, who had returned from India, and was about to join his brothers and a caravan of eight hundred Nubians of Sennaar, accompanied by a large number of women: elephant-teeth, and gold-dust were the merchandizes which they brought to Kaira, to barter for coffee, sugar, shawls, cloths, lead, iron, senna, and tamarinds. The French had much conversation with this young prince, whom they found full of vivacity, cheerfulness, ardour, and understanding, qualities that were written on his countenance: his complexion was more than brown; his eyes very fine; his nose a little prominent, but small; his mouth much flattened, but not flat; his legs, like those of all Africans, lank and bowed: he told the French that his brother was in alliance with sultan of Bùrnû, that he traded with that country, and that he carried on perpetual war against Sennaar; he said that from Fûr to Siût was a journey of forty days, during which water could be found, either in the cisterns or the väses, only at places eight days asunder. The profits of these caravans must be incalculable, to indemnify those who conduct them in the charges they sustain, and remunerate their excessive fatigues. When the female slaves are no cap-

captives but purchased merchandize, their price is a bad musket a head. The price of the male is two. The prince related that it was very cold in his country, during a part of the year; and, having no word to express *ice*, he said that his countrymen ate a great deal of a thing which was hard when it was taken into the hand, and which escaped from the fingers after it had been held a little while. The French mentioned Tombuctoo, with which city he was, well acquainted. He described it as lying to the south-west of his country; and said that its inhabitants came to trade with Fûrese. Their journey takes up six months. The Fûrese sell them all the different articles which they fetch from Kaira, and receive gold-dust in exchange: that country is called, in their language, *paradise:* he added, that Tombuctoo was seated on the banks of a river which flows to the west, and that its inhabitants were small and civilized. The French regretted the early departure of this traveler, whom they could not resist questioning, even to folly, and who was extremely communicative, having nothing of the gravity of a moslem, and delivering himself with energy and facility. He said, further, that the sovereignty of Fûr, though hereditary in the royal family was elective as to the individual; that it was the military and civil chiefs among whom that son or relation of the deceased sultan was chosen whom they most approved as his successor;

sor; and that no example had yet occurred of a civil war being produced by an adherence to this practice. The whole of the above is a correct account, word for word, of the information received from this foreign prince. He added, that Africa stood in need of many of the goods of the French, that that country would readily become commercially tributary to them, without injury to its internal trade, that all the wants of the Africans were of such a nature as to attach them to the interests of the French, that the commerce of India might be opened by the way of Mekka with equal advantage; that city, or Kosseir, being made the staple; in the same manner as Aleppo was the staple for the turkish states, notwithstanding the length of the marches on either side to reach this point of contact.

The French waited for the barks which ought to have followed their march, and which contained their provisions, their ammunition, and the clothing of the troops: the wind, contrary to what was usual at the season, had been constantly favourable, and yet the barks had not returned. Several expresses were sent to gather information; of these the first had perished in passing through the revolted village, and the latter were still unreturned. The proper season was wasted in inaction; the country had cause to think that they were afraid of the mamlûks, and this idea encouraged it to new resistance: the payment of the
miri

miri was refused, the people giving for reason, that they ought to wait for the battle, and pay it to the conqueror.

On the eighth of January,* the tenth day of their encampment at Djirjieh, general Desaix resolved to send his cavalry to Siût, to learn definitively the fate of the aquatic convoy; a battalion had been sent through Djirjieh to Bardis, in search of provisions; and on the evening of this day, the officer who commanded it sent information of a report that on the tenth the mamlûks would march to Hô to arrive there on the eleventh; that they were desirous of coming to battle: this news was confirmed from all parts; and, though unconvinced of the reality of this good fortune, Desaix the more reproached the barks for having deprived him of his cavalry, by which he was left without the means of profiting by his victory, if he should obtain one; for the infantry, alone, could only accept a battle from the mamlûks, without the power of forcing or prolonging it.

Another evil with which the French were troubled was that of perpetual robbery, so completely organized that no military rigour could defend the arms and horses. Every night, the inhabitants entered the camp like rats, and left it like bats, almost always carrying away their prey. Those sur-

---

* 19 Nivose.

prized

prized, had been sacrificed to the immediate anger of the soldier: it was hoped that this severity would have taken effect; the guard was doubled; and, the same day, two artillery-forges were taken: the robbers were seized and shot. In the very night of this execution, the horses of the general's aid-de-camp were stolen: the general betted that he should not be robbed; the next day they took away his horse, and they would have demolished a wall, to reach himself, if the light had not come to his succour.

On the tenth, the French learned that Mûrat-bey had invited the arabian shechs of the villages which had submitted to march against them, appointed them a rendezvous at Djirjieh. On the eleventh, the day on which he was to attack them, several of these shechs sent letters assuring them of their fidelity to the treaty. Those who had promised to join the bey were denounced; but the cavalry had previously met them, and put them to the route.

On the eleventh, the weather was cloudy; and, though the day was as mild as a fine April-day in Europe, the French, reckoning upon warmth in Egypt, imagined they suffered the cold of a severe winter's day. On this day, however, the tendrils of the vines were as green as in the month of June; in this country, the leaves only crispen, redden, and dry, while the ends of the branches perpetually renew their verdure; it is the same with

with the everlasting-pea; its stem becomes ligneous: it sometimes attains a height of forty feet, reaching to the summits of trees.

The French learned that there had arrived at Mekka an innumerable multitude of foot-soldiers to join Mûrat-bey, and that they were on their march to attack them.

On the twelfth, they received intelligence that their cavalry had fallen in with a party of people at Menshieth, and put a thousand of them to the sabre: a lesson less *fraternal* than any thing else, but which their situation, perhaps, rendered necessary: this province, which, at all times disposed to revolt, had acquired the reputation of being terrible, had to learn that it was not when it measured its strength with the French that this term could be applied: it was necessary, besides, to conceal that their resources were small and scattered; perhaps it was also necessary that the people should be made to believe that they were as vindictive as merciful; perhaps, in short, not having time to catechize them, it was necessary through the misfortune of the case, to inflict severe punishment on those who resisted the belief that all the French were doing would be beneficial to themselves.

The army prepared to march the instant the cavalry should return, whether the barks might at length arrive, or whether all hope of them were to be renounced; for to wait longer was only
to

to aggravate its evils, and those to which it was obliged to expose the inhabitants of its neighbourhood, by suffering the continuance of a state of warfare, uncertainty, and inorganization.

On the twelfth, there was the same want of news as before. The French listened to arabian tales, to deceive the time and moderate their impatience. The Arabs tell their stories slowly, and the French had interpreters who, if they could not keep exactly the same, retarded the pace of their narratives but little: they have preserved the same passion for tales as that with which we have been acquainted ever since the sultan Skehersade of the thousand and one nights; and in this particular, Desaix and Denon were almost sultans themselves: the prodigious memory of the former did not lose a single phrase of what he heard; and the latter committed no part of the tales to paper, because Desaix promised to repeat them to him, word for word, whenever he wished: but M. Denon observed that if these histories are not rich in real and sentimental incidents, a merit which appears to belong peculiarly to the narrators of the north, they abound in extraordinary events, and striking situations, produced by passions always elevated; seizures, castles, grates, poisons, daggers, nocturnal scenes, mistakes, treasons, all that can complicate a history, and seem to render an unravelment impossible, is employed by these story-tellers with great boldness; and yet the history always ends

ends naturally, and in the clearest and most satisfactory manner. Thus much is the merit of the inventor; there still remains for the relator those of precision and delivery, to which the auditors attach great value: hence it happens that the same story is told repeatedly by different narrators before the same audience, with an equal success; the one shall have better told and delivered the sentimental and amorous part, another shall have better described the battles and their terrible effects, a third shall have commanded laughter; in a word, this is their drama: and in Europe, as we go to the theatre at one time to see the piece, and at another for the performance of the actors, the repetitions do not weary. These histories are followed by discussions; praises are disputed, and talents excited to improve: hence, he that is admired enjoys high reputation; he is the happiness of a family, of an entire horde. The Arabs have likewise their poets, and even their improvisators, who are invited to their feasts, and by whom they appear to be enchanted: M. Denon has heard these; but, when their songs are not apologetic, they must lose too much by translation to be worthy of recital: they appeared to him to be mere conceits or insipid playings upon words: the arabian poets have also a singularity of manners, and convulsive motions, by which they are characterized in the eyes of their fellow-countrymen, but which, to the French, gave them

an

an air of lunacy that inspired pity and repugnance: it was not the same with the story-tellers, who appeared to have talents more true and more allied to nature.

M. Denon had regretted the delays of the army the less, for that they gave him time to lessen the inflammation which preyed upon his eyes; but he shared the anxiety of Desaix, who had reckoned upon all the supplies of the convoy, the absence of which paralized his operations on every side, leaving him in a state of afflicting privation: happily, the sick and wounded were not numerous; for the surgeons, destitute of drugs, were only in the army to tell what ought to have been given, without the power of administering any thing: an hospital, however, was established, as well as ovens, a magazine, and a barrack sufficiently well fortified to withstand an attack of the peasantry, and to enable the general to leave three hundred men in security at this key of the port of the Nile.

Not knowing what to resort to for the benefit of his eyes, M. Denon thought of trying the baths of the country, and found them beneficial. The reader will find their description in the elegant pages of Savary, whose brilliant imagination has at once given the picture of the recommendations those baths possess, and of the pleasures of which they are susceptible.

On the thirteenth, it was cold enough in the morning to render a fire desirable; but it was the coldness often felt in Europe during the month of May: the same evening it thundered, an event very extraordinary in this country; one, in short, which only happens in the course of an age, through a concourse of circumstances which it is easy, perhaps, to describe. The north-wind, the most constant of the winds which prevail in this part of the world, brings the clouds of a colder region from the sea, and precipitates them into the valley of Egypt, where they are rarefied by an ardent sun, and reduced into vapours: this vapour being driven into Abyssinia, the south-wind, which crosses the lofty and frozen mountains of that country, sometimes brings it in little clouds, which experiencing but a slight change of temperature on repassing into the humid valley of the Nile at the time of its inundation, remain condensed, and produce at times, without thunder or storms, little momentary rains; but both the winds of the east and west, which ordinarily produce storms, crossing thirsty deserts which absorb the clouds they carry, or which raise the vapours to such an height that they pass over the narrow valley of upper Egypt without capability of experiencing detonation from the pressure of the waters of the river, the phenomenon of thunder becomes so extraordinary to the inhabitants of Egypt that even the learned of the country do not think of attributing

buting it to a physical cause. General Desaix having put some questions concerning thunder to a professor of the law, " It is well known," replied the latter, with the confidence of certitude, " that the thunder is an angel, but one of so small " a bulk that he cannot be seen in the air: he " has the power, however, of bringing clouds " from the Mediterranean into Abyssinia; and, " when human wickedness has arrived at its " height, he makes his voice heard, which is that " of rebuke and threat ; and, to prove that pu- " nishment is at his disposal, he causes the gate " of heaven to open, whence darts the lightning: " but, the mercy of God being always infinite, " his anger is never further manifested in upper " Egypt." It is always confounding to hear a sensible man, with a venerable beard, deliver so puerile a story as this. Desaix attempted to explain the phenomenon differently ; but the lawyer considered his explanation as so inferior to his own, that he did not even take the trouble to hear it out. To conclude, during the night, it rained violently ; and, in consequence, the streets became muddy, slippery, and almost impracticable. Here ends the history of the egyptian winter, of which we shall have no further occasion to speak.

On the fourteenth, egyptian ovens were constructed ; and, on the fifteenth, they were used for baking biscuit. It were to be wished that the quickness and address of the workmen could be described.

described. It may be said that individually, the Egyptian is industrious and adroit; and that, wanting, like the savage, every species of instrument, it is astonishing how much he does with his fingers, to which he is reduced, and with his feet, by which he aids himself wonderfully: he has, as a workman, a very valuable quality, that of being without presumption, patient, and willing to recommence till he has nearly accomplished all that is desired. It is uncertain to what degree he might be rendered valiant; but we are not to see without alarm all the military virtues he possesses; eminently sober, swift as a running-footman, a rider like a centaur, a swimmer like a triton; and yet it was over a population of several millions of men of this description, occupying four hundred miles of country, that four thousand insulated Frenchmen exercised an absolute dominion: so much is the habit of obeying, like that of commanding, a peculiar mode of being, a second nature, till, the one dozing in the abuse of power, the other is awakened by the clanking of its chain.

On the seventeenth, the cavalry returned: it brought news of the arrival of the barks, and details of a battle which it had had to sustain against some mamlûks and their agents, who had spread a report that they had destroyed the French; and that those who were seen returning were the remains, endeavouring to gain Kaira.

Two

Two thousand Arabs on horseback, and five or six thousand peasants on foot, thinking themselves able to complete the destruction, had posted themselves before Tata: when the cavalry had descried them drawn up for battle, it had made a movement to form; the enemy had thought they declined the battle, and had charged with his accustomed disorder, that is to say a few valiant men in the front, the rest in the middle, attacking, but never exposing their own persons; at the second discharge, astonished to see the cavalry act with fire-arms like a battalion, they had begun to give ground; and, after having lost about forty of their comrades, and had an hundred wounded, they had dispersed, abandoning the poor infantry, which, as usual, had been sabred, and which would have been wholly cut to pieces, but that the night came to its assistance.

On the nineteenth, the barks, at length, arrived: some accommodations that they brought, and above all the band of one of the brigades, playing french airs, excited a sensation so uncommonly voluptuous for the place at which it was felt, that it calmed all the irascibility which impatience had introduced into the minds of the army. It was, alas! the song of the swan; but let us not anticipate events; in war, the moment present must be enjoyed, for that which is to follow belongs to none.

For

For one-and-twenty days the French had been fatigued with indolence. M. Denon had known that he was near Abrdiu, where Osmianduë had built a temple, and where Memnon had resided. He frequently begged Desaix to send a reconnoitring party to El-Araba where he had repeatedly been told there were ruins; but Desaix always replied that he would lead him thither himself; that Mûrat-bey was within two days march, that he would arrive the next day but one, that then a battle would take place, and that after this nothing would be to be thought of but antiquities.

At length, on the twenty-first of January*, the army left Djirjieh at night-fall.

It passed before the ruins of El-Araba, and a village which it afterwards found to be called El-Besera, for, at the time of its arrival, there was not a single inhabitant to tell its name. I always loved, says M. Denon, to meet with these abandoned villages, that I might not hear the cries of the people whom we were obliged to ravage. The army left nothing but the walls, carrying away even the doors and door-posts; and a village which had been forsaken six hours assumed the appearance of the ruin of an age.

On the twenty-second, the army had scarcely began its march before the mamlûks were per-

---

* 2 Pluviose. In the original it is 2 *Nivose*; but the dates are confused in several parts of the work.

ceived;

ceived; they were advancing with a front of immense extent: the French formed in squares, two of infantry on the wings, and one of cavalry in the center, flanked by eight pieces of artillery at the angles; they marched in this order, following their road as far as Samanhùt, a village on an eminence, against which they endeavoured to support themselves. The mamlûks, opening and turning the French at three points, commenced their fire and their cries before the French had leveled their cannon. A body of volunteers of Mekka was posted in a ravin, between the village and the French, whence it fired from under cover, upon the square of the twenty first: Desaix sent a detachment of infantry to dislodge them, and a detachment of cavalry to pursue them when they should fly. The cavalry, from excess of ardour, commenced its attack too soon, and with disadvantage; one of the French was killed, and another wounded; and aid-de-camp Rapp received a cut from a sabre, and would have fallen if a volunteer had not parried four other blows with which he was menaced; the Mekkans, however, were repulsed.

The chasseurs were sent to the village to dislodge those by whom it was occupied; the mamlûks put themselves in motion to attack the left of the French, while others spread along their right: they had a favourable moment presented them for charging; but they hesitated, and it did

not

not return; they wheeled about the French, displaying their splendid arms, and their manœuvring horses, with all the eastern pomp: but the northern austerity of the French presented a severe aspect not the less imposing because it was less gay; the contrast was striking, iron seemed to be trying its strength with gold; the plain glittered, and the spectacle was admirable. The French artillery was discharged on all sides at once: the mamlûks made a false attack on the right; several of them perished; a chief, overthrown by a bullet, had fallen too near the French to be assisted by his own party; his horse, surprized to see him hanging from his saddle without falling from him, would not draw nearer to the French; blazing with gold, he excited the avarice of the artillery-men, who repeatedly attempted to make him their prize; tossed about by fate, and carried here and there by his horse, this unfortunate man did not die till he had suffered the horrors of a thousand deaths.

Other chasseurs had been sent to Samanhût to dislodge those who were posted there; the latter were soon put to flight: in the number of the fugitives was Mùrat, who had stationed himself in reserve; he took the road to Farshiut. This movement completely divided the enemy's army: Desaix seized the circumstance, caused his troops to march on the ground which was abandoned,

abandoned, and ordered the cavalry to charge those who still remained on his right: in an instant, they fled into the desert, where they climbed the steep aclivity of a mountain with astonishing swiftness: the French thought that when they had attained the summit they would resist the approach of their troops; but, terror and disorder in their ranks, they attended to nothing but unity in their flight; some of their stragglers were killed, and a few camels taken; a small body fled to the left: the fire ceased at mid-day; at one, no enemies were within sight. The French marched to Farshiùt, which Mùrat-bey had already abandoned.

This unfortunate town had been pillaged by the mamlûks a few hours before their arrival. The shech was a descendant of the shechs Ammam, powerful and beloved sovereigns in the Saïd, who, at the commencement of the present century reigned with justice, and defended their subjects from the vexations of the mamlûks. This latter, beaten by Mûrat, and reduced to a state of feebleness and poverty, had expected with pleasure the arrival of his avengers, and prepared them a supply of biscuit: Mûrat, overcome, and obliged to fly, had, before he left Farshiùt, sent in search of the aged prince, loaded him with reproaches, and, in his fury, cut off his head with his own hand. The French, on their arrival, completed the pillage of the magazines; the generale was beat, to stop

stop this disorder: the whole army being in fault, it was necessary to punish all: a forced march was ordered; and, to avoid the reproachful looks of the people, it was commenced at midnight.

The darkness was frightful, and the cold so severe that the troops were obliged to light fires every time they were stopped by the artillery. Sheltered behind a wall, and surrounding one of these fires, Desaix, his aid-de-camp, and M. Denon, were warming themselves when they suddenly received a volley of musketry from above the wall. It was still the volunteers of Mekka who attacked them, for they were destined to meet these every where; they were twenty in number; eight were killed, while the rest escaped by favour of the night. These volunteers, who pretended to the distinction of nobility, wore the green turban, as descendants of the race of Aly*;

nearly

---

* This is wrong. It is the race of Mohammed. It is in Persia only that the name of *Ali* nationally is revered. This error calls to mind one of a similar nature which has been current in the english newspapers. It was said that Bonaparte, during his stay in Egypt, had assumed the surname of *Ali*, and this was represented as an hypocritical pretention to mohammedism; but the truth is that Bonaparte never pretended to be a mohammedan, and that the name or addition which he did assume had no connection with any religious profession. That he wished to favour mohammedans as much as christians is certain; but he always caused himself to be considered among the number of

the

nearly vagabonds, occupied in robbing the caravans on the coast of Jidda*, and impelled by a laudable zeal for religion, they had made use of a dead season to attack an european nation which they believed covered with gold, and willingly come at their own risk and charge, to load themselves with booty from the French.

Armed with three javelins, a pike, a dagger, two pistols, and a carabine, they attacked with boldness, resisted with obstinacy; and, though mortally wounded, seemed unable to cease to live: subsequent to this surprize, M. Denon again saw one of them fight, and wound*t* two soldiers while they held him nailed against a wall with their bayonets.

---

the latter: this is evident from an expression which general Reynier represents as frequent in the mouths of the mohammedan inhabitants of Kaira, after Menou (who sincerely became a mohammedan) was placed in the rank of commander-in-chief: he relates that they said, *they experienced less kindness from a mohammedan general than they had from a christian general.* The addition really assumed by Bonaparte was that of *aäli,* which has long been equally used by the East-India-Company in Indostan, and which signifies, *the magnificent*. To have taken upon him the name of *Ali,* the most detestable of all others in the ears of mohammedans in Egypt and in all the turkish states, would have been as absurd as for an english prince to seek popularity by professing himself a papist.

* The name of this port is also written *Gidda, Gedda, Jedda, Joddu,* and *Zeiden.*

At

At one o'clock in the day, the French reached Hô; the mamlûks had retired from this place, one party of the beys having taken to the desert with their camels to gain Esneh, which they were to do in a day and an half, while the others followed the Nile, a route which compelled them to separate.

Hô, or the antient Diospolis-Parva, is in a fine military situation: it has no remains of antiquity.

The French halted at Hô, which they left an hour before midnight. They were aware that the night, as they had experienced on the preceding, would be dark, and perilous to the march of the artillery; but the conquest of Egypt, which had commenced so brilliantly with the battle of the pyramids, was to be completed by the battle of Thebes, had it been possible to obtain it from the *Fabius*, Mûrat-bey. How many forced marches, continues M. Denon, did not this battle cost us! but Desaix was not the spoiled child of fortune, and his star was nebulous: experience could not convince him of the insufficiency of his resources to gain upon the swiftness of the enemy whom he pursued; he would hear nothing that could weaken his hopes. The artillery was too heavy; the light cavalry scarcely seconded his wish; and I am sure that he lamented his not being a plain captain that, in the ebullition of his ardour, he might have led his company to attack and

and fight with Mûrat-bey: at length, we set out, and, after having witnessed the false light of an aurora-borealis, and waited for the moon till half past ten o'clock, we arrived at eleven o'clock at a large village of which I have never learned the name, and at which, unfortunately for it, and to the great injury of its inhabitants, our soldiers thus wandered. . . .

On the twenty-fourth of January, the French set forward at day-break. The tongue of cultivated land tapers on the right bank of the Nile, where they then were, and widens in the same proportion on the opposite bank.

At length, they entered the desert: at a small distance, they saw a wild beast which, from its size and remarkable form, they judged to be an hyena; they pursued it, but their horses were unable to rival its swiftness.

Arrived at Tintyra*, the first object was a little temple on the left of the road, the style and proportions of which were so bad that, at a distance, it appeared to be only the ruins of a mosk. Turning to the left, buried among the most dismal ruins, was a door, constructed of enormous masses, covered with hieroglyphics; and, through this door, M. Denon perceived the temple. I wish, he observes, it were in my power to excite in the reader the sensation that I experienced. I was

---

* Or Tintyris.

too much amazed to exercise judgment; all that I had hitherto seen of architecture was insufficient, here, to set bounds to my admiration. This edifice seemed to me to bear a primæval character, a character which, by excellence, was that of a temple. All encumbered as it was with rubbish by which it was degraded, the silent respect with which it impressed me seemed to me a proof of this; and, without partiality for the antique, it struck the whole army.

Before we enter into any detail, let us endeavour to explain the extent and ordonnance of this edifice, its present state, and picturesque appearance. These buildings stand at the very edge of the desert, on the last flat of the libyan chain, to the foot of which reaches the inundation of the Nile, at the distance of two miles from its bed. The libyan chain forms the back ground of the landscape. Near the ruins are a few palm-trees the remotest productions of the waters of the Nile.

The grand door of the temple opens opposite the center of the portico, and is covered with hieroglyphics. The portico is more elevated than the nave, or body, of the temple; an austere simplicity reigns throughout the architecture, which is enriched with innumerable hieroglyphics that do not interfere, however, with its beautiful lines: a large cornice majestically crowns the whole edifice; a torus, which appears to surround it, in-

creases

creases the appearance of the solidity of the talus which exists throughout, and serves to complete the junction, taking away the poverty of repeated angles, without taking away the precision and solidity of the whole, since this solidity manifests itself where it ought, that is to say at the extremity of the cornices. Three sphinx-heads project from the side of the nave; and, from their form, and the holes between their paws, it is probable that they were gutters by which was discharged the water thrown upon the flat roof of the temple to cool the apartments within it; for, under the ruins of the arabian buildings which still remain on this roof, there are little private temples, decorated with the most elaborate and scientific hieroglyphics. The modern habitations of these ruins, which are still seen, were doubtlessly erected at this elevation in the hope of placing them out of the reach of the bedûins, and living on this edifice as within a fortress; or, rather, to escape a burning soil, and seek coolness in the loftier atmosphere. The quantity of roman coin of the time of Constantine and of Theodosius, which is daily found here in digging for nitre, seems to show that Tintyra was still inhabited at that era. M. Denon himself found roman lamps of burnt earth, mingled in the ruins with little egyptian divinities in glass and in porcelain, with a blue varnish.

On the plinth of the cornice which crowns the sanctuary of the temple, there is an inscription in the

the greek character, but too much injured by time, and at too great an elevation, to allow M. Denon, from the height at which he saw it, to copy it. M. Denon thinks it a dedication posterior to the erection of the temple, made by one of the governors of the province for the Ptolemies: another greek inscription, placed in the same manner over the southern door, may support this opinion. In the center of the cornice is an head of Isis, which, every where repeated, shows that this temple was dedicated to that goddess. Below, on the entablature, is the winged globe which occupies this place in all the edifices of Egypt: the same figure is in this instance repeated on all the stones of the plat-bands which form the cieling of the portico. The capitals of the columns, very peculiarly decorated, produce, in their execution, an effect as noble as it is rich. The square part represents a temple, with a divinity under the portico of its sanctuary: to this four faces of Isis, with the ears of a cow, and the head-dress of the egyptian women.

Nothing can be more simple and better adapted than the small number of lines which are comprized by this architecture. The Egyptians having borrowed nothing from others, have employed no foreign ornament, nor any thing beyond what was dictated by necessity: ordonnance and simplicity have been their priciples; and they have carried these principles to sublimity! arrived at this point,
they

they attached equal importance to its preservation, and to the care that, much as they loaded their edifices with bass-relief, inscriptions, and historical and scientific pictures, none of these ornaments should destroy a single line. These lines have been respected; they seem to have been sanctified; all that is decorative, rich, and sumptuous, at hand, disappears at a distance, and leaves nothing visible but the principle, which is always grand, and always directed by a powerful reason. It never rains in this climate; nothing therefore was wanting but plat-bands to cover and overshadow; from this cause, there are no pitched roofs, nor no pediments: the talus is the principle of solidity; and they chose it for every part by which any thing was borne, esteeming security as the first sentiment which architecture ought to inspire, and its constituent beauty. With them, the immortality of God was represented by the eternity of his temple. Their ornaments, always founded upon reason, always agreeing with each other, and and always significative, equally evinced fixed principles, a taste founded upon truth, and a concatenation of profound reasonings; and, though we have not acquired evidence of the eminent degree at which they had arrived in the abstract sciences, their architecture alone, in the state in which we have found it, should give us an idea of the antiquity, the refinement, the character, and the gravity, of this people.

I have

I have not, continues M. Denon, words, as I have said, to describe my feelings while I stood below the portico of Tintyra. I thought myself, I really was, in the sanctuary of the arts and sciences. At the sight of an edifice like this, what a succession of epochs presented themselves to my imagination! how many ages must have been occupied in leading a creative nation to these results, to this degree of perfection and sublimity in the arts! how many other ages to bring about the oblivion of such a multitude of things, and to reconduct man, upon the same soil, to the state of nature in which we had found him! never was there so much space in a single point; never were the steps of time more strongly marked, or better followed. What uninterrupted power, what wealth, what abundance, what superfluity of resources must have belonged to a government that could raise an edifice like this, and that could find in its nation men capable of conceiving, executing, decorating, and enriching it with all that speaks to the eyes and to the mind!

M. Denon wished to make drawings of all the parts of this temple, but he trembled on putting his hand to the work; he felt that, unable to raise his design to the elevation of that which he admired, he should disfigure what he desired to imitate: no where had he been surrounded by so many objects fitted to exalt his imagination. These edifices, which impress the respect due to the sanctuary

sanctuary of the Divinity, were books by which science was developed, or morals dictated, or useful arts explained; all spoke, all was animated, and all constantly expressed the same. The embrasure of the doors, the angles, the most obscure line, equally presented a lesson, a precept, and all in admirable harmony; the lightest ornament on the gravest member of architecture displayed in a vivid manner the most abstract dogma that astronomy has to express. Painting, further, added a charm to the sculpture and architecture, and produced in the union an agreeable richness, which took neither from the simplicity nor the gravity of the whole. Painting, in Egypt, at this period, was used merely for ornament; according to all appearance, it was not even a peculiar art: sculpture was emblematic, and, so to say, architectural. Architecture, then, was *the* art, by excellence; the art dictated by utility; this alone, therefore, might remove the doubt, if not of the primogeniture, at least of the superiority of the architecture of the Egyptians compared with that of the Indians, because while it participated in nothing with the latter, it has yet become the basis of all that we have since admired, of all that we have thought exclusively belonging to architecture, the three grecian orders, the doric, the ionic, and the corinthian. We must be careful therefore to think, not, as it is vulgarly believed, that the architecture of Egypt is the infancy of the art, but, that it is the type.

M. Denon.

M. Denon could not hope to find any thing more complete or more perfect than Tintyra. He was agitated by the multiplicity of objects, amazed by their novelty, and tormented with the fear that he should not behold them again. On the ceilings, he had seen planetary systems, zodiacs, and celestial planispheres, represented with an ordonnance full of taste; on the walls he found endless representations of the rites of the egyptian worship, the proceedings in agriculture and the arts, and the precepts of morals and religion: he saw that the supreme Being was every where represented by emblems and by his qualities: all these it was equally important to collect; and M. Denon had only a few hours for observation, reflection, and drawing. Our french impatience, he observes, would have been shocked at the constant dispositions of the people who executed these edifices: throughout, there are the same research and care; a fact which leads to a conclusion that the works were not performed by the kings, but at the expense of the nation, under the direction of the priests, and by artists on whom they imposed invariable rules. Among the latter, a lapse of time would have produced some extension of faculty; but each temple has so complete an equality in all its parts, that all seem to have been sculptured by the same hand; there is nothing better, nothing worse; no negligence, no effusion of distinguished genius; unity and harmony reign throughout

throughout. The art of sculpture, enchained to architecture, was circumscribed in its principle, in its method, and in its mode : a figure expresses nothing by its sentiment ; it was to have such an attitude to express such a thing ; the sculptor had his pattern, and was not permitted to make an alteration, by doing which he might have changed its true meaning : it was with these figures as with our playing-cards, of which we preserve the imperfections, lest we should take from the facility with which they are recognized. The perfection which they have given to their animals sufficiently proves that they had an idea of style ; they have marked their character with a few lines, upon a grand principle, and a system which tended to the beautiful in gravity, and the beautiful in idea, as has already been seen in the two sphinxes of the capitol, and which exist in the style of those which are on the side of the temple.

As for the character given to the human figure, borrowing nothing from other nations, they have copied their own, which was rather agreeable than fine. The figures of women resemble their handsome women of the present day: their lines are round and plump ; the nose little ; the eyes long, but little open, and raised at the exterior angle, like those of all nations among which this organ is fatigued by the ardour of the sun or the whiteness of snow ; the flesh of the cheeks rather full, the lips thick, the mouth wide, but smiling and gracious :

gracious: throughout, the african character, of which the Negro is the extreme, and perhaps the original.

The hieroglyphics, executed in three manners, are also of three kinds, and may likewise belong to three eras: from examining the different edifices which he beheld, M. Denon was enabled to form an opinion that the most antient are those which have only a simple outline, cut without relief, and very deep; the second, and those which produce the least effect, are merely in very low relief; and the third, which seem to be of a better age, and which are more perfectly executed at Tintyra than at any other place in Egypt, are in relief within a hollow contour. Across the figures which compose the subjects, there are little hieroglyphics, which appear to contain their explanation; and which, with simplified forms, seem a more rapid manner of expression. a sort of *running-hand*, if this expression may be used, in speaking of sculpture.

A fourth kind seems to have been devoted to ornament; it has been called, improperly, and it is difficult to say why, *arabasque*: adopted by the Greeks, in the time of Augustus it was received among the Romans, and in the fifteenth century, on the revival of the arts, it was transmitted to us as a fantastic decoration, of which the taste was all the merit. Among the Egyptians, equally employed with taste, each object had a meaning or a moral a moral, and was at the same time made a decoration of the frises, the cornices, and the substructions of their architecture. There are at Tintyra representations of caryatide-peristyles of temples, such as were executed in painting at the baths of Titus, copied by Raphaël, and every day aped in our chambers, without a thought that the Egyptians furnished the first models.

Amidst the anxieties with which the number of interesting objects filled the mind of M. Denon, who had so short a period of time for their examination, he discovered a little apartment containing a celestial planisphere. This apartment was one of those which lay under the ruins of the arabian fabrics on the roof of the temple. He had entered this chamber before he perceived, with the declining light of day, that he was alone with general Belliard, who would not leave him in so desert a place, and with whom he was obliged to hasten, at full gallop, after the division.

The army had already reached Dindera, a place at about the distance of a mile and an half from Tintyra, where it was to sleep. Every officer and soldier, not restrained by his duty, had delighted himself by a visit to Tintyra.

In the evening, Latournerie, an officer of the most brilliant courage, and great delicacy of mind and taste, observed to M. Denon: " From the time I came to Egypt, deceived in every thing,

thing, I have constantly been melancholy and unwell: Tintyra has cured me; what I have seen to-day has repaid all my fatigues; whatever may happen to me in the sequel of this expedition, I shall applaud myself all my life for having undertaken it, on account of the recollections which it will have indelibly imprinted on my mind."

On the twenty-fifth, a new scene presented itself: dûm-palm-trees, much larger than those described before, gigantic tamarind-trees, villages of half a league in length, and at the same time, ground which, though it had been inundated, was left uncultivated. Was this because the inhabitants cultivated no more than was necessary for their sustenance, and thus deprived their tyrants of the superfluity? In the afternoon, crocodiles were mentioned, on being opposite to the low islands of sand which they frequent; upon inspection, something long and brown, among a multitude of mallards was discovered. This turned out to be a crocodile, lying asleep, and eighteen feet in length: a musket being fired, he entered the water leisurely, and returned a few minutes afterwards; a second musket being fired, he went into the water again, and again returned: the belly of this animal was much larger than those stuffed specimens of the species which M. Denon had seen.

The French learned that a party of mamlûks had passed the right bank of the river, and that another

another had taken the route of Esneh and Syeneh. Desaix dispatched his cavalry at midnight, to endeavour to cut off these latter.

On the twenty-sixth, the French began their march at two in the morning; at eight, they found a dead crocodile on the banks of the river: the body was still fresh, it was eight feet long; the upper jaw, the only moveable one, but ill fitted with the lower; but a gullet supplied its place, which yielded like a purse, and the elasticity of which answered the purpose of a tongue, which it was wholly without: its nostrils and its ears closed like the gills of fishes; its small eyes, at but a little distance from each other, added much to the horribleness of its physiognomy.

At nine o'clock, turning the end of a chain of mountains which formed a promontory, the French suddenly beheld the seat of the antique Thebes, in all its developement; Thebes, of which Homer has painted the extent in a single word, the *hundred-gated* Thebes, a poetic and empty expression, confidently repeated through a series of ages. Described in a few pages dictated to Herodotus by the egyptian priests, and copied ever since by all other historians; celebrated for a succession of kings whose wisdom has placed them in the rank of gods, for laws which were revered without being understood, for sciences confided to pompous and enigmatic inscriptions (those learned and earliest monuments

numents of the arts, which time itself has forborne to injure); this abandoned sanctuary, insulated by barbarism, and returned to the desert whence it was conquered; this city, in a word, perpetually wrapped in that veil of mystery by which even colossuses are magnified; this exiled city, which the mind no longer discovers but through the mists of time, was still a phantom so gigantic to our imagination, that the army, at the sight of its scattered ruins, halted of itself, and, by one spontaneous impulse, grounded its arms, as if the possession of the remains of this capital had been the object of its glorious labours, had completed the conquest of the egyptian territory.

The situation of Thebes is as beautiful as fancy can conceive it; the extent of its ruins leave no doubt that it was as vast as its renown has represented: the width of Egypt not being sufficient to contain it, it has rested its extremities on the two chains of mountains by which it is bordered, and its tombs fill the valley to the west, far into the desert.

Four little towns divide the relics of the edifices of Thebes, and the river, by the meanderings of its course, would seem to be proud of flowing amidst its ruins.

Between twelve and one o'clock the French arrived in a desert which was the burying-ground: the rock, cut on its inclined plane, presented, on
three

three sides of a square, regular apertures behind which double and treble galleries and chambers have served for sepulchres. Denon and Desaix entered this place on horseback, believing that it could only be an asylum of peace and silence; but they had scarcely committed themselves to the darkness of the galleries before they were assailed with javelins and stones by enemies whom they could not discover: an end was thus put to their observations; and they afterwards learned that these obscure retreats were inhabited by a considerable population, being part of the people of Kûrnû, in company with their flocks; that, contracting, apparently from their abodes, ferocious habits, they were almost always in rebellion against authority, and were become the terror of the neighbourhood: too much in haste to form a more ample acquaintance with these people, they fled with precipitation; and, for this time, they saw Thebes only as they galloped.

It would have been interesting to examine these tombs more particularly, but when the French returned to it a second time they were fired upon; on a third occasion, they came in actual hostility to the neighbourhood; and when tranquillity was restored, they forbore to risk its disturbance by the attempt.

M. Denon complains that it was his lot to sojourn for months at Zaoyëh, at Benésùef, and at Djirjieh, and to pass without stopping at the
places

places of which he came in search. A moment, after leaving the field of the dead, he reached a temple which, from its dilapidations, its decided tint of decay, the inferiority of its execution, the excessive simplicity of its ornaments, the irregularity of its lines and dimensions, and the rudeness of its sculpture, he judged to be of the highest antiquity. He made a sketch of this building, and then, galloping after the troops, which had continued on their march, he arrived at a second edifice much more considerable than the former, and in much better preservation. On the road, he saw a statue of black granite; he uses the term *granite* till it shall be decided what the substance is which has long been called basaltes, and of which are formed the magnificent egyptian lions which are at the feet of the stairs of the capitol.

This second edifice is that which it is agreed to call the Memnonium. It lies east and west, and reaches to the foot of the libyan chain. At its entrance, two square moles flank an immense gateway: on the wall of the interior are sculptured in two low-reliefs the victorious battles of an hero; their sculpture is of the most crude composition, destitute of perspective, design, and distribution, and similar to all other first conceptions of the human mind, which always proceeds by the same steps. M. Denon has seen at Pompeia some designs by the roman soldiers on the stucco

stucco of the walls; and these perfectly resembled those now under his contemplation, and those made by every child who attempts to represent his first ideas, before he has seen, compared, and reflected. In these sculptures, the hero is gigantic, and the enemies with whom he fights are five-and-twenty times smaller than himself: if this was among the first essays of the arts in flattery, it was flattery very falsely understood, since it must have been shameful for the hero to fight with pygmies.

At some paces from this gateway are the remains of a vast colossus; it has been mischievously broken, for the scattered parts have so completely preserved their polish, and the fractures their edges, that it is evident that if the devastating spirit of man had suffered him to leave to time alone the charge of ruining this monument, we should still enjoy it in its state of completion. To give an idea of its magnitude, it will be sufficient to observe that the width of its shoulders is twenty-five feet, which gives nearly seventy-five for its height; exact in its proportions, the style is middling, but the execution perfect: in its descent, it has fallen on its face; and thus this interesting part is prevented from being seen: the head-dress being broken, it cannot be ascertained whether it was the figure of a king or of a divinity: was it the statue of Memnon or of Ossimandue?—The descriptions hitherto given, compared with the
monuments

monuments themselves, throw more confusion into our ideas than they enlighten them. If this statue were that of Memnon, which is the more probable idea, all the travelers of the preceding two thousand years have been deceived in the object of curiosity, as is seen by the inscription of their their names on another colossus shortly to be mentioned.

There remains a foot of this first statue, detached and in good preservation, very well adapted for carriage, and which would supply Europe with a scale of comparison for monuments of this kind. The enclosure within which this figure stood was either a temple or a palace, or perhaps both at once; for if the low-relief correspond with the palace of a sovereign, eight figures of priests before two porticoes agree, also, with a temple, unless, indeed, this group were placed to remind the sovereign that, conformably with the laws, the priests were always to serve and assist his dignity. To conclude, this ruin, seated on the declivity of a mountain, and never having been inhabited in latter times, is so well preserved, in all its parts yet standing, that it has less the look of a ruin than of an edifice which has been building and of which the works have been suspended: there are several columns visible to their bases; the proportions are grand; but the style, though purer than that of the first temple, is nevertheless not to be compared with that of Tintyra, either for the

the majesty of the whole, or for the delicacy of the execution of the parts. It would require time and reflection to form an idea of the plan of this edifice, and it was now necessary to leave it at full gallop.

The French were attracted into the plain by the sight of two large figures, between which, according to the descriptions of Herodotus, Strabo, and those who have copied these writers, was the famous statue of Ossimandue, the tallest of all the colossuses: Ossimandue himself was so vain of the execution of this bold undertaking, that, on the pedestal of the figure, he caused an inscription to be engraved in which he challenged the power of man to attempt a monument like that of his tomb, of which the pompous description appears to M. Denon to be but a fantastic dream. The two statues still remaining are doubtlessly those of the mother and son of this prince, of whom Herodotus makes mention; that of the king has disappeared; time and envy having eagerly disputed its destruction, there exists only a formless rock of granite; it requires the persisting eye of an accustomed observer to distinguish some parts of this figure escaped from destruction, and, when found, they are so insignificant that they cannot give any idea of its dimension: the two which are still existing are fifty-five feet in height; they are seated, with their hands on their knees: what remains affords sufficient

cient testimony that the style was as rugged as the attitude is correct. The low-reliefs and little figures which compose the chair of the southernmost figure are not wanting, however, either in grace or delicacy of execution. It is on the leg of the northernmost, which it has been agreed to call that of Memnon, that are written in greek characters the names of the antient and illustrious travelers who have come to hear the sounds of this statue*. It is here that we may receive conviction of the dominion of celebrity over the mind of man, since, in the age when the antient government of Egypt and the jealousy of the priests ceased to forbid strangers to approach these monuments, the love of the marvelous still prevailed over the minds of those who came to visit them; since, in the age of Adrian, enlightened by the rays of philosophy, Sabina, the wife of that emperor, and herself literate, sought, together with learned men who accompanied her, to hear those sounds which no cause, physical or political, could any longer produce.

The figures are each formed of a single block; they are placed upon elevated ground, and may be

---

* It was said that the statue of Memnon emitted certain musical sounds at the rising of the sun. Some have attempted, but probably upon insufficient grounds, to account for these sounds as being produced by the action of the sun-beams on the pores of the basaltes or metallic stone of which, according to them, the statue is formed.

seen

seen at the distance of ten miles. In the morning, their shadows stretch across the plain, and lie on the sides of the libyan mountains.

M. Denon had scarcely begun to make drawings of these figures when he perceived that he was left alone with his magnificent originals; alarmed at his situation, he hastened after his curious companions, who had already reached a large temple, near the village of Medinet-Abû. In passing, he observed that the scite of the tomb of Ossimandue was cultivated, and that, consequently, the inundation came thus far; a proof, either that the bed of the Nile has risen, or that antiently there was some quay or bank to prevent the river from overflowing this part of the city, which, at the time the French passed it, was a large field of very green wheat, promising an abundant harvest.

To the right of and adjoining the village of Medinet-Abû, at the foot of the mountain, is a small palace united with a vast temple built and enlaged at various epochs. All that could be discovered by an hasty review, made on horseback, was that the back of the palace, which lies on the mountain, was covered with hieroglyphics, very deeply cut, and without any relief; that christianity, in the fourteenth century, employed the temple for a church, adding too ranks of columns, in the style of the times, for the support of a roof. The palace is the only edifice remaining that was not built for a temple, and even this adjoins a temple.

ple. It has a raised story, square windows, small doors, a stair-case, and balconies. On one side are fabrics reconstructed with more antient materials, before which are a skeen and court which have never been completed. This palace is as solidly constructed as the sacred edifices, and equally covered with low-reliefs.

The army advanced to Hermontis, now called Ermenta, where M. Denon was lodged in a temple, in the examination of which he employed the small portion of day that remained. From the figure of Typhon or of an Anubis, which is frequently repeated in the interior, it may be believed that it was consecrated to this divinity, or evil genius. He is represented standing, with the belly of a hog, surmounted by hanging breasts like those of the elder egyptian women of the present day. To the east, at an hundred toises from the temple, is a large reservoir, lined with fine stone, and furnished with four flights of steps by which it may be descended. This antique bason receives the water of the Nile at the time of the inundation, and still retains it, notwithstanding the state of ruin into which it has been suffered to fall. The nilometer of which Aristides the sophist speaks was certainly in the center; there remains nothing of the column on which it is said the degrees of the inundation were marked. Above the bason is an open flight of stairs, in good preservation, of which the steps are very low, and cut

in

in an enormous block of granite: this flight ascends to a platform. According to appearances, this platform served for a terrace to the temple which is behind. The sanctuary is completely preserved; what has been added, and which has never been finished, has experienced more injury. The portico has never been fronted; the sculpture of the capitals has never been completed; and the hieroglyphics which were to have covered the whole edifice are only in an early state of performance. The sanctuary has been entirely finished: it was divided into three parts; the first opened, by a lateral door, on a stair-case, which led to the roof; the second received light only through the door; and the third was wholly without light, and receives none at present but through a small dilapidation near the roof: before this was made, it received air only by a very low and small lateral door; this obscure apartment, nevertheless, is decorated like all the rest. It cannot be doubted but that, in the earlier times, sanctuaries only were built; and that afterwards open porticoes, surrounding apartments, and galleries, were built, whether to render the ceremonies more august, or to lodge the priests, and perhaps the king.

At two hundred toises further, in the same direction, are the ruins of a church built in the fourteenth or fifteenth century, with the most beautiful egyptian remains; superb columns of granite decorated the nave: but the whole is fallen; nothing

thing continues standing but the skreen of the choir and some parts of the walls of the enclosure: this destruction has taken place at the hands of man; the edifice was too well constructed not to have withstood the elements.

The light departed, and M. Denon returned, with a head full of the profusion of objects which had passed before his eyes within so short a space of time; he thought that this prolific day had been the product of a dream; and, in truth, he would have been deliciously fed for a whole month upon that which he had been obliged to take within a few hours, and without being able to promise himself even on the morrow a single moment for reflection.

On the twenty-seventh, at eight in the morning, he saw a tamarind of uncommon height, planted on the banks of the Nile; it had been undermined by progressive inundations, and at length overturned; the greater part of the upright roots had produced leaves; the old branches which it had received from the earth, and which had run into it in the fall, served for roots; so that its enormous trunk, horizontally suspended, had, by the confusion of the circulating system, vegetated in every direction; a phenomenon by which it had been rendered so extraordinary an object that the people in its neighbourhood by no means omitted to make it a miraculous tree: M. Denon would

would have made a drawing of it had he not been somewhat behind the division, and had not the subject required, for its adequate representation, a scrupulous detail of its parts.

On halting, the French found another *choking* of the Nile. The libyan chain, suddenly turning to the east, the Nile is forced upon the arabic. Pressed between these two obstacles, the river has triumphed over that which opposed the lesser resistance. In its increase, the current has undermined and broken through a bed of gravel which it has found under the plane of the libyan chain: the upper part, wanting a base, has tottered, and, in breaking loose, formed two points of rock. This rock, called Djibelin*, or the Two Mountains, serves for the boundary of a division of upper Egypt; and, during the latter government, it served for a barrier against the rebellious beys who were exiled into the upper Saïd; a barrier which they could not pass without becoming outlawed. It was thus that, a few years ago, Osmanbey, after being sent to Kosseir, accompanied by men who had secret orders to kill him instead of embarking him for Mekka, whither he was sentenced to be banished, overcame his assassins, ran away with the bark, richly laden, took refuge in upper Egypt, and collected a number of mamlûks suffi-

---

* Or Gibelin.

cient

cient to force Mûrat to treat, and to yield him the sovereignty of the whole space between Djibelin and Syeneh.

At this place, there is the tomb of a santon which enjoys very high reverence, and which performs miracles daily.

After this choking of the course of the Nile, the valley widens without any thing being added to the cultivated space: vast fields, cracked by the stay of the waters, have expected in vain the loan of that which they would have returned with such high interest.

On the twenty-eighth, the French arrived at an early hour at Esneh, the furthermost village of any magnitude in Egypt. Mûrat-bey had been obliged to evacuate on the preceding evening, a few hours before the arrival of the French cavalry, burning a part of his tents, and of the heavy baggage, which would have slackened his march. They were now authorized to suppose that he was determined to leave Egypt and penetrate into Nubia, in the expectation of fatiguing and scattering their strength: the country affording nothing to feed the bulk of their army, he might hope to reassemble his forces, and come by the way of the deserts to attack their detachments.

Esneh* is the antient Latopolis; on the banks of the Nile may be seen some wrecks of its port

---

* Or Isna.

or quay, which has often been restored, and which, well as some of the reparations have been performed, is in a deplorable state. There is also in the town the portico of a temple, which may be considered as the most perfect remain of antient architecture: it is situate near the bazar, in the great square, and would make the most incomparable ornament, if the inhabitants had any idea of its merit; instead of this, they have hid it with frightful and ruinous buildings, and abandoned it to the meanest uses: the portico is in high preservation, and has great richness of sculpture; it is composed of eighteen columns with widened capitals; these columns appeared to M. Denon excessively elegant, though their effect could be viewed only in the manner most disadvantageous to architecture; it would be necessary to remove the rubbish in order to ascertain if any part of the *cella* is still in existence: the hieroglyphics, in relief, with which it is covered within side as well as without, are of very elaborate execution; among the more remarkable are a zodiac, and large figures of men with the heads of crocodiles; the capitals, though almost all different from each other, have a fine effect; and, what might be added as a proof that the Egyptians borrowed nothing from other nations, all the ornaments of which these capitals are composed are taken from productions of the country, such as the lotus, the palm, the vine, the reed, &c. &c.

In

In considering those egyptian capitals of which opportunity permitted examination, and which offered remarkable peculiarities, M. Denon expresses entire astonishment that we should have supinely believed, upon the mere authority of the people themselves, that the Greeks were the inventors of architecture, and that three orders are the only truths of the art; it may be said that nothing is wanting to each of the egyptian capitals but an history like that of the urn of the priestess of Corinth to give it an equal celebrity, or, rather, that it has no want of an history similar to that of the corinthian capital, in order to be esteemed a superb production. The Egyptians have copied nature; they have copied their own; and the Greeks have only added fables to the robberies which they have committed on them. Here, the calyx of a flower above a bundle of its stems, has furnished the form of a column, of its base, and of its capital; in this country, this plant expressed the inundation, it was the emblem of the entry of the Nile into their canals, of a grand blessing of nature upon Egypt; the Egyptians made it a part of the decoration of their temples, as an homage of their gratitude to Isis, who presided over this blessing; as goddess of the earth, they dedicated to her all its productions, stems of the lotus, reeds, palms, vines, &c. &c.

Among these significant capitals, which adorned in an explicative manner the worship of the divinity

nity whose temple they decorated, may be particularized one from which spring the leaves and stems of the papyrus or reed; a second, composed of the branches and leaves of the palm-tree, and the different stages of its fruit, is perhaps the most elegant of all known capitals, and one which, without having in Europe that interest which belongs to it in Egypt, it would still make the most splendid of decorations for a banqueting or ball room; a third is composed of several calyxes of the flower of the lotus, grouped with the leaves of the plant; a fourth, of a bunch of the tufts of palm-trees, when, in spring-time, the branches and flowers are not yet developed, and the whole tree resembles the bud of a flower; a fifth is ingeniously made up of the root of the plant lotus, its stem, and its flower alternately open and in bud; a sixth, of branches of the vine mingled with those of palm-trees. This variety of capitals, thus richly compounded, enable us to give credit to the pompous descriptions which have been transmitted to us of those of the temple of Solomon, which are spoken of in the scriptures as corinthian capitals with leaves of the palm-tree.

The head of Isis, with all her attributes, crowns the columns of the temple of Tintyra. In the temple of Hermontis, which appears to have been dedicated to Typhon, his figure is represented on a die, which is no more than a prolongation of the column; this member of architecture,
which

appears to be peculiar to the egyptian column, disengages the capital, prevents its appearing to be crushed by the architrave, and produces so fine an effect when the eye is near the column, that it is astonishing it should never have been imitated.

On the twenty-ninth, after a march of three hours, on the borders of the desert, and at the distance of a mile and a half from the river, the French found a smaller pyramid of from fifty to sixty feet in base, and built with rough stones, too small to have preserved their places; whence the coating is destroyed from the top to the bottom. This is the furthermost of the pyramids: it is seated at two hundred and sixty miles from those of Jiza, and stands near a village: much smaller than any of the buildings of a similar kind, and built of more irregular masses, it has not been able to oppose the same resistance to time, or rather belongs to an anterior period: broken in all its parts, it no longer offers any other spectacle than that of an heap of stones, which, however, is seen to have been graduated and raised in a regular manner.

The families of the arab-cultivators on the border of the desert, where the French now were, present an image of that tranquil monotony which is never disturbed by the shock of a single novelty, of that calm which leaves a length of time between each event of life, of that quiet where every thing succeeds peaceably in the soul, where

where little by little an emotion becomes a sentiment, or an habitude a principle, where, in a word, the lightest impression is analized; and this to the degree, that, in conversing with this description of men one is altogether astonished to find in them the most nicest distinctions, and the most delicate sentiment, by the side of the most absolute ignorance.

A few sides of walls, to which they add a cover of straw, suffice for their habitation. Within a few paces is a dove cot, built of earth dried in the sun, and divided into compartments in the interior, for the accommodations of each family of pigeons. The door is circular, at the bottom of the dove cot. In the middle, is a little opening for the admission of air; this is shut every night, to secure the colony from the shacals. Near this is the fowl-house, less elevated, and smaller, having no division within. The hut is the principal apartment, that of the women, and that to which the men retire when they are apprehensive of a cold night. To the establishment belong dogs, who make no part of the family, and who live separate from it as defensive allies, a ghazal, and a kite, both of which are also free associates; the pigeons and chickens are the only domestics. The *bardaks*, which are drinking-pots, the *ballasses**, or jars for clearing

---

* Or hamâm.

the water of the Nile, and a few poringers, are nearly all the utensils of the house.

The colocynthus is a plant of the desert: it germs and developes during the season of the cool nights which succeed the inundation, and when some rains on the mountains send a little water into the plain; this plant, having spread, and its melons being formed, a part of the leaves is ate by the ghazals, and the rest consumed by the drought. Defended by its bitterness, the fruit remains till the next year, when the seeds it contains sow themselves and perpetuate this vegetable, the most remarkable of the few that grow in the desert.

At half past two, a little on this side Edfû, the French approached the remains of Hieracónpolis, which consist in the remains of the entrance of an edifice which, from the size of its stones, the extent of its wrecks, and the diameter of its decayed capitals, which are scattered here and there over the ground, appears to have been considerable: the nature of the stone with which Hieracónpolis has been built is so friable that the edifice has not retained any form, and that all its particulars are indistinguishable. At some toises further, another, still more perished, is, with difficulty discovered: the remains of the city are no more than heaps of bricks, much burnt, and a few fragments of granite.

On the other side of the Nile, the French saw two hundred mamlùks with their baggage, coming

ing down: they afterwards learned that this body was composed of Elfy-bey and his followers; Elfy (having been wounded at the battle of Samanhût) not chusing to pass the cataracts with the other beys. Approaching, they admired the superb and advantageous situation of Apolinópolis the great, overlooking the river and the whole valley of Egypt, while its magnificent temple rose above all, like a citadel that might command the country: an idea so naturally attendant on its appearance that is known in its neighbourhood by no other name than that of *the fortress.* Foreseeing with regret that the army would arrive late and depart early the next morning, M. Denon put his horse on the gallop to gain the start of the advanced-guard of the army, and to reach the temple before the day was wholly closed. At this time, he had only opportunity to ride round the edifice, the magnitude, the nobleness, the magnificence, and the preservation of which surpassed all that he had yet seen in Egypt or elsewhere, and made an impression upon his mind, vast like its dimensions. This edifice is a long suite of pyramidical entrances, courts decorated with galleries, porticoes, and covered cellas, constructed, not with stones, but with whole rocks. Night was already fallen before he had been able to complete the tour of this surprizing building; and he renewed his sorrow at being obliged to glance so rapidly over that
which

which deserved so much scrutiny. The preservation of this antique edifice contrasts in a wonderful manner with the gray ruins of the modern habitations constructed within it: a part of the population inhabit the temple in huts, built in the courts and on the ruins, and which, like the nests of swallows on our houses, project without hiding or disfiguring them. In short, this mixture, vexatious at the first view, produces a picturesque contrast which gives a scale at once of the people and of time: besides, are the French justified in ridiculing ignorant people who have sought support for their feeble constructions, unmolested by the fear of concealing beauties which have never caught their eyes, while they themselves leave the arenas of Nîmes encumbered with ruined houses?

Beyond Edfû, the country diminishes in width, leaving scarcely half a mile between the desert and the river. At noon, the French halted on the banks of the Nile. The cavalry proceeded onward; but, at the moment the infantry was about to commence its march, intelligence was received that the space immediately before them consisted of a desert, fourteen miles across; and, the day being too far gone to allow of the commencement of a march of this length, the night was passed in an abandoned village, where there was happily a supply of wood.

On

On the thirtieth, they set forward at three o'clock in the morning: after marching an hour through a cultivated country, they reached a mountain composed of rotten slate, freestone, white and rose-coloured quartz, brown pebbles, and some white coral. After five hours march in this desert, their shoes torn to pieces, the soldiers fastened about their feet what linen they had: they were devoured by a raging thirst; no water was to be had but in the Nile, of which the banks were as arid as the desert: the division was harrassed, and, to reach the river, it was necessary to turn aside for a league: thirst, however, commanded this procedure, and the Nile was gained, where the troops arrived in a state of exhaustion. The baggage, the animals that carrried which had had no food the preceding evening, weakened by hunger, could only follow in parcels. What was the distress, says M. Denon, when it became necessary to tell the soldiers that there was nothing to eat! we looked sorrowfully on one another; no one uttered a murmur; but the silence, the tears, sad harbingers of despair, were still more terrible. This frightful situation had lasted a few minutes, when a camel, bearing a light burden of butter, came up, with a few of those whose provisions had been ate. The sacks were searched to the bottom, and shaken, and enough flour was found to give each

an

an handful. It was proposed to make fritters, and a tree supplied fire-wood. Occupation drove away melancholy ideas, and french gaiety renewed their courage among the troops. Lightly ballasted, they set forward at a quick pace; but their poor horses, who had not tasted the fritters, rolled under them with ananition; it became necessary to lead them; it became necessary to support or to abandon them; it was necessary to march, a thing which M. Denon professed he should have thought impossible but for the necessity of the case: but *there was unalterable necessity*; and they had learned the extent of the resources which these words caused to be found.

An hour and an half after passing the first desert, the French found the ruins of Silsilis, which consist in fragments, bricks, and the remains of a temple, of which the most elevated walls do not at present rise more than three feet above the ground. The cella of the temple, covered with hieroglyphics, may yet be recognized: it was surrounded by a gallery, to which, in later times, a portico, without hieroglyphics has been added. The French entered the desert for the third time, followed, for many hours, by an hyena.

The rock grew granitous, with pebbles of all colours and all species, and of a hardness which rendered them susceptible of a brilliant polish. M. Denon found coralines, jasper, and serpentine-stone: the sand is composed only of the inadherent

rent primitive and constituent particles of granite. The French ascended an elevated flat, whence they had a wide prospect of the windings of the Nile, which river, after flowing along the Mokatam returns to the north-west, to resume its northerly course. At this angle, there were perceptible the ruins of a pharos, which was once perhaps serviceable to the tortuous navigation of that part of the river; at another, there were distinguisable the heights of Ombos, elevating their beautiful remains of antique edifices; at the elbow of the flood, one of its branches formed an island which it inundates, and on which alone, amid forty square miles of surrounding country, it bestows that blessing: the situation of this island equally preserved it from the incursions of the mamlûks and the French; the inhabitants of the continent fled to it, giving up the large village of Binban, embraced by the desert, and as dismal as that. At this moment, a scene presented itself containing a striking contrast between the most ferocious brutality and the most generous sensibility. At the instant in which M. Denon was remarking that if avarice is ingenious in discovering an hiding-place, want is perhaps still more so in discovering it, a soldier came out of an hole, dragging with him a goat which he had found: he was followed by an old man with two suckling infants in his arms; the old man laid them upon the ground,
fell

fell upon his knees, and, without uttering a word, pointed, while he shed a torrent of tears, that his children must die if the goat were taken from them. Blind and surly want was not stayed by the sight of this distressing picture, and the goat was instantly killed: at the same point of time, another soldier came up, bringing in his arms another infant, which a mother, in flying before the French, had doubtlessly been obliged to abandon in the desert: notwithstanding the burden with which this brave man was laden, his knapsack, his musket, his cartridges, the weariness of a forced march of four days continuance, the desire of saving this little uufortunate creature had made him tenderly take it up; he had carried it four miles in his arms; at a loss what to do with it in this abandoned village, he descried a single inhabitant, he descried two infants, and, without considering any thing else, he deposited beside them the object of his solicitude, with the enthusiasm of a creature who had done a good action.

If I had been struck with horror, adds M. Denon, at seeing hunger render an individual of my species as ferocious as a beast of prey, the other soldier had soothed my feelings, had reconciled me with humanity. What sensations are those produced by the display of the softer virtues amidst the horrors of war! they revive the drooping soul; they are a glass of fresh and cool water in the
midst

midst of the desert. I had money and biscuit to give to the old man; but, unable to do any thing for the infants, I fled to deliver myself from the sight of a misfortune to which it was not within my power to afford any relief.

On the thirty-first, there were still a continuance of deserts to cross. The rock was alternately of granite and of free-stone, the decomposition of which formed a friable and grating crust on the surface, resembling scoriæ. In the valley, which abounds with sand, the surface is close and delicate like that of snow, so that the traces of animals are imprinted on it with the same facility, and that it is recognizable by what they have been crossed since the preceding wind. The traces with which they had been impressed were generally those of the ghazals: these pretty animals, more timid than wild, after taking their food on the banks of the river, hasten to hide their fears in the depth of the desert. M. Denon remarked with compassion, that the footsteps of an animal of prey almost always followed those of this elegant and feeble creature: the swiftness of its course does not always secure its escape from its enemy. In the course of the day, the French saw two of these animals, the most beautiful and the most delicate of the extensive family to which they belong.*

---

* The *ghazal*, or *antelope*, is a species of animal related both to the goat and to the deer.

The

The march was slow and painful; each stopping every moment to re-adjust the clothing of his feet, and to take breath: in the afternoon, M. Denon discovered in the open desert the traces of an antique road, lined on each side with large masses of cut stone, and leading direct to Syeneh. The troops were now so completely fatigued that on leaving the desert they were permitted to stop at the first place that could furnish forage for their horses; and, on recommencing the march, it seemed almost impossible to force the animals from the herbage, or to cause the soldiers to re-assume their legs. M. Denon was so wholly exhausted that he remained the whole night upon the spot where he had first sat down. The next day, they marched but a mile and a half before they rejoined the cavalry, which, in preceding them, had ate up all the food of the country. At length, the army reached Esûan or Syeneh, the end of its march. The soldier forgot his fatigues, as if he had reached the promised land, as if, to return to a country which could feed him, he had not had to retrace the road which he had just traveled with so much pain; but the past was already nothing, and the enjoyment of the present scarcely allowed a glimpse of the uncertain future. M. Denon thought few, however, had reason to be so rejoiced as himself; since he, for the first time was about to breathe and seat himself in a country where every thing was interesting.

The

The first good news received was that the mamlûks had not burned the barks with which they had attempted to pass the cataracts: the French encamped for the night at Contra-Esûan. The next morning, M. Denon ascended to the convent of saint Lawrence, which is a bad ruin. Above this, is the Tower of the Winds, which is a gazebo whence the most singular of views is discovered:* it is the end of the world; or, rather, it is a chaos, with the air already disengaged, and the water also beginning, by veins, to separate itself from the earth, and to promise fecundity to nature; in truth, its first benefactions are manifested on rocks of granite, or heaps of sand and mud deposited in hollows, where they form bases for vegetation, increasing by degrees. At Elephantine, itself, the culture, the trees, and the habitations, present a picture of nature in her perfection; the origin, no doubt, of its arabic name, Kesiret-èl-Sag, or the *flowered isle*.

On the first of February,* the French crossed the river, to occupy Esùan, or Syeneh, which lies on the right bank. Mûrat-bey had passed the cataracts, and extended himself through a long space, for the sake of subsisting his mamlûks and their horses: the French were obliged to pursue a similar plan.

---

* The entry of the Nile into Egypt.   † 14 Pluviose.

On the third, Desaix departed, with his cavalry, in search of Elfy-bey, whom he had left behind him, on the right of the river. I had not previously been separated from him, says M. Denon, since our departure from Kaira.* I may presume to say, and with some degree of pride, that this was an occasion of sorrow to us both; many and sweet were the moments we had passed together, marching side by side, for twelve or fifteen hours at a time; we did not converse, we thought aloud; and often, after these long sittings, we said to each other: How many things shall we not have to talk of, all the rest of our lives!—How many ideas of polity, wisdom, and philanthropy, entered his large mind when the clangour of the trumpet and the rolling of the drum ceased to fill him with the fever of the warrior! How many interesting notes would not his astonishing memory have furnished me with at this moment! with what advantage should I not have consulted him! with what interest would he not have seen my work, which he might have regarded as his own! In leaving me for a few moments, he has seemed as if willing to accustom me by degrees to his absence.

M. Denon accompanied general Belliard, who was directed to take possession of the government

---

* Here is a slight forgetfulness in the author; he had been left with the army at Benéshuef, while Desaix repaired to Kaira.

of Syeneh. The ruins of this place date their origin at various epochs. Those of the earliest are easily distinguished: if, as appears probable, the edifices on the right bank of the Nile and on the island of Elephantine belonged to one and the same city, this, at the epoch of their erection, must have been a considerable place. The separation is produced by the river alone, which at this part, is rather deep and wide. The arabian ruins are grouped on a rock to the eastward: lower down, and in the island of Elephantine, there are some remains of roman fabrics. To all this, in a still later age, has succeeded a large village, better built, and with streets more regularly laid out, than the ordinary villages; a superiority which must be attributed to the presence of the stone, and of a quantity of antient materials. In the midst is a turkish castle, masked on all sides, and incapable of affording any defense.

The first concern of the French was that of providing for their establishment. They obtained very excellent head-quarters: these were at the house of the kiashef, built in stone, with a raised story, terraces, and vaulted cielings: the French made themselves beds, tables, and stools: to undress, be seated, and go to bed, appeared to M. Denon to be effeminacy, absolute voluptuousness: the soldiers had the same accommodation. On the second day of their establishment, the streets of Syeneh were already filled with french taylors, shoemakers,

shoemakers, goldsmiths, and barbers, with all their insignia; and cook-shops and taverns, with fixed prices. The station of an army, adds M. Denon, presents a picture of the most rapid developement of the sources of industry; each individual sets his whole strength to work, for the good of society: but that which peculiarly characterizes a french army, is the establishing the superfluous at the same time and with the same care as the necessary: we had gardens, coffee-houses, and gaming-tables, with cards made at Syeneh. At the end of the village, an alley of trees lay in a north direction: here, the soldiers placed a mile-stone, with this inscription: *Road to Paris, no. eleven, one hundred and sixty-seven thousand three hundred and forty:* it was a few days after a distribution of dates for the whole of their rations that they entertained ideas thus jocular, or thus philosophical. Death alone could put an end to so much bravery and cheerfulness; the greatest misfortunes were ineffectual.

On this side of the river, there is no other remain of the egyptian city than a little square temple, surrounded by a gallery; and even this is so much destroyed, and so deprived of form, that nothing can be distinguished but the embrasure of two intercolumniations, with the capitals, and a small part of the entablature: this fragment is that which Savary, who confesses he never was at Syeneh, indicates, upon hearsay, as the remains of
the

the observatory, in which, according to him, we must look for the nilometer.

Near this ruin, among the palm-trees, are the fragments of an edifice which, it is probable, must be given to greek christianity: there are still two columns of granite, two door-posts of the same material, and some columns against two faces of a single pilaster, which two last remnants are overthrown.

The island of Elephantine became at once the country-house, and the scene of delight, observation, and research to M. Denon: he thinks he turned every stone and examined every rock it contained. It was at the southern part that the egyptian city and the roman and arabian habitations which succeeded it, were placed. The roman occupation is recognized only by the bricks, the broken pottery, and the little deities of burnt earth, and of brass, which are still found. That of the Arabs is recognized only by the dung with which they have covered the soil, and which forms the ordinary ruins of their edifices. As for the whole of those of posterior times, they have scarcely left any trace of their existence: all have perished before the egyptian constructions, formed, as these were, for posterity, and resisting, as they have, the efforts of man and of time. Amid the vast field of bricks and burnt earth which has been mentioned, still arises a square temple of great antiquity, surrounded by a gallery, with pilasters, and two
                                                columns

columns of a portico. Only two columns, at the left angle, are wanting to this ruin. Other edifices have been added posteriorly: of these, nothing remains but a few remnants, incapable of demonstrating their form, and which only serve to prove that the accompaniments were much larger than the sanctuary: this latter is covered within and without by hieroglyphics in relief, tolerably well preserved, and excellently sculptured. M. Denon drew the whole of one side of the interior part, and of which that on the opposite side is nearly a copy; he also drew one side of the exterior, and a single pilaster, the rest being, in like manner, almost a repetition. The species of picture which the side of the interior composes is so much the more interesting as it contains food for discussion, and as it has an unity M. Denon had not hitherto observed in this sort of decoration, which is ordinarily divided into compartments. The whole of the pictures seem to represent the consecration of the temple by an hero, or sacrifices to gain the favour and protection of the divinities. The picture on the side of the interior of the sanctuary, represents a sacrifice of wild and domestic quadrupeds, birds, fishes, flowers, and fruits; the hero who presents the offerings holds a censer in one hand and a vessel of lustral-water in the other. On an high altar is a bark, in which is a temple, apparently unable to contain that to which it is consecrated. On one side, under

der a sort of table of promission, are flowers of the lotus, palm-branches, and figures of Isis. In a group, on the other side, is the apotheosis or the protection granted to the hero by the two great divinities: in the picture opposite to this, the only differences are in the figure which offers the sacrifice, and which holds, instead of a vessel of lustral-water, a group of pigeons by the wings.

It is doubtful whether this were the temple of Kneph, the good genius, or the egyptian god who most approaches our ideas of the supreme Being, or whether that temple, mentioned by historians, were not rather the one which stands six hundred paces further, which is more ruinous, and of which all the ornaments are accompanied by a serpent, the emblem of wisdom and of eternity, and particularly of the god Kneph. Judging by comparison with all the other egyptian edifices, this latter is of the order most antiently employed; and it is precisely of the same kind with the temple of Kûrnû at Thebes, which appears to be the most antient of that city. What is more peculiarly observable in the sculpture of this temple is, that the figures have greater action or freedom, and the robes a greater length and better fashion. Three figures, in a low-relief, seem to thank an hero for having delivered a fifth personage, which is almost effaced, but which may be discovered to have been prostrate. The hero appears to have killed a robber; and the three figures are either returning

returning him thanks, or vowing fidelity. Had not this piece been found in the place it was, it would have been to be doubted whether it were egyptian sculpture. The clothing of these figures resembles that of no others, and does not appear to be egyptian; and the expression in the grouping of the figures is equally singular. In another piece of sculpture within the same temple, there appears to be represented a subsequent scene of the same event. Here, incense is offered to the hero: the peculiarities of the costume, and the unusual freedom of the figures is the same. It is a question whether these sculptures, in which there is a sort of picturesque composition, and perspective, were executed before or after the Egyptians had established laws for their figures, in order to render them, like writing, characters which, at the first sight, might manifest their signification, almost without requiring to be looked at. Nothing remains of this edifice but one column of the portico, and the whole of one side of a gallery, with pilasters.

In the center of the island are two chambranles of a great outward door, formed of blocks of granite, ornamented with hieroglyphics: these fragments have doubtlessly belonged to some edifice of great magnificence, of which a superficial digging might discover the extent. To the east, is another fragment of an edifice, very small, and very elaborate: it consists in the western side of a narrow a narrow chamber, or perhaps of a very small temple; and what remains of the hieroglyphics is admirably sculptured: the ornaments are surcharged with the lotus, and, among others, are the flowers of this plant, of which the withering stem appears to be re-animated by a figure who waters it, as in another sculpture at Latópolis. This chamber or temple communicates with a passage still narrower than itself, which, as may be judged from a series of fabrics, terminated in a gallery that opened on the Nile, and finished by a large embankment, which defended the eastern part of the island from being injured by the action of the current of the river: there still remain three porticoes of this gallery, and a flight of steps, in granite, which descend into the water. It suggested itself to M. Denon, that this gallery, this decorated chamber, and this flight of steps, belonged to the nilometer for which travelers have searched in vain in Syeneh. Prepossessed with this idea, he carefully sought, but was unable to discover, any mark upon the facing of the steps which could at all resemble graduation: nevertheless, the very steps might have answered this purpose; or, the upper part being covered, the degrees might have been marked on the stones which he was not able to examine*. All

---

* Strabo, who observed Syeneh with care, and who has described it with minuteness, says that the nilometer was a well which

All these fabrics are seated on masses of rock, and are covered with hieroglyphics, sculptured with more or less care: further on, advancing towards the north, are found two portions of a parapet, between which is an opening, to allow of a descent into the river: on the interior side of the portion to the right, is a bass-relief in marble, representing the figure of the Nile, four feet in height, and in the attitude of a colossus which is at Rome, and which represents this same river. This copy of the same idea proves that the building is roman, that it is posterior to the time when this grecian masterpiece was carried to Rome, and that the Romans, having been able to add the ornaments of luxury and superfluity to constructions of the first necessity, had not merely a military station at Syeneh, but a powerful colony: the baths and precious utensils of bronze which are still daily found, give further support to this idea of the wealth and derivation of this colony.

The island of Elephantine, defended to the south by shelves, is doubtlessly much augmented to the north by alluvion: this alluvion is daily transformed into cultivated ground and pleasant gardens, which, perpetually watered by little fur-

---

which received the water of the Nile, and that the marks by which the inundation was estimated were engraved on the sides of this well.

rows,

rows, produce four or five harvests a year: hence, the inhabitants are numerous, rich, and very courteous. M. Denon hailed them from the opposite bank; they came to him with their boats, and he was presently accompanied by all the children, who brought and sold him relics of antiquity, and rough cornelians: with a few crowns, he was able to make a multitude of little people happy, and their parents became his friends; they gave invitations, and prepared him a breakfast in the temple which he had come to examine: in a word, he was as the benevolent proprietor of a garden wherein every thing that it is attempted to imitate existed in reality; islands, rocks, deserts, fields, meadows, gardens, thickets, hamlets, deep groves, rare and various plants, a river, canals, mills, and sublime ruins: a scene so much the more enchanting as that, like the gardens of Armida, it was surrounded by the horrors of nature, of those, in short, of the Thebaïd, the contrast with which made the luxury of its charms apparent. The senses and the imagination equally employed, M. Denon never passed hours more delightfully spent than those which he bestowed in his solitary walks in Elephantine. This island alone supplies the whole territory of the city.

The population of Syeneh is numerous: its commerce, nevertheless, is reduced to senna and dates, which two articles pay for all the wants of the inhabitants, and the maintenance of a kiashef, a governor,

governor, and a turkish garrison: the senna which grows in the neighbourhood of Syeneh is of a middling quality, and it is not sold without being fraudulently mixed with that of the desert, which is brought by the Barabrans, and which they sell for about one hundredth part of the price which is paid for this article in Europe: it is true that several duties are levied on it in its way, and that it is one of the most important articles at the custom-house at Kaira, and at that at Alexandria. The second article of exportation is that of dates; these are dry and small, but produced in such abundance that, besides forming the food of the principal part of the inhabitants, it is daily sent down the Nile, into lower Egypt.

The French learned by their spies that the mamlûks ascended as little as possible above the cataracts, that they were ravaging both banks of the Nile, which still supplied them with a little forage; that they then procured flour and dates from Dahirût and Breebehs, but that the aga who resided there had sent them word that the supply would shortly fail; that they occupied ten leagues of space on the one and the other bank; that their rear-guard was only eight leagues from themselves, where they were informed of every thing they did, by the same means as the latter were told of their movements, and perhaps by the

the same emissaries, who faithfully served either party with the same punctuality.

General Daoust had met Hassein-bey on the right bank, opposite to Edfû, at the moment of his approach to the Nile for water: the imminent danger of losing his baggage made him charge with fury; the eagerness of the cavalry to possess themselves of it, and a portion of contempt for their enemy, which they had taken up at the battle of Samanhût, occasioned them to attack with too much negligence. This combat between two hundred cavalry on the one side, and two hundred cavaliers on the other, was rather an afray than a battle; both parties exhibited unheard-of valour. The charge lasted an hour and an half; at the end of which the French became masters of the field, but Hassein-bey attained his object, that of saving his baggage: the former had forty killed and as many wounded, the latter, twelve killed and wounded: Hassein himself was wounded in the leg; and neither side could gratulate itself on this recontre.

From Syeneh, the French went in search of the barks with which the mamlûks had attempted to ascend: the project was, to see the cataracts at the same time. Among the rocks of granite, they found the quarries whence those enormous masses were taken, which served to make the colossal statues which have been the object of
admi-

admiration during so many ages, and of which the ruins still strike the beholder with astonishment; it would seem as if it had been designed to record the masses which they have produced, by leaving hieroglyphical inscriptions in their place, which contain, perhaps, their memorial. The operation by which these blocks were detached must have been the same as that now employed for similar purposes; that is to say, that there was primarily formed a cleft, after which the mass was disjoined by means of a number of wedges, struck at the same time. The marks of these operations are preserved with such freshness on this unalterable material, that the works seem to have been suspended only yesterday. All the rocks with plane superficies bear marks of these operations, and all appear as if the workmen had left them only the preceding evening. The quality of this granite is so hard and so compact, that the rocks which lie in the current, instead of being worn away and demolished, have acquired lustre from the friction of the water. The most beautiful of the granites, and that which is in the greatest abundance, is the rose-coloured; the gray is often too brittle: between these blocks are found veins of very brilliant quartz, beds of a red stone, the substance and hardness of which approach to those of porphyry, and other beds of that black and hard stone which has long been taken for basaltes, and which the
Egyptians

Egyptians often employed for the material of their statues of the middle size.

At a league and an half beyond the quarries, the rocks multiply, and form a sort of bar, whereat the French found the barks of the mamlûks fixed between the rocks, at the lowest height of the river. Here they left the little vessel in which they had arrived. Proceeding on foot for a quarter of an hour, they discovered what it is agreed to call the *cataract* : this is only a shelf over which the river flows amidst the rocks, forming, in several places, cascades of a few inches in height : these falls are so very insensible that they could scarcely be expressed in a draught; but they would make a fine picture, if represented with the colours by which they are characterized. The mountains, entirely set with black and sharp projections, are reflected in a sombre manner in the mirror of the waters of the river, which are pent up and crossed by numerous peaks of granite that interrupt the surface, and stripe them with long white lines: these rugged forms and colours are contrasted by the tender green of the groupes of palm-trees scattered here and there among the rocks, and by the azure vault of the most beautiful sky in the world: this picture, well executed, would have the singular advantage of presenting at once a true image of nature, and a striking novelty. Beyond the cataracts, the rocks encrease in elevation, and have their summits formed

formed of blocks of granite which seem to pyramid and balance for the production of picturesque effects.

It is across this barren and rugged landscape that the eye suddenly discovers the superb monuments of the isle of Philoë, which form a brilliant contrast, and one that produces the most wonderful surprize that a traveller can experience. The Nile makes a turn as if to come in search of and embrace this enchanted island, on which the edifices of antiquity are separated only by a few clumps of palm-trees, or by rocks which seem to have been preserved only to group the richness of nature with the magnificence of art, and make an assemblage of all that is most picturesque and most noble. The enthusiasm which a traveler feels on beholding the monuments of upper Egypt may appear to the reader but a continual emphasis, a monotony of exaggeration; but it is only the unstudied expression of that sentiment which the sublimity of their character inspires.

There were no inhabitants on the continent; and even those of Philoë had fled, and retired to a further and larger island, whence they raised wild cries, which were said to be the cries of fear: the French made every effort to persuade them to send a bark which lay on their bank, but could obtain nothing. They returned, very well satisfied by their journey; but this glance was not sufficient for objects of antiquity thus important,

for

for relics thus considerable, thus well preserved, and of which the details must be interesting.

Some days afterwards, the French learned that the mamlûks of the right bank had come to forage within two leagues of their station: in consequence, they set out, four hundred strong, and advanced to Philoë by land, across the desert: a route which has this peculiarity, that its having been traced is evident; it was raised in the manner of a causey, and, formerly, was much used: this is the only space in Egypt where a high way was a thing of absolute need; here, the Nile, in consequence of the cataracts, suffering an interruption in its navigation, all articles of commerce from Ethiopia, which were landed at Philoë, were necessarily carried by land to Syeneh, where they were embarked afresh. All the blocks which are met with on this route are covered with hieroglyphics, and seemed to be there for the entertainment of passengers. One of the more singular of these presents the form of a seat, which has been completed by the fabrication of steps up to the foot of the stool; the whole covered with hieroglyphics, of which the greater part are highly elaborate, while others are only traced. The inscriptions are of two kinds, of which that first mentioned is engraved to the depth of an inch: they were doubtlessly consecrations or dedications. This extraordinary rock was perhaps consecrated to five divinities of which the figures are traced

traced above its inscription. It is possible that the Egyptians, always colossal in their undertakings, had intended to place a gigantic figure on this seat.

Another peculiarity on this route are the ruins of lines constructed in brick baked in the sun, of which the base has from fifteen to twenty feet in thickness: this intrenchment runs along the valley, bordering the road, and terminating at the rocks and forts at the distance of nearly three leagues from Syeneh. Though these walls were constructed of a material little precious, there has been an expense in the fabrication which proves the importance attached to the defense of this point: it may be that this is the remnant of the famous wall raised by a queen of Egypt called Zuleikha, daughter of Ziba, one of the Pharoahs, and which extended from the antient Syeneh to the present El-A'rysh, where the fragments are called by the Arabs *haïf-él-adjûz*, or the wall of the city.

The inhabitants of Philoë were now returned to their habitations, but as unwilling as before to receive a visit; this the French again attributed to the fears they entertained, and continued their route. Beyond Philoë, the river is entirely unincumbered and navigable. After passing an arabian fort, and a mosk of the same age, the banks of the Nile gradually became impassable; instead of a profusion of monuments and inscriptions, nothing was any longer to be seen but a naked landscape, with, on the rocks, a few habitations, which resembled the huts of savages. One of the most sumptuous of these will afford, in its description, a favourable picture of the whole: this, like all the rest, was built of earth, with some pieces of the wood of the palm-tree, which served for chambranles to the doors or apertures by which the inhabitants passed into the chambers or magazines, the whole being covered with faggots of dûrac-straw, which is employed for fuel. When the houses are devoid of trees, and constructed in the rocks, they disappear to the eye as soon as the rising sun ceases to throw shadows. M. Denon has often, while in the midst of it, hunted at noon for a village which he had seen in the morning. One of the strange sensations of the tropic is to find oneself at noon as in the center of the light of which it is the source, and to see objects which cast no shadows, objects which flatten and cease to have apparent projections, thus giving a new aspect to a whole country, the forms of which become lost or irrecognizable.

On one side of this house was a magazine for grain of different kinds, which building was closed hermetically with a sort of stakes which were withdrawn to the number necessary, through small holes at the bottom. On either side of the door were severally a hen-house and a pigeon-house. Necessity, which is the distributor of the localities and architecture of these houses has given all a general resemblance, without making any two precisely the same. On one side was the kitchen, which is always in the angle of one

of

of the walls, to the end that the fire may be sheltered from two winds, and that the inhabitants may not be incommoded with smoke by the other two. The chamber of the women can neither be entered nor inhabited but on the knees. This apartment conceals the most sorry and ugly children that can be imagined: for it appears that the orientals increase in beauty till they are forty-five years of age; and that they do not begin to be handsome till they are twenty. The date-palm and dûm-palm trees form the only decorations of these houses: but it is interesting to see, in the same country, the extremes of the results of industry, man aggrandizing himself with the majesty of his palaces and the superfluous ornament which he can raise around him, and man almost returned into the class of animals, by re-approaching nature, and reducing his desires to his wants alone.

The people of this country are called *Goubli* or *of the other side*, or Barabrans, which is the generic name of all the nations of Egypt that lie on *the other side* the Cataracts: their costume, as far as it regards the males is absolute nakedness, to which they add a morsel of woollen or cotton cloth, which they wind at will round so much of their bodies as they wish to cover; their hair, which is of tolerable length, though crisped, is further frizled in long curls, in the manner of the antient egyptian figures; they anoint their head-dress with oil of cedar, of which they love the odour, and which at the same time saves them from the
inconvenience

inconvenience of vermine, which, but for this, would lodge themselves irremovably in hair which it is impossible to comb. The women and children wear two curls at each ear, the one above, and the other underneath; necklaces with fringes formed of little stripes of leather, terminated with beads of coloured glass: a girdle of the same materials and fashion, descending half-way to the knees, suffices, till the time of their marriage, to tranquilize all the alarms of modesty. The women *of the other side* are well made, with rounding and firm muscles; they have a delicate skin, cool to the touch, and in this latter have a peculiar merit, highly valued by men with whom love is palpable, and pleasure wholly material; who calculate and appreciate physical qualities, and who purchase in the women *of the other side* the enjoyments of summer, a provision of luxury which Europeans have hitherto extended only to their clothing: the Russians build their houses for winter, and the Italians for summer; the Orientals, like the Kamtschadales, think they have need of one habitation for winter, and another for seasons of ardent heat.

The French entered a desert, cutting an angle of the Nile, to shorten their journey; and, after descending valleys for some hours, as deep as if they had been in a country subject to storms and torrents, they opened on the Nile by a ravine which led them to Tôdy, an indifferent village, on the banks of the river: on their approach, the
mamlûks

mamlûks had just abandoned the village, leaving their dishes, their kettles, and even the soup which they had prepared, and which they were going to eat as soon as the sun had set; for this was the month of ramadan, during which, the mohammedans holding a species of lent, even soldiers do not eat while the sun is above the horizon.

During the night, the French dispatched a spy; and, at day-break they were informed that the mamlûks, thinking themselves too near even at Demmiet, at four leagues from Tôdy, after baiting their horses, had recommenced their flight at midnight. The object of driving them off being gained, the French resumed their route for Syeneh. I had already, says M. Denon, had enough of Ethiopia, of their Goublis, and of their women, the extreme ugliness of whom can only be compared with the furious jealousy of their husbands: I had seen some of them: as I inspired their husbands with less fear than the soldiers, they placed a certain number of them under my safeguard in an hut, before the door of which I had fixed myself for the night. Surprized by the return of our march, they had not had time to fly or to conceal themselves in the rocks, or to swim across the river; they had absolutely the wild, stupid look of savages. A barren soil, fatigue, and insufficient nourishment, robs them, no doubt, of all the charms of nature, and gives, even in their youth, the impression and haggardness of decrepitude. It would seem as if the men were of another

ther species, for their features are delicate, their skin fine, their physiognomy animated and intelligent, and their eyes and their teeth admirable. Full of life and understanding, their language is remarkable for clearness and concision; a short expression always contains a complete answer to the question proposed: their vivacious character is more analogous to that of the French than to that of their fellow-orientals; they understand and perform with quickness; steal still more swiftly; and have an avarice for money, which can be justified only by their excessive poverty, and compared only with their frugality. It is to all these reasons that we should attribute their meagreness, which does not proceed from ill health; for their colour, though black, is full of life and blood, only their muscles are mere tendons: I have never seen one individual fat, or even fleshy*.

---

* The reader will find it difficult to reconcile the account of the women *of the other side* in this paragraph, with that given a page or two before; but he will not be displeased to have in the one a counterpart to the apparently harsh terms of the other. The women between Syeneh and Tôdy may be somewhat inferior to the rest of the Barabrans; but the author has said, in general terms, that the women *of the other side* are well made.

END OF VOL. I.

www.ingramcontent.com/pod-product-compliance
Lightning Source LLC
Chambersburg PA
CBHW021818300426
44114CB00009BA/223